Macromedia®
Flash™ MX 2004:
A Beginner's Guide

Brian Underdahl

McGraw-Hill/Osborne

New York   Chicago   San Francisco
Lisbon   London   Madrid   Mexico City
Milan   New Delhi   San Juan
Seoul   Singapore   Sydney   Toronto

The McGraw·Hill Companies

McGraw-Hill/Osborne
2100 Powell Street, 10th Floor
Emeryville, California 94608
U.S.A.

To arrange bulk purchase discounts for sales promotions, premiums, or fund-raisers, please contact **McGraw-Hill**/Osborne at the above address. For information on translations or book distributors outside the U.S.A., please see the International Contact Information page immediately following the index of this book.

Macromedia® Flash™ MX 2004: A Beginner's Guide

1234567890 FGR FGR 019876543

ISBN 0-07-222982-9

Publisher   Brandon A. Nordin
Vice President & Associate Publisher   Scott Rogers
Acquisitions Editor   Nancy Maragioglio
Project Editor   Lisa Wolters-Broder, Patty Mon
Acquisitions Coordinator   Athena Honore
Technical Editor   Jim Kelly
Copy Editor   Jan Jue
Proofreader   Susie Elkind
Indexer   Valerie Robbins
Composition   Tara A. Davis, John Patrus
Illustrator   Kathleen Fay Edwards, Melinda Moore Lytle, Lyssa Wald
Series Design   Jean Butterfield
Series Cover Design   Sarah F. Hinks

This book was composed with Corel VENTURA™ Publisher.

This book is dedicated to everyone who is willing to spend a little time learning something new. The effort is always worthwhile.

About the Author

Brian Underdahl is the award-winning author of more than 65 books on a wide range of computing-related topics, as well as numerous magazine and web site articles. He has appeared on a number of television programs and has taught a number of college-level computer classes.

When he is not at the keyboard, Brian may often be found preparing gourmet meals in the kitchen of the home he and his wife built in the mountains overlooking Reno, Nevada.

Contents at a Glance

Contents

Acknowledgments

Writing a successful book really takes a team effort. My name may be on the cover, but there are a lot of other people who played vital roles in making it happen.

A few of these very important people include Nancy Maragioglio, Athena Honore, and Lisa Wolters-Broder. I'd really like to thank them and all the other fine people at McGraw-Hill/Osborne for making this book possible. I'd also like to add very special thanks to Heather Hollaender at Macromedia for putting up with the ranting from people like me.

Introduction

Macromedia Flash is one of the best tools you will find for adding some special effects and animation to your web site. Not only does it produce highly efficient content, but virtually everyone who surfs the web is already equipped to view your Flash movies. Add the fun of seeing your own animated productions creating some multimedia splash, and you have a real winner!

Who Should Read This Book

This book was written on the assumption that you want to learn how to use Macromedia Flash MX 2004 but that you don't want to be intimidated by one of those books which is aimed at experienced Flash developers. I won't assume that you already know how to use Flash. Rather, I'm going to take a lot of care in making certain that I really do tell you what you need to know. If you want to learn how to make use of Flash to create content for your web site, this is the book you need.

How to Read This Book

This book was written to be read one module after the other, in succession. However, this is not necessary to your understanding of Macromedia Flash MX 2004. If you want to jump to a specific topic, please do so. Each module can stand alone, independent of all other modules. Modules will reference relevant topics in other modules as they come up.

The files that are referenced throughout the book can be downloaded from the McGraw-Hill/ Osborne web site at www.osborne.com.

What This Book Covers

This book is divided into 14 Modules and an appendix.

Module 1: Understanding Flash MX 2004

This module introduces you to Flash and gives you some ideas how you can use Flash.

Module 2: Learning the Flash Tools Panel

Here you will learn the basics of creating objects using the Flash toolbox. You will see how each of the drawing tools really function.

Module 3: Learning the Flash Panels

The Flash panels are essential to almost any task you wish to accomplish in Flash. In this module you learn how to use the panels as well as how to determine which panel you really need.

Module 4: Using the Timeline and Layers

Because Flash is far more than just a drawing program, you need ways to work with independent objects and to control the flow of your movies through time. In this module you learn how the timeline and layers work, and you see how to use them in creating your Flash animations.

Module 5: Drawing Objects

In this module I teach you how to create objects using the Flash tools. In addition, you learn how to manipulate those objects in your movies.

Module 6: Creating Animations

Animation is what changes Flash productions from simple, static images into exciting, interactive movies. In this module you learn how to create Flash animations and you also learn how to determine the type of animation you need for different purposes.

Module 7: Using Guides and Masks

When you want to move beyond the simplest level of Flash animations, you need to understand motion guides and masks. In this module you see how you can use these objects to create some very interesting effects such as scrolling text banners.

Module 8: Creating Symbols and Using the Library

One of the very important elements in making Flash so popular is the small file sizes of Flash movies. This efficiency means that Flash movies are easily downloaded without creating long download times. In this module you learn how to use some important Flash features to maximize the efficiency of your Flash movies.

Module 9: Using Imported Graphics

As great as Flash is, there are times when you may want to use imported graphics—such as images from your digital camera—in your Flash movies. In this module you not only learn how to do that, but you also learn some tricks for creating fancy effects by treating text as graphics.

Module 10: Adding Sounds to Your Movies

Sound is often an important element of a multimedia production. In this module you learn how to use sounds to add some audible interest to your Flash movies.

Module 11: Publishing Flash Movies

Flash movies are a whole lot more fun when you can share them with other people. In this module you learn what you need to know to publish your Flash movies and to place them on your web site.

Module 12: Learning Basic ActionScript Concepts

ActionScript is the programming language which you can use to control your Flash movies and to add some interactivity to them. In this module I introduce you to the basics of the ActionScript language.

Module 13: Learning Basic ActionScript Programming

In this module I show you how you can make use of basic ActionScript programming to gain more control over your Flash movies. You will see how even very simple ActionScript statements can do a lot for you.

Module 14: Learning More ActionScript Programming

In this module I take you a bit further along the way to using ActionScript in your Flash movies. You will learn such important tasks as how you can control the properties of objects using ActionScript, and how you can make your movies function the way you want with a little ActionScript programming.

Appendix A: Answers to the Mastery Check

Here you will find the answers to the questions I pose at the end of each chapter. In this way you can check to make certain that you have fully grasped the subjects you learned in each module.

Special Features

There are many special features in this book. All modules (chapters) open with a list of critical skills that each chapter sets out to fulfill.

Modules include *Notes* and *Tips*. These are short asides that relate to the topic at hand. *Ask the Expert* sections are in-depth explorations of related topics that take you beyond the normal text.

One or more *Projects* are located in each module, guiding you, step-by-step, through the creation of specific code. Annotated code listings are sprinkled throughout the text and projects to illustrate specific concepts and to emphasize portions of a template.

To help you quiz yourself along the way, simple *Progress Checks* are located throughout the text. A *Mastery Check* is included at the end of every chapter, providing a deeper analysis of what you have learned.

Module 1

Understanding Flash MX 2004

I f you're going to have a web site, you probably want people to visit it. To make this happen, your web site needs to be interesting—nothing will drive visitors away faster than a boring web site. Macromedia's Flash MX 2004 is a very popular tool for creating interesting and dynamic web sites. With Flash MX 2004, you can add animation and interactivity to your web site, and make people want to return. Of course, you need to learn how to use Flash MX 2004 to create all of that neat and interesting content for your web site. In this module, you will learn what you can do with Macromedia Flash MX 2004 movies to liven up your web site. In addition, you will learn about all of the basic elements of the Flash MX 2004 interface so that you will be ready to begin creating Flash MX 2004 movies right away.

Flash MX 2004, of course, is just one of the many tools that you may use in creating and maintaining your web site. In addition to Flash MX 2004, you will probably use a page layout program such as Macromedia Dreamweaver or Microsoft FrontPage. You may even use graphics editing software or sound editing software to create web page content. Even so, you will find that Flash MX 2004 has some pretty amazing capabilities all on its own.

CRITICAL SKILL
1.1 What Can You Do with Flash MX 2004?

Flash is everywhere. As you browse various web sites, you probably aren't even aware just how often you are viewing a Flash movie. You may be surprised to learn that the vast majority of web sites that contain animation use Flash. If you visit a web site and you see objects slide into place, you're probably viewing a Flash movie. If menus appear when the mouse pointer rolls over a particular point on the screen, that's probably a Flash movie, too. Just why is Flash so popular? It's because Flash can enable you to do so much with so little work.

TIP

Macromedia has a number of players available on their web site in the event that you need a different version. You will find them at www.macromedia.com/shockwave/download/alternates/.

Let's take a look at some of the things you can do with Flash MX 2004.

Create Web Images

The World Wide Web—or just "the web"—is a part of the Internet that truly cries out for visual creativity. When you surf the Web, you see thousands of different ideas about what makes an interesting web site. And yet, even with all of these divergent opinions, one notion is almost universally accepted—images and color are pretty much a requirement when you are creating a web site.

Ask the Expert

Q: I've heard the term "Shockwave" used. How does this relate to Flash MX 2004?

A: When the second version of what was to become Flash was introduced, it was called Shockwave. Later, the name was changed to Flash. Indeed, Flash MX 2004 movie files use an SWF file extension, which stands for Shock Wave Flash. Today, however, Macromedia has both a Flash Player and a Shockwave Player, and the term "Shockwave" is primarily used for content that is created using Macromedia Director MX. Though there has been considerable confusion along the way, none of the modern versions of Flash should be referred to as Shockwave.

Q: Do I need to be concerned about the earlier versions of Flash MX 2004?

A: Old Flash movies still sit in some of the moldy corners of the Web, but you won't encounter them very often. If you do, they will play just fine in the current version of the Flash Player. Your new movies may not always play in older versions of the Flash Player, but that probably won't be of much concern to you. For one thing, if any of your visitors are using an old version of the Flash Player and your movie requires a newer version, they can quickly and easily download the new version for free. In fact, depending on the browser they are using, they will probably be given the opportunity to automatically download a newer version of the Flash Player.

Flash MX 2004 has the tools you need to create colorful web images with very little effort. For example, here is a company logo I created for a web site in just a few minutes using Flash MX 2004. In this case, the illustration does not quite do justice to the logo because the actual logo uses simple Flash MX 2004 animation techniques to bounce the "radio signal" back and forth between the two antennas.

1

Understanding Flash MX 2004

NOTE

Flash MX 2004 offers a benefit that you may be unaware of. Images that you draw in Flash MX 2004 are created using *vector* graphics rather than *bitmaps*. Vector graphics are far superior to bitmap images in a number of important ways. Not only do vector graphic image files generally create far smaller file sizes than the equivalent bitmap images, but vector images can easily be scaled up or down in size without losing quality. When you scale bitmap images to a larger size, they tend to look very blocky (or *pixilated*).

Although this may come as a bit of a surprise, you cannot simply add Flash MX 2004 images to your web site. Many different programs can easily display various types of bitmap images, but vector graphics typically must be viewed using a special program. For Flash MX 2004 images, this special program is the Flash Player, which most people already have installed in their web browser. Flash MX 2004 images are saved as part of a Flash MX 2004 movie, and that Flash MX 2004 movie is what is placed on your web page. When your web browser encounters a Flash MX 2004 movie on a web page, the browser automatically loads the Flash Player so that the Flash MX 2004 movie (and the images it contains) can be viewed.

You do need to add a bit of HTML to the web page, but Flash MX 2004 automatically creates the necessary HTML code when you publish a Flash MX 2004 movie. You'll learn more about publishing Flash MX 2004 movies in Module 11.

TIP

Even though you must create a Flash MX 2004 movie in order to use graphics that you created in Flash MX 2004 on a web site, you will probably find that the Flash MX 2004 movie is smaller than a bitmap image file would be.

Animate Your Web Site

Let's face it, plain old web sites that simply sit there are boring. A little bit of animation can make quite a difference. Some nicely done animation—even if it is simply moving menu elements into place—makes your web site stand out from the rest.

Flash MX 2004 makes animation easy to create using a process known as *tweening*. Essentially, in this process you tell Flash MX 2004 where you want the animation to begin, and you tell it where you want the animation to end. Once you have done this, Flash MX 2004 automatically generates all the in-between frames. So, if it takes 24 frames to complete your animation, you may end up creating two of the frames, while Flash MX 2004 creates the other 22 frames. Obviously, this greatly reduces your workload.

For example, take a look at this animated sequence. Here, I'm moving the truck across the stage. I needed to create only one instance of the truck. I told Flash MX 2004 where I wanted the truck to begin, and then I told it where the truck should end. Once I did this, Flash MX 2004 took care of all the rest and generated all of the frames necessary to make it appear as though the truck were smoothly driving across the screen from one side to the other.

NOTE

In this illustration, I have turned on the *onion skin* view. This is a feature in Flash MX 2004 that enables you to see how your animations will look over the course of several frames. See Module 4 for more details on onion skin view.

Flash MX 2004 actually offers several different ways to move and reshape objects. As you will learn in Module 7, you can create a *motion guide* when you want to move an object along a path that isn't straight. In addition to *motion tweens,* which are used to move objects, you can also create *shape tweens.* These enable you to change the shapes of objects. You will learn about both types of tweens in Module 6.

TIP

In most cases, you're far more likely to use motion tweens than shape tweens. If you aren't sure which type of tween you need to use, you will almost always be correct to choose the motion tween.

Build Interactive Movies

In addition to using simple animation, you can use Flash MX 2004 to build interactive web sites. You could, for example, create a Flash MX 2004 movie that enables the visitor to choose between several different movie clips or even between different soundtracks. Because Flash MX 2004 is *object-oriented,* your movies already know how to interact with users. All you need to do is to tell your movies what you want them to do when the user does something like click a button. By the way, "object-oriented" is a programming term. In this context, it means that the things (objects) in your Flash movies have built-in capabilities that you can use without knowing how to create those capabilities.

NOTE

Interactivity can be defined in several different ways. Typically, however, when Flash MX 2004 developers talk about interactivity, they are talking about making their movies react to something that the user does. Other definitions might include a program that queries a database and acts based on the information found there, or programs that monitor a process (such as in an industrial chemical plant) and control machines or valves to maintain the proper operating conditions—but these latter definitions are well beyond the scope of this book.

It does take a small amount of ActionScript programming in order to add most interactivity to Flash MX 2004 movies. (ActionScript is the programming language that you can use to control various aspects of your Flash movies.) Don't let this worry you. As you'll learn later, Flash MX 2004 makes adding some ActionScript commands very easy because you can essentially just click and then make selections from list boxes. You don't have to become an expert ActionScript programmer to add simple interactivity to your Flash MX 2004 movies.

Here are some of the things you can do with interactivity in Flash MX 2004 movies:

- Enable web site visitors to select the movie they want to view
- Create games that allow users to drag and drop objects
- Add rewind buttons and other controls to allow users to control the playback
- Load different movies depending on when a visitor comes to your web site
- Allow visitors to mute the soundtrack of a movie
- Send information requests from visitors to an e-mail address

Of course, interactivity can take many other forms, too. If you can dream up an idea about how you would like your Flash MX 2004 movies to interact with a visitor, there is probably a fairly simple way to make it happen.

Display Buttons

Buttons, of course, are an interface element that virtually everyone understands. You probably don't have to explain to visitors that selecting (or clicking) a button will cause something to happen.

You can easily add buttons to your Flash MX 2004 movies either by creating your own buttons or by using some of the buttons that come along with Flash MX 2004, as shown next.

When you add buttons to a Flash MX 2004 movie, those buttons already know how to act. That is, they know that when a user clicks the button, something should happen.

Of course, when you add a button to a Flash MX 2004 movie, the button doesn't really know what you want to happen, only that it should respond to a mouse click. You have to tell the button what you want it to do. For example, if you want to create a button that rewinds the movie and starts it playing again at the beginning of the movie, you might add a line of ActionScript code that looks like this:

```
gotoAndPlay(1);
```

Believe it or not, that is all of the ActionScript programming you need to add to create your rewind button! Flash MX 2004 automatically handles all of the other details for you.

TIP

Flash MX 2004 comes with a number of prebuilt objects that you are free to use in your movies. For example, if you select Window | Other Panels | Common Libraries | Buttons from the Flash MX 2004 menu, you will be able to choose from a series of buttons you can drag and drop into your movies.

Transform Shapes

One of the animation techniques in Flash MX 2004 allows you to change an object from one shape into a totally different shape. This process is known as a *shape tween.* Here I am transforming a rectangle into a circle (and once again I am using the onion skin view so that you can more easily see how the tween is transforming the object):

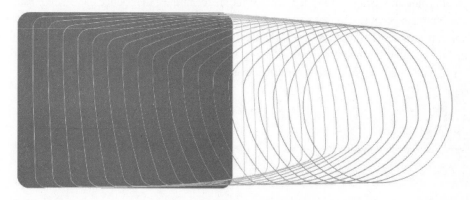

Ask the Expert

Q: Now I'm confused. I thought that shape tweens and motion tweens were totally different, but the example shows the rectangle to the left and the circle to the right. Is this a shape tween or a motion tween?

A: I can understand how this example might confuse you. When you are changing the shape of an object so that it becomes a different object, you use a shape tween. The original object and the final object don't have to be in the same position, however. In fact, when you consider that the two objects don't have to look anything like each other, it's easy to see why it would be very difficult to place them in precisely the same position. The thing to remember is that you use a motion tween to *move* an object and a shape tween to *morph* an object. Really, though, you won't need to worry about this until much later.

TIP

You can also transform an object back into the original shape or move it back into its original position. Often, this can create a very interesting effect. To accomplish this effect, you simply create a second tween that reverses the effect of the first tween. You will learn more about using tweens in Module 6.

Display Rolling Banner Text

You have no doubt seen rolling text banners on a number of web sites. These are often used to create a tickertape-style effect, where text scrolls into a text box from one side and scrolls out of the box on the other. This effect is used to display stock market results and news headlines, among other things.

In Flash MX 2004, creating a rolling text banner is quite easy. Basically, the effect requires you to combine a couple of Flash MX 2004 movie techniques to produce the desired result. You start with a motion tween that moves a text block across the stage. Then you add a *mask* that controls how much of the text is visible at any one time. When you do this, users cannot tell that the whole text block is moving—all they see is the portion of the text block that is currently visible through the mask, and this creates exactly the effect that you want.

NOTE

Masks are covered in Module 7.

It is quite easy to display predefined text in a rolling text block, but displaying something like a stock ticker or a scrolling headline ticker is quite a bit more involved. You will need to learn some advanced ActionScript techniques as well as some server-side programming to be able to supply the constantly updated text to your Flash MX 2004 movie. From a practical standpoint, you will probably find this project to be a lot harder than you might expect, and one that you will want to postpone until you have considerably more experience both with Flash MX 2004 and with programming in general.

Okay, so now that you have an idea about some of the things that you can do with Flash MX 2004, let's take a look at the various things you will see when you use Flash MX 2004.

Progress Check

1. What is the Flash MX 2004 term for an animation?

2. What type of images can you create in Flash MX 2004?

3. What type of view enables you to see several animation frames at once?

CRITICAL SKILL
1.2 Understanding Flash MX 2004's Basic Elements

As with any other program you might use on your computer, Flash MX 2004 has a number of basic elements that enable you to accomplish the tasks for which the program was designed. Here is an overview of some of the most important elements—we'll look at each of these in more detail shortly.

---

1. Tween
2. Vector
3. Onion skin

Tools panel   Layers   Timeline   Stage   Panels

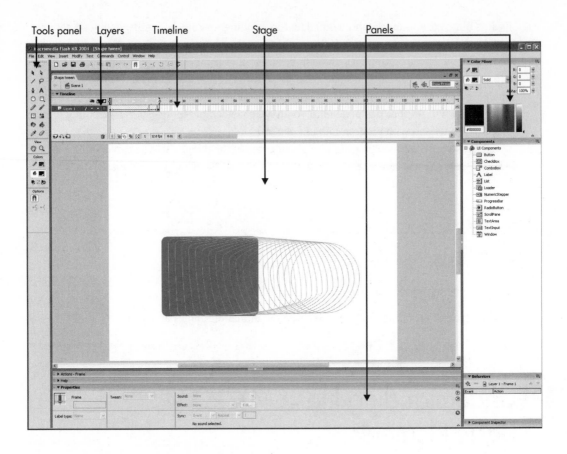

The Flash MX 2004 Stage

The stage is the area where you create your Flash MX 2004 movies. This is the white area that takes up most of the middle of the Flash MX 2004 window. When your movie plays, anything that is on the stage will be visible in the movie.

NOTE

By default, the Flash MX 2004 stage measures 550 pixels wide and 400 pixels high. "Pixel" is short for "picture element"—the smallest addressable dot on your computer display screen. The screen resolution of your computer monitor is also measured in pixels, with 800x600, 1024x768, 1280x1024, and 1600x1200 being some of the more common sizes.

Ask the Expert

Q: Can I change the size of the Flash MX 2004 stage?

A: Yes, you can modify the size of the stage to suit your needs. To do so, you can select Modify | Document from the Flash MX 2004 menu (or right-click the stage and choose Movie Properties from the pop-up menu). In any case, you will display the Document Properties dialog box shown here. You can then use the Width and Height boxes to set a new size for the stage.

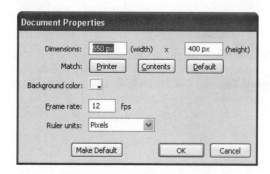

Q: Is there any reason why I can't simply make the stage the same size as my screen?

A: Actually, there are a lot of reasons why you wouldn't want to set the stage that large. For one thing, larger stage sizes result in larger movie files that take longer to load and may not play back smoothly. In addition, keep in mind that some users may be using a lower screen resolution, and this would cause your movie either to be distorted or to spill off the edges of their monitor screen. Finally, working with a stage that is too large can be difficult because either you will have to scroll a lot as you work on your movie, or you will have to zoom out so much that it will be difficult to position objects precisely.

The stage is surrounded by a gray area known as the *workspace*. It is perfectly acceptable for you to place objects in the workspace off the edge of the stage. Objects that are in the workspace but not on the stage won't appear in the movie unless they are moved onto the stage—just as actors in a play cannot be seen until they move out onto the stage.

TIP

Placing objects offstage can be very useful. If, for example, you want an object to cross the stage, the effect may be more realistic if the object starts from a completely offstage position. That way, the object will appear gradually as it moves onto the stage rather than suddenly appearing with no lead-in. Likewise, objects can complete their movements off the stage, too.

You can use the zoom control above the right side of the timeline to zoom in or out. You can also use the View menu to zoom in or out, or to select a specific magnification level.

TIP

The Show Frame and Fit In Window options in the zoom control are similar in that they both make the stage as large as possible given the currently visible workspace. However, the Show Frame option also makes scroll bars visible, and this can make it somewhat easier for you to work with offstage objects.

Progress Check

1. What is the normal size of the Flash MX 2004 stage?

2. What happens when an object moves off the stage?

The Timeline

The timeline is the Flash MX 2004 element that controls when things happen during the movie playback. Here I've marked off the important items you see on the timeline. (In this case, I have not shown the layers area that is always attached to the left side of the timeline—we will look at that element shortly.)

---

1. 550 by 400 pixels

2. It disappears from view.

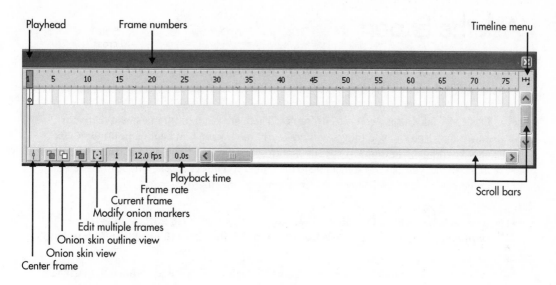

Playhead   Frame numbers   Timeline menu

Playback time
Frame rate
Current frame
Modify onion markers
Edit multiple frames
Onion skin outline view
Onion skin view
Center frame

Scroll bars

Here is a brief description of these important timeline elements:

● **Playhead**   You can drag the playhead to different frames to view the contents of those frames. You can also click a frame in the timeline to select that frame—this automatically moves the playhead to that frame.

● **Frame numbers**   These are your guide to working with the timeline, since they enable you to place objects in the correct frame.

● **Timeline menu**   This provides access to a number of options where you can choose timeline view settings.

● **Center frame**   This moves the current view of the timeline so that the current frame is centered in the visible area of the timeline.

● **Onion skin view**   This displays several frames before and after the current frame, using lightly shaded versions of the objects on the stage so that you can get a feel for the animation sequence.

● **Onion skin outline view**   This also displays an onion skin view of several frames, but it uses wire-frame outlines rather than filled objects.

● **Edit multiple frames**   This enables you to edit the animation in several frames.

● **Modify onion markers**   This displays a menu that allows you to choose how many frames to display in onion skin view.

● **Current frame**   This shows the frame number of the currently selected frame.

Ask the Expert

Q: When I try to select a frame in the timeline, the playhead stays at frame 1. Why can't I make the new frame the current frame?

A: Flash MX 2004 uses two types of frames. There are plain old frames, and there are *keyframes*. You can add things only to keyframes. When you begin a new movie, the only keyframe is in frame 1. If you want to select another frame and make it the current frame so that you can add something to the frame, you must add a keyframe to the selected frame using the Insert | Timeline | Keyframe command.

Q: I opened the Insert | Timeline menu, and I see there is also a Blank Keyframe command. Why would I choose this command rather than the Keyframe command?

A: When you add a keyframe using the Insert | Timeline | Keyframe command, Flash MX 2004 copies the contents of the previous keyframe into the new keyframe (and into all of the plain frames between the two keyframes). In most cases, you want to copy the contents in order to make creating an animation sequence easier. But if you don't want to copy the contents of the previous keyframe, just use Insert | Timeline | Blank Keyframe, and you will create an empty keyframe where you can add whatever you want.

- **Frame rate**   This shows the number of frames per second that are displayed in the current movie.

- **Playback time**   This shows how many seconds will have elapsed when the current frame is played.

- **Scroll bars**   These enable you to see frames or layers that are not currently displayed.

TIP

Most animations are easier to create if you start by completely creating the object in the first keyframe before you add the second keyframe. That way, you won't have to copy and paste the object, since Flash MX 2004 will automatically copy it if it exists before the second keyframe is added to the timeline.

Progress Check

1. What type of frame can you use when you want to add something to your movie?

2. What does the playhead position represent?

Layers

Layers are like transparent overlays on the stage. They enable objects to act independently of objects on other layers, and they also control whether objects are visible—objects on layers that are in front of other layers hide the objects on those other layers when they cross in front of them.

Here is a closer look at the layers area (this is actually an integral part of the timeline and cannot be separated from the timeline):

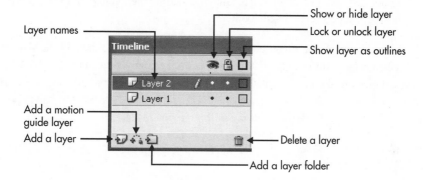

Let's take a look at each of these items:

● **Layer names**   These are the names of the layers. You can change the names by double-clicking the layer name. Most Flash MX 2004 developers name the layers to indicate their contents or purpose.

● **Add a layer**   Click this button to add a new layer. Since all objects on a single layer must have the same animation effects, this enables you to create objects that function independently of each other.

---

1. A keyframe
2. The current frame of the movie

● **Add a motion guide layer**   This enables you to create a guide layer so that you can move objects in a path that is not necessarily a straight line. Objects on guide layers do not appear in your movie once it has been published.

● **Add a layer folder**   This enables you to add folders to help organize the layers.

● **Delete a layer**   This removes the currently selected layer and any objects it contains. Use this with caution so that you don't accidentally delete objects you need.

● **Show or hide layer**   Clicking in this column toggles the visibility of the layers. Hiding layers may make it easier to create objects by reducing the visual confusion. Clicking the icon toggles all layers. To toggle a single layer, click in this column within the layer itself.

● **Lock or unlock layer**   Click in this column to lock the layers to prevent any changes. Locking a specific layer is a good way to avoid accidentally making changes to that layer—especially if you inadvertently select the wrong layer to work in.

● **Show layer as outlines**   Click this column to show the objects as wire-frame outlines rather than as filled objects. This may be useful when you want to see how objects on different layers relate to each other.

Extra layers do not affect the size of the published movie, since Flash MX 2004 flattens published movies into a single layer. That is one reason you need to save your Flash MX 2004 movie project in addition to publishing the movie—your movie project file (the FLA file) contains all of the layers so that you can make whatever modifications you want. If you import a published movie file (the SWF file), everything will be in one layer.

TIP

Always double-check to make certain you have selected the correct layer before making any changes. It is very easy to accidentally make changes to the wrong layer if you don't remember to check before you modify something.

The Tools Panel

The Flash MX 2004 Tools Panel contains all of the tools you need for drawing or selecting objects. Here is a closer look at the Tools Panel.

NOTE

For this illustration, I *undocked* the Tools Panel by dragging it away from the left edge of the Flash MX 2004 window. Depending on your screen resolution setting, you may find either the docked or the undocked option preferable.

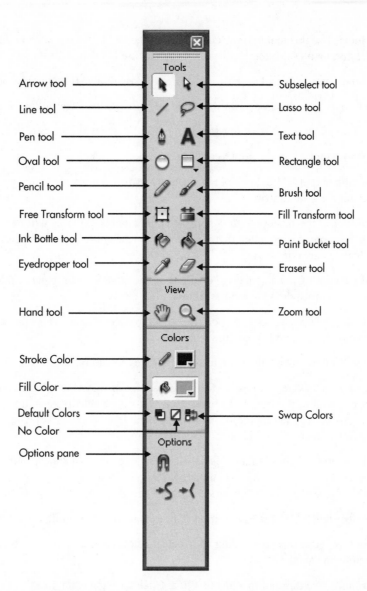

Let's take a look at the purpose of each of the tools in the Flash MX 2004 Tools panel:

- **Arrow tool**   Use this tool to select objects. You can click an object to select it, double-click to select the object and all of its components, or drag the Arrow tool to create a selection box to select everything within the box.

- **Line tool**   Use this tool to draw lines. Hold down SHIFT as you draw to draw lines that are perfectly horizontal, vertical, or at 45 degrees.

- **Pen tool**   Use this tool to draw curved lines. The Pen tool draws *Bézier* curves, which are curved lines with selection handles that you can use to control the curve.

- **Oval tool**   Use this tool to draw oval objects. Hold down SHIFT to draw perfect circles.

- **Pencil tool**   Use this line to draw individual points or lines that follow an irregular path.

- **Free Transform tool**   Use this tool to modify the shape of objects.

- **Ink Bottle tool**   Use this tool to modify the color of a line.

- **Eyedropper tool**   Use this tool to select a color from an object so that you can match the same color in your drawings.

- **Hand tool**   Use this tool to drag the stage (and all objects). This will be most useful if you have zoomed in so much that you cannot see the entire stage and you want to work in a different area of the stage.

- **Stroke Color**   Click this icon to open the stroke color selector pane so that you can choose a color for drawing strokes (lines).

- **Fill Color**   Click this icon to open the fill color selector pane. This enables you to select a fill color or gradient fill for drawn objects.

- **Default Colors**   Click this icon to set the stroke color to black and the fill color to white.

- **No Color**   Click here to change the current stroke or fill color—depending on which of the two is currently selected—to none. You may not be able to select this when it makes no sense—such as setting the stroke color to none (that is, invisible) when you are drawing a line rather than a filled object.

- **Options pane**   Many of the tools have optional settings that appear in the Options pane of the Tools Panel. To see what an option does, hold your mouse pointer over the option icon briefly until a tool tip appears next to the mouse pointer.

- **Subselect tool**   Use this tool to modify lines that you drew with the Pen tool.

- **Lasso tool**   Use this tool to drag an irregular selection area. This selects any objects that are within the area.

- **Text tool**   Use this tool to add a text box. Click once to create a text box that can expand horizontally, or drag to create a text box that has a fixed width.

- **Rectangle tool**   Use this tool to draw rectangles. Hold down SHIFT to draw perfect squares. Depending on the options you choose, the rectangle may have either square or rounded corners.

- **Brush tool**   Use this tool to draw freehand brushstrokes. This tool has a number of options that control the effect that is created.

- **Fill Transform tool**   Use this tool to modify the shape and positioning of gradient fills.

- **Paint Bucket tool**   Use this tool to add or modify the fill color or gradient fill inside an object.

- **Eraser tool**   Use this tool to erase areas of a drawing.

- **Zoom tool**   Use this tool to zoom in or out on a drawing.

- **Swap Colors**   Click this icon to swap the fill and stroke colors.

NOTE

In Module 2, you will learn the specifics of using each of the tools in the Flash MX 2004 Tools Panel.

If you find that you have made a mistake, select Edit | Undo immediately to undo the error. Some actions cannot be undone, but most things that you might do with the tools in the Flash MX 2004 Tools Panel can be undone.

TIP

You can set the number of *undo levels*—the number of changes that can be undone— by selecting Edit | Preferences and entering a number in the Undo Levels box. Don't set this value too high, though, because Flash MX 2004 must save all of the changes in memory in case you might want to undo a whole series of actions. In most cases, 100 undo levels should be more than you would ever need.

In most cases, a tool remains selected after you have used it once so that you can reuse the same tool, but this is not always the case. Get in the habit of taking a quick glance at the Tools Panel to see what is selected, and you will find yourself needing to rely upon the Edit | Undo command much less often!

The Flash MX 2004 drawing tools create vector images rather than bitmap ones. This is important to you for a number of reasons. Vector drawings generally take far less file space, so your movies load faster and run a bit more smoothly. In addition, objects that are drawn as vector images can be scaled up or down freely without losing quality.

Because the Flash MX 2004 drawing tools create vector images, you may notice that Flash MX 2004 sometimes "cleans up" the lines that you draw. When it does this, it is attempting to simplify the lines so that they have fewer curves, since this takes less memory.

Ask the Expert

Q: When I try out the Line tool, the line that appears is too thin. But I don't see an option for changing the line width. What can I do?

A: Like many things in Flash MX 2004, the options are there if you know where to look. In this case, you may need to open the Properties panel using the Window | Properties command to set the options for line drawing. The line drawing options appear in the Properties panel whenever a tool that draws lines is selected, or when a line that has already been drawn is selected. You may not need to use the Flash MX 2004 menu to display the Properties panel, though, since it normally appears near the bottom of the Flash screen. The panels are described in the next section.

TIP

When you draw objects in your Flash MX 2004 movies, don't forget to place objects that you want to act independently of each other on separate layers.

The Panels

Flash MX 2004 makes extensive use of *panels*. These are very similar to dialog boxes, but there are some differences. For example, panels do not have OK or Close buttons. That's because a panel does not need to be closed in order to apply any selections that you may have made in it.

It's not really important that you study the purpose of each panel in detail at this point. As you progress through the modules, you will become familiar with the panels as you need to use them. You will probably find yourself using the Properties panel most often since it enables you to modify the properties of whatever object is currently selected. You will no doubt also make use of the Help panel, too.

TIP

Many of the panels have keystroke shortcuts that you can use to open the panel without going through the Flash MX 2004 menus. One of the best ways to learn these shortcuts is to watch the menus as you open and use them. When a keystroke shortcut is available, it will be listed to the right of the command on the menu.

CRITICAL SKILL

1.3 Create Your Own Animations

One of the best ways to get a feel for how Flash MX 2004 helps you create animations is to try it yourself. It isn't necessary to get fancy with this first project, but at least you will get a chance to get your feet wet.

Project 1-1 Creating a Simple Animation

In this case, you will create a simple Flash MX 2004 movie that has a box that moves from one corner of the stage to another corner. Although this is a very simple animation, it does provide you with the basics that you will use later as you create more complex movies.

Step by Step

1. Make certain that you have Flash MX 2004 open and that there is nothing on the stage. If necessary, select File | New from the Flash MX 2004 menu to open a new, blank movie. (If the Start page appears, click New Flash Document to display an empty stage.)

2. Click the Rectangle tool in the Tools Panel so that this tool is selected. You must select a tool before you can draw with it.

3. Near the lower-left corner of the stage, draw a small rectangle. The exact positioning and size are not important for this project.

4. Click the Arrow tool to select it (this also deselects the Rectangle tool since only one tool can be selected at a time).

5. Double-click the rectangle you just drew so that both the fill and the stroke are selected. You may find it easier to simply draw a selection box that surrounds the entire rectangle. Either way your goal is to make sure that you have selected the entire object.

6. Select the Modify | Group command. The object needs to be grouped in order to have a motion tween applied.

7. Click frame 24 in the timeline to select the frame. You can tell when the frame is selected because the frame will then change to dark blue. The choice of frame 24 is arbitrary. In this case, we want the animation to last for 2 seconds, and at the default frame rate of 12 frames per second, frame 24 will produce the desired result.

8. With frame 24 still selected, choose Insert | Timeline | Keyframe from the Flash MX 2004 menu to add a keyframe to frame 24. Remember that you can only make changes within keyframes.

(continued)

9. Drag the rectangle from the lower-left corner to the upper-right corner of the stage. This will be where the rectangle finishes its movement in frame 24.

10. Click the timeline between frames 1 and 24 to select a frame in that range. You do not have to select all of the frames between frame 1 and frame 24—selecting any of the frames between the two keyframes is good enough.

11. Select Insert | Timeline | Create Motion Tween from the menu. This will add a solid arrow that points from frame 1 to frame 24 in the timeline.

12. Select Control | Test Movie to try out your animation. Your rectangle will move from the lower left to the upper right of the stage and then jump back and start again. Don't worry about the fact that your movie repeats endlessly; you will learn how to control this behavior to suit your needs in later modules.

13. Click the lower Close button to close the Flash Player and return to the Flash MX 2004 development environment.

Project Summary

Believe it or not, you have just created your first Flash MX 2004 movie! In this project, you selected tools from the Tools Panel, used those tools to create an object, added a keyframe to the timeline, and created a motion tween. With these few simple steps, you have used the basic elements of Flash MX 2004 to produce an animation in almost no time.

For reference, your movie should look something like this (I've turned on the onion skin view so that you can see the animation effect). Don't worry if your movie looks a little different from the illustration—as long as it is somewhat similar, you have successfully completed the project.

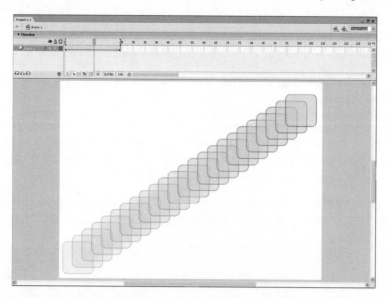

✔ *Module 1 Mastery Check*

1. The area in Flash MX 2004 where you draw objects you want to appear in your movie is the _____.

2. The tool that you use to select objects is the _____ tool.

3. Which of the following is not something you can do with Flash MX 2004?

    A. Create interactive buttons

    B. Move objects across the stage

    C. Lay out a trip route using a GPS receiver

    D. Display a scrolling text banner

4. To create a perfect circle with the Oval tool, you hold down the _____ key.

5. The dialog box–like objects that you use to set options in Flash MX 2004 are called _____.

6. The two types of tweens you can create in Flash MX 2004 are _____ and _____ tweens.

7. If you want to animate two objects independently of each other, you would place them on separate _____.

8. Before you can place an object in frame 24 of the timeline, you must insert a _____.

9. When a button in your movie responds to a user's mouse click, that response is known as _____.

10. To draw a box on the stage, you would use the _____ tool.

11. The _____ panel enables you to change the characteristics of drawn objects.

12. If you use the standard settings, a 48-frame movie will take _____ seconds to complete.

13. You can reverse most actions that you have performed in Flash MX 2004 by using the _____ command.

14. The view of the stage that shows how an animation will appear over the span of several frames is called the _____ view.

15. For someone to view a Flash MX 2004 movie that you have placed on your web site, they must have a copy of the _____ installed on their computer.

Module 2

Learning the
Flash Tools Panel

When you create a movie using Flash, it's likely that you will draw nearly all of the objects in your movie by using the tools in the Flash Tools panel. Most of these tools are relatively easy to understand and use, but if you want to get the best results from your efforts, it is important to know exactly what to expect from each tool. In this module, you will learn how to get the results you want from those tools so you can produce the best possible movie.

CRITICAL SKILL
2.1 Learning the Tools Panel

The Flash Tools panel holds all of the tools that you use to draw objects within Flash. As this shows, the Tools panel is divided into four different areas:

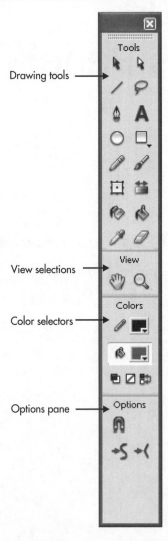

Drawing tools

View selections

Color selectors

Options pane

TIP

If the Tools panel does not appear in the Flash window, select Window | Tools from the Flash menu to display the Tools panel.

For most purposes, of course, you will make extensive use of the drawing tools area of the Tools panel. This does not mean, however, that the rest of the Tools panel is just taking up space. Each of the Tools panel areas serves a very useful purpose that you will learn about in this module.

Selecting the Tools

The Flash Tools panel is really intended to be used with the mouse. That is, you simply click the tool that you want to use in the Tools panel, and this selects the tool. The currently selected tool has a depressed appearance as though it were pushed in. When you move the mouse over a tool, the tool's button looks as though it were above the surface of the Tools panel. In addition, a tooltip that gives the tool's name appears briefly as you move the mouse over a tool.

If you do not see a tooltip after you hold the mouse pointer over a tool for a brief time, the tooltips may be turned off. To re-enable the tooltips, select the Edit | Preferences command to display the Preferences dialog box, as shown here. Click the Show Tooltips check box to select it, and then click the OK button to close the dialog box.

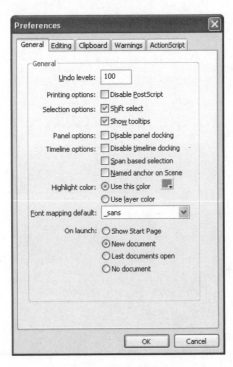

Though the Tools panel is primarily designed for use with the mouse, you can use keyboard commands to select the tools. Table 2-1 lists the keyboard shortcuts that you can use to select each of the tools.

Selecting Tool Options

When you select certain tools from the Tools panel, various items may appear in the Options pane. In fact, half of the tools have options that you can use to modify how the tool functions. For those tools that have options, you simply select the option that you want to use with the tool.

TIP

All of the options have tooltips that appear when the mouse pointer is over the option icon.

Tool	Keyboard Shortcut
Arrow tool	V
Line tool	N
Pen tool	P
Oval tool	O
Pencil tool	Y
Free Transform tool	Q
Ink Bottle tool	S
Eyedropper tool	I
Hand tool	H
Subselect tool	A
Lasso tool	L
Text tool	T
Rectangle tool	R
Brush tool	B
Fill Transform tool	F
Paint Bucket tool	K
Eraser tool	E
Zoom tool	M or Z

Table 2-1 Keyboard Shortcuts for Selecting Tools Panel Tools

In some cases, the options are toggles. That is, you can click the option icon to turn the option on or off. If an option icon is depressed, that means the option is selected. Some tools have multiple options that you can select in combination with each other.

You will see several different types of options in the Options pane. For example, the options for the Brush tool shown here are of three different types. Clicking the icon at the top left displays a list of choices. The top-right icon is a simple toggle that can be either on or off. Clicking the arrow to the right of one of the boxes in the lower section displays different sizes and shapes that you can choose. You will learn more about the specifics of each of these options later in this module.

NOTE

Some of the tool options are available only in certain circumstances. For example, the Smooth and Straighten options for the Arrow tool apply only when you have already selected a line. These options wouldn't make any sense when you are using the Arrow tool to make a selection, so they are unavailable when nothing is currently selected.

We will look at the individual tool options as we examine each tool in detail in the next section. Remember that the options are specific to the individual tools.

Progress Check

1. What do you call options that switch between on and off each time you select them?

2. What two methods can you use to select tools?

---

1. Toggles
2. Clicking the tool or pressing the tool's hot key

CRITICAL SKILL
2.2 Using the Tools

To create a drawing, you begin by selecting the appropriate tool from the Tools panel. Next you choose the options from the Options pane. Let's take a look at each of the drawing tools to see how each works.

TIP

It is always a good idea to check the current color selections before you begin using one of the drawing tools. That way, you can be sure that you have selected the correct stroke and fill colors before you begin drawing. Remember that the color selections remain the same as you select different tools (rather than reverting to the colors that you were using the last time you used the newly selected tool).

Drawing with the Line Tool

The Line tool draws straight lines as you hold down the mouse button and drag the mouse from the starting point to the ending point of the line. When you draw with the Line tool, Flash draws the line using the currently selected stroke color, width, and style. You can use the Stroke height slider in the Properties panel to set the line width.

TIP

Remember to check the Properties panel to see the current line drawing settings for color, width, and line style. Doing so before you begin drawing can save you a lot of frustration.

If you want the line to be perfectly horizontal, vertical, or at a 45-degree angle, hold down the SHIFT key as you draw the line. As you hold down SHIFT, the line will snap to the 45-degree angle that is closest to the mouse pointer. That is, the line can be at 0 degrees, 45 degrees, 90 degrees, 135 degrees, and so on. If you do not hold down SHIFT, the line will simply extend from the starting point of the drag to the current mouse pointer position.

TIP

To choose a custom line style, click the Custom button in the Properties panel. You can open this panel using the Window | Properties command.

Ask the Expert

Q: When I try to draw a line, Flash automatically connects the line to the nearest existing line. Why is this and what can I do to prevent this from happening?

A: By default, Flash snaps the starting point of a line to the nearest line so that you don't have to be quite so precise when you are drawing with the mouse. This is intended to make drawing with a mouse somewhat easier, but it can also make it difficult for you to create just the effect you want if, for some reason, you don't want the lines to automatically connect. You can control this behavior using the Preferences dialog box shown here. You can display this dialog box using the Edit | Preferences command. Then click the Editing tab to choose the drawing settings you prefer. Click OK to close the dialog box when you have made your selections. You can also use the Snap To Objects icon in the Options pane to turn the snapping on or off without changing the selection in the Preferences dialog box.

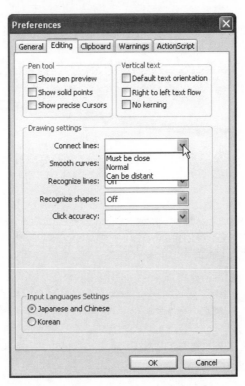

(continued)

Q: Sometimes when I am drawing a line I see a large circle at the end of the line. What does this mean?

A: Flash indicates the "snap to" position with a large circle. As you are drawing a line, when the large circle appears, it means that if you release the mouse button at that point, the line will snap to the point in the center of the large circle—even if this point is some distance from the end of the mouse pointer. This is intended to make it easier for you to draw objects, since you don't have to be quite as precise in your placement of the mouse pointer, and you can still connect the lines.

Once you have drawn a line, you can add to the line by clicking the endpoint of the line with the Line tool and then dragging to the new ending point, as shown here. By doing this, you can create a series of straight line segments that are connected via their endpoints.

 TIP

To move an existing line, select it with the Arrow tool, and then drag it to the new location. To modify the angle of the junction between two joined lines, use the Subselect tool to drag the junction to a different position.

Progress Check

1. How can you make a line be perfectly vertical, horizontal, or at a 45-degree angle?

2. How do you join lines?

---

1. Hold down SHIFT as you draw.
2. Click the end of the existing line and drag from there.

Drawing with the Rectangle Tool

You use the Rectangle tool to draw rectangular boxes—objects that have two vertical and two horizontal sides. The rectangles can have square or rounded corners depending on the settings you choose.

When you select the Rectangle tool, the Options pane displays the Round Rectangle Radius icon. This option enables you to create rectangles with rounded corners rather than square ones. When you click this icon, Flash displays the Rectangle Settings dialog box shown here. You can enter a value in the text box to specify the amount of rounding you want. Specify 0 for square corners, or a number up to 999 for round ones. You can also use the UP ARROW and DOWN ARROW keys while you are drawing with the Rectangle tool to change the roundness of the corners.

Rectangle Settings
Corner radius: [ ] points
OK
Cancel

NOTE

The corner rounding value you enter is a "sticky" value. That is, Flash will remember the value you last entered and use it the next time you draw a rectangle—even if it is not during the same session.

The Options pane also displays the Snap To Objects icon when the Rectangle tool is selected. This option works in exactly the same manner as it does when the Line tool is selected.

To draw a rectangle with equal-length horizontal and vertical sides, hold down SHIFT as you draw the rectangle. If you have set the corner rounding to 0, this will produce a perfect square.

When you draw a rectangle, the lines around the rectangle are separate from the fill. Depending on the corner rounding setting, there may be four, six, or eight separate line segments around a rectangle:

- There will be four line segments if the corners of the rectangle are square.

- There will be six line segments if the rounding value is very high and the opposite sides of the rectangle are too close to allow for a straight line between two corners. The reason this makes for six segments is that even though the rounded ends of the rectangle do not have straight lines between the corners, each of the four rounded corner segments remain independent of each other.

- There will be eight line segments for most rectangles with rounded corners because each corner will have a curved line segment and each side will normally have a straight line segment.

The reason the number of line segments around a rectangle is significant relates directly to how those segments act when you select the rectangle object. If you click once inside the rectangle, you will select the fill without selecting any of the lines. If you double-click inside the rectangle, you will select the entire rectangle, including any lines that surround it. But if you click one of the line segments, you will select only that one segment. For example, here I have selected several of the eight line segments around this rectangle and dragged them away from the edges of the rectangle.

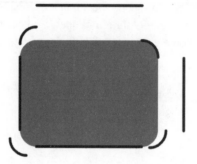

TIP

You can use the Subselect tool to modify the curves and lines of objects that you draw using the Rectangle tool. For example, you can change a square-cornered rectangle into a triangle by dragging one of the corners onto an adjacent corner with the Subselect tool.

Progress Check

1. How can you round the corners of a rectangle?

2. How many lines segments can there be when you draw with the Rectangle tool?

Drawing with the Oval Tool

The Oval tool draws objects that are either ellipses or circles, depending on how you use the tool. As with the other drawing tools, you draw with the Oval tool by dragging the mouse

---

1. Using the Rectangle Settings dialog box or the UP ARROW and DOWN ARROW keys
2. There can be four, six, or eight.

pointer from the starting point to the ending point. As you drag, Flash displays an outline view that shows where the object will appear.

TIP

Remember to hold down SHIFT if you want to draw a perfect circle.

Drawing an ellipse or a circle can be a little confusing at first. The reason for this is that the points where you begin and end the drag are not actually on the resulting ellipse or circle. Rather, the starting and ending drag points are at the corners of the *bounding box*. This is a normally invisible box that extends to the *bounds*—the outer edges—of a drawn object. All objects you draw in Flash have a bounding box, but you normally aren't aware of the bounding box because it doesn't appear on the screen unless you make a special effort to display it.

To get a better feel for how the bounding box relates to an ellipse or a circle, try this exercise:

1. Select the Oval tool and draw a fairly large ellipse on the stage. You will want this ellipse to extend almost to the edges of the stage with just a small white space around each side.

2. Select the Arrow tool and draw a selection box around the entire ellipse so that both the fill and the stroke are selected.

3. Use the Modify | Group command to group the fill and the stroke. Doing so will display the bounding box shown here (whenever a grouped object is selected, the bounding box appears).

4. Select the Oval tool again (you may also want to select a different fill color to make the end result stand out a bit more clearly).

5. Carefully place the mouse pointer over one of the corners of the bounding box, and then drag the mouse pointer to the bounding box corner that is diagonal from the corner where you started. Notice how the new ellipse outline exactly matches the existing ellipse. This clearly demonstrates how the bounding box is related to the ellipse.

TIP

You may want to try this exercise with a slight modification—placing the two ellipses on separate layers. That way, you can toggle the visibility of one of the layers to see that the two ellipses are indeed identical. To toggle the visibility of a layer, click the dot in the column below the eye symbol in the layers area to the left of the timeline.

Progress Check

1. Which objects have bounding boxes?

2. How can you display the bounding box?

Adding Text with the Text Tool

Text is often an important part of any web site. Flash provides the Text tool that you can use to add text to your movies. Text can be stand-alone, or it may be something that you add to another object.

There are two different ways to use the Text tool:

- If you select the Text tool and then simply click where you want the text to begin, Flash creates a text box that initially is one character wide. As you type, the text box expands horizontally to fit whatever text you add, even if it has to expand off the stage, as shown here. Unless you press ENTER, all of the text will appear on a single line that may extend well past the right edge of the stage. This type of text box is easy to identify by the small circle in the upper-right corner of the text box.

This text box can expand horizontally

1. All drawn objects
2. Group the object.

Ask the Expert

Q: Which type of text box do I need to create for a scrolling banner?

A: That actually depends on the direction you want to scroll the text. If you want a single-line banner that scrolls right to left, use a text box that can expand to the right to fit all of your text, and then make certain that you type everything on one line. If you want to create a scrolling banner that scrolls lines up from the bottom, create a fixed-width text box.

Q: I want to use a different font and type style in my text box. How can I control the appearance of the text in my text box?

A: Use the Properties panel to control all aspects of text appearance. You open this panel using the Window | Properties command. Be sure to change the settings before you begin adding text, because otherwise they will not apply to the current text. To change the properties of an existing text box, select the text in the text box and then modify the settings in the Properties panel.

● If you drag out a text box rather than simply clicking, Flash creates a text box with a fixed width. When you add text to this type of text box, words wrap to the next line if they cannot fit on the current line. This type of text box expands downward to accommodate additional lines of text as necessary. You can identify this type of text box by the small square in the upper-right corner of the text box, as shown here:

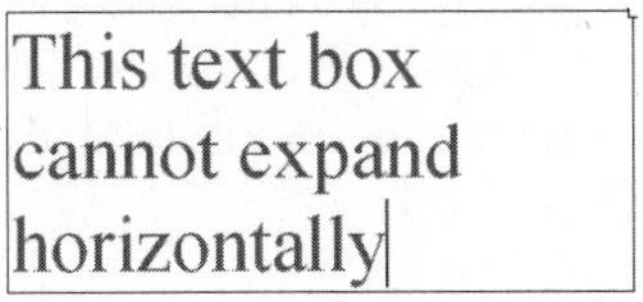

This text box
cannot expand
horizontally

When you are creating text for use in your Flash movies, it is important to remember that Flash does not automatically check the spelling of your text. If you misspell a word, Flash won't provide you with any clues to let you know that something is incorrect. To avoid having spelling errors appear in your movies, use the Text | Check Spelling command. You may need to modify the spell check settings using the Spelling Setup dialog box, as shown here. To display this dialog box, select the Text | Spelling Setup command. You will need to select the Check Text Fields Content option if you want Flash to check the spelling in your text boxes.

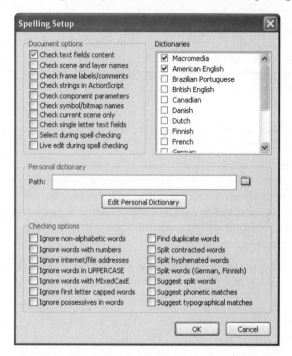

Flash uses the current text option settings whenever you add a new text box to the current movie. That is, if you used the Properties panel to select a different type size or font, Flash will use that same font and type size for subsequent text boxes until you make another change in these settings. You will learn more about the panels in Module 3.

Progress Check

1. If you want to set a specific width for a text box, how should you create the text box?

2. How can you tell if a text box will expand horizontally?

1. Circle in Drag the box to the width you want.
2. It has a small square in the upper-right corner.

Drawing with the Pencil Tool

The Pencil tool draws any shape of line that you want. Unlike the Line tool or the Pen tool, the Pencil tool follows whatever path you want—no matter how crooked it might be. This is the tool that you will want to use to add small details to objects when the other drawing tools seem just a little too confining.

When you select the Pencil tool, you will have three optional settings for how the tool functions, as shown here:

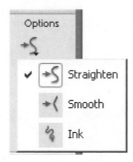

These three options are

- **Straighten** When you select this mode, Flash converts the lines you draw into connected straight line segments.

- **Smooth** When you select this mode, Flash converts your lines into smooth curves.

- **Ink** In this mode, Flash applies the least amount of smoothing to the line so that it remains fairly close to what you actually drew.

In most cases, you probably won't notice too much difference between the three options. The Straighten option will probably produce the best results if you want fairly straight lines, while the Smooth option will help the most if you are trying to draw curves. The Ink option will generally produce the most ragged-looking lines, but it will also allow you to create the finest detail.

NOTE

Flash always applies some smoothing to any lines that you draw. This is done to reduce the complexity of the lines and thereby reduce the size of the published movie file. Lines that are smoother require less space to define mathematically. In the vector drawings you create in Flash, all lines and fills are defined mathematically, so simplifying the lines is an important factor in making your movies smaller and faster loading.

It is very important that you understand that Flash applies the current settings from the Properties panel to all lines that you draw, no matter which tool you are using. If you have selected settings in the Properties panel for use with the Line tool or the Pen tool, those same settings will also apply to the Pencil tool.

Drawing with the Brush Tool

The Brush tool acts like a paintbrush. With this tool, you can draw any type of object that you want. The Brush tool uses the fill color selection, and this means that you can paint with gradient fills if you want (gradient fills are multicolor fills that you can use in place of solid colors).

You can choose any of five different painting modes when you use the Brush tool as shown here. These include the following:

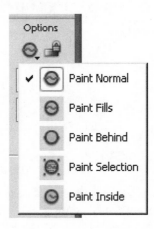

- **Paint Normal**   Choose this mode to simply paint wherever you drag the Brush tool.

- **Paint Fills**   In this mode, the Brush tool paints only when it is over the fill of an object. The lines are untouched.

- **Paint Behind**   Use this mode when you want to paint the background while leaving any objects untouched.

- **Paint Selection**   When you choose this mode, the Brush tool paints only objects that are selected.

- **Paint Inside**   This mode paints inside the first object that you click with the Brush tool, but leaves other areas untouched.

TIP

Rather than using the Paint Behind mode, you might want to consider painting your background on a separate layer that sits behind the layers where the objects are. That way, you will have more flexibility to move the objects without having to redo the background.

In addition to choosing the painting mode for the Brush tool, you can select the brush size and brush shape from the drop-down boxes. Both of these boxes offer a wide variety of choices that should suit all of your needs.

The fourth Brush tool option deserves some special attention. The Lock Fill option is a toggle, so the only choices are on or off. This option serves a useful purpose only if you are using a gradient fill.

When the Lock Fill option is on, the first place that you begin painting with the Brush tool becomes the anchor for all subsequent areas that you paint with the Brush tool. That is, as you paint additional areas, the fill continues as if the two areas were connected rather than restarting the fill in the new area. You may, however, find the Lock Fill option a bit hard to use because it begins the fill at the last place you painted when you turned on the option. This may not be what you want in all cases.

TIP

I strongly recommend that you practice with the Lock Fill option until you become comfortable with it. First, draw some rectangles or circles, and then select the Brush tool. Use the fill color selector to choose one of the gradient fills. Finally, try painting with the Lock Fill option on and with it off to get a feel for how the two settings differ.

Drawing with the Pen Tool

The Pen tool enables you to draw smooth curved lines. The name for this type of line is a Bézier curve. When you draw with the Pen tool as shown here, each point on the curve has both an anchor position (the place where you click) and a handle that you drag to produce the curve.

Creating a smooth curve in the exact shape you want can be a tricky proposition. Each time you click and drag, you are creating both a direction and a *force vector* for the curve. The further away from the initial click point that you drag the handle, the stronger the force vector that is produced at the initial click point. Stronger force vectors make the line (on the opposite side of the click point) stay closer to the departure angle for a longer distance. By moving the handle around and away from the click point, you can shape the curve just the way you want.

When you are drawing with the Pen tool, you can create a closed shape by clicking the initial point on the line. When you do, Flash creates a smooth curve to that point from the last point on the curve. If you have selected a fill color or gradient, Flash also fills the shape with that color or gradient.

It can be difficult to get exactly the effect you want with the Pen tool, but Flash offers another tool that is designed specifically for modifying curves. The Subselect tool works along with the Pen tool to enable you to modify curves that you have drawn with the Pen tool. When you click the Subselect tool, you can click any of the points on the curve (these are the places where you clicked the Pen tool and are identifiable by a small box that appears on the curve at each point), and then drag the point or handles to modify the curve.

TIP

You can also add new points to an existing curve by reselecting the Pen tool and then clicking the curve when the mouse pointer shows a small plus sign. Don't add points you don't need, however, because additional points on the curve will increase the size of your published movie file. Also, if you add unnecessary points and then remove them later, Flash may modify the curve automatically.

Progress Check

1. What happens if you click the first point on the line a second time when you are using the Pen tool?

2. What tool do you use to modify a curve?

1. Flash creates a closed object.
2. The Subselect tool

Adding Fills

A *fill* is the color or gradient that fills the inside of closed objects. When you use the Pen, Oval, or Rectangle tool to create an object that is completely surrounded by lines, Flash automatically fills the object with whatever fill is currently selected.

To choose a fill, you click the fill selector to display the selector pane shown here. When you do, the mouse pointer becomes an eyedropper that you can use to select a color or gradient from the selector pane or from almost anywhere on the screen.

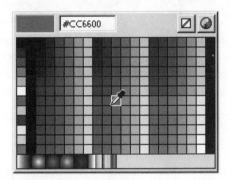

You can also change the current fill in an object or add a fill to an unfilled object by clicking the Paint Bucket tool. When you do, Flash fills any objects you click with the new fill. You can also use the Ink Bottle tool to change the color of any lines you click to the current stroke color.

Another way to change the fill or the stroke is to click the Eyedropper tool. This tool picks up the color of the next object that you click and then opens the Paint Bucket tool or the Ink Bottle tool—depending on whether you clicked a fill or a stroke with the Eyedropper tool.

In addition to using a solid color or gradient fill, you can also use a *bitmap* fill. This is a fill that you create by importing a bitmap image and then using the Modify | Break Apart command before you click the bitmap image with the Eyedropper tool. You will learn more about using imported bitmap images in Module 9.

TIP

Only fills can use gradients or bitmaps. Strokes are limited to solid colors unless you convert the stroke to a fill using the Modify | Shape | Convert Lines To Fills command.

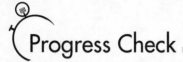

Progress Check

1. What types of objects can have fills?

2. What happens when you click an object with the Paint Bucket tool?

Using the Eraser Tool

You will probably find that your attempts at drawing objects using your mouse don't always produce precisely the results you might hope for. Everyone makes mistakes, and no one ever claimed that a mouse was the ideal drawing tool, anyway. But even if you don't make any mistakes in your drawing, you may find that you have a need to erase objects—either partially or completely.

TIP

The quickest way to erase an object you just drew is to use the Edit | Undo command immediately. This method offers the advantage of leaving the rest of the objects on the stage untouched.

The Flash Eraser tool provides you with the ability to selectively erase portions of a drawing. This tool has several modes that you can select using the Eraser Mode option that appears in the Options pane when you select the Eraser tool, as shown here:

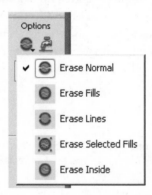

---

1. Closed objects
2. The fill is changed to the currently selected fill.

- **Erase Normal**   This mode makes the Eraser tool remove everything under the Eraser tool as you drag it across objects.

- **Erase Fills**   Choose this mode when you want to erase fills but leave any lines untouched.

- **Erase Lines**   Use this mode to erase lines but leave all fills alone.

- **Erase Selected Fills**   This mode erases only fills that were selected before you selected the Eraser tool. This mode does not erase all of the selected fills—only those areas where you drag the Eraser tool.

- **Erase Inside**   Use this mode to erase only within the area where you begin dragging the Eraser tool.

You can use the drop-down Eraser Shape list box to choose a size and shape for the Eraser tool. Unlike the Brush tool options, the Eraser Shape option sets both the size and the shape of the Eraser tool.

The final Eraser tool option is the Faucet option. This is a toggle, so this option is either on or off. When you select this option, the Eraser tool erases a complete line or fill with a single click. You can tell when the Faucet option is active by the shape of the mouse pointer—it looks like a water faucet.

When you use the Eraser tool, Flash smoothes the edges of the remaining object. As with all of the other drawing tools, this smoothing reduces the complexity of the object by drawing the edge with as few points as possible. The end result is a smaller published movie file, which provides faster downloads once your movie is placed on a web site.

NOTE

The next two tools that we discuss can also be used to remove part or all of an object. Before you decide to use the Eraser tool, make certain that you fully understand how both the Arrow tool and the Lasso tool function, because in many cases, one of those tools will actually be more appropriate than the Eraser tool.

Selecting with the Arrow Tool

The Arrow tool is probably the one tool in the Flash Tools panel that you will use most often. This tool enables you to select, move, and reshape objects in your movies. Once you have drawn objects, you will use the Arrow tool to place them precisely where you want them.

When you click the Arrow tool, you will notice that this tool has several different mouse pointers associated with it. This shows you how those pointers change for different purposes.

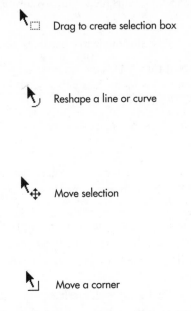

Drag to create selection box

Reshape a line or curve

Move selection

Move a corner

You can use any of three methods to select objects with the Arrow tool:

- Drag a selection box around the objects that you want to select. Everything within the selection box will be selected. Keep in mind, however, that if you are selecting ungrouped objects, only those portions of the objects that are actually within the selection box will be selected. This means that you can select a part of an ungrouped object without selecting the entire object.

- Click an object to select the item you clicked. If you click a line, the current line segment will be selected. If you click a fill, the fill will be selected.

- Double-click an object to select both the fill and any lines that outline the object.

TIP

Regardless of the selection method you choose, you can hold down SHIFT and make additional selections by any method to add to the current selection.

When the Arrow tool pointer shows a curved line, you can use the Arrow tool to reshape the line or curve. To do so, point to the line or curve, hold down the mouse button, and drag the line or curve. Flash will automatically adjust the fill if you are dragging one of the outlines of a filled object.

If the Arrow tool pointer displays a four-headed arrow, you can drag the currently selected objects. Simply hold down the mouse button and drag the objects to their new locations. Remember, though, that if multiple objects are selected, all of them will move—not just the object you are pointing to.

Finally, if the Arrow tool pointer shows a line with a 90-degree corner, you can use the tool to drag a corner point to a new location. This will also reshape the lines that are attached to the corner.

TIP

Remember that if you want to change the angle of the corner without moving the corner point, you should use the Subselect tool.

Progress Check

1. How can you add new items to a selection?

2. What happens if you drag when the Arrow tool pointer shows a curved line?

Selecting with the Lasso Tool

As useful as the Arrow tool may be, it is not always the most convenient tool if you want to select several objects out of a group, or if you want to select an irregular area of an object. For example, if you have a bottle on the stage and want to create the effect of the bottle being broken, it would be a very difficult effect to create with the Arrow tool. For this more free-form approach to making selections, the Lasso tool may be a better option.

---

1. Hold down SHIFT while you click.
2. You bend the line.

Learning the Flash Tools Panel

2

The Lasso tool enables you to draw an irregular selection area around or through objects. When you complete the selection drag, everything that is inside the area you dragged is selected. As this shows, the selection does not necessarily have to include the whole object. (The selected area is the area with the cross-hatching effect in the upper section of the illustration.)

Another use for the Lasso tool is to select a number of objects where you want only some of the objects in an area and where it would be impossible to select them by dragging a selection box using the Arrow tool. Of course, you might be able to use the double-click method to select tightly spaced objects, but the Lasso tool offers another option.

CRITICAL SKILL
2.2 # Use Tools to Create an Object for Your Movies

Now it is time to put together all of the information you have learned about the Flash drawing tools in this module and do something useful with those tools. You will use the drawing tools extensively as you create your Flash movies, so it is important that you become comfortable using them.

Project 2-1 Drawing a Truck and Adding Some Text

For this project, you will use several of the drawing tools to create a drawing of a delivery truck and to place some text on the side of that truck. Along the way, you will see how those tools interact, and you will get a better idea about what it takes to make a realistic-looking drawing in Flash.

Step by Step

1. Open a new, blank movie. (If you already have objects on the stage, use the File | New command.)

2. Click the Rectangle tool to select it.

3. Click the Round Radius Rectangle icon in the Options pane to display the Rectangle Settings dialog box, as shown here:

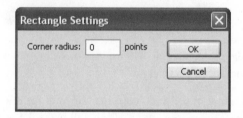

4. Make certain that the Corner Radius box is set to **0** so that your rectangle will have square corners, and then click OK.

5. Choose a stroke color and a fill color as shown here using the color selectors. To display the color selector, click the Stroke Color or Fill Color icon in the Colors area of the Tools panel. Then click on the color you want to use.

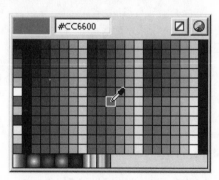

(continued)

6. Make certain that the Snap To Objects icon is selected in the Options pane. This will help when you start to draw the small rectangle at one side of the large rectangle, since the side of the new rectangle will snap to the side of the existing one.

7. Draw a large rectangle and then a small one, as shown here:

8. Click the Arrow tool to select it. You will use this tool to remove one of the corners of the small rectangle to make it into a triangle.

9. Drag the upper-left corner of the small rectangle down to the lower-left corner, as shown here. When you release the mouse button, Flash will make the rectangle into a triangle.

10. Use the Rectangle tool to draw another rectangle to the left of the large rectangle. Make this rectangle line up with the bottom of the large rectangle, and leave room between the top of this new rectangle and the triangle for the truck's windows.

11. Click the Line tool to select it, and then draw a vertical line from the front of the triangle to the top of the lower rectangle to make the windshield. Remember to hold down SHIFT to create an absolutely vertical line.

12. Click the Text tool to select it.

13. Use the Text | Size command to display the text size options menu, as shown here. Select 36 to make the text much larger than the default 12-point type.

14. Select a contrasting color in the fill color selector. If you do not select a contrasting color, Flash will draw the text using the existing fill color, making your text invisible on the side of the truck.

15. Click the side of the truck to create a text box. Make certain that you click near the front of the large rectangle so that there will be room to add your text.

16. Type **Bob's Trucking** in the text box. (You can substitute your own name if you like.) You truck should now look something like this:

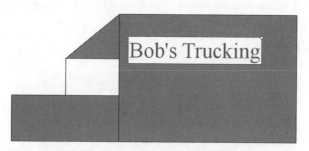

17. Click the Oval tool to select it so that you can add some wheels to complete your truck.

18. Select black for the stroke color.

(continued)

2

Learning the Flash Tools Panel

Project
2-1

Drawing a Truck and Adding Some Text

19. Select Window | Properties to display the Properties panel. You will want to increase the width of the stroke so that the tire portions of the wheels look more realistic.

20. Enter **10** in the stroke height list box, as shown here. You can either enter the number directly or drag the slider to the top of its range.

21. Draw a wheel under the front of the truck. Remember to hold down SHIFT to create a perfect circle.

22. Click the Arrow tool to select it.

23. Double-click the wheel to select both the fill and the stroke. When both are selected, you will see a cross-hatch appear on both parts of the selected object.

24. Select Edit | Copy to copy the wheel. By copying the wheel, you can make certain that both wheels will end up the same size.

25. Click outside the wheel to deselect it.

26. Choose Edit | Paste to paste a copy of the wheel onto the stage.

27. Drag the new copy of the wheel to a position under the back of the truck. Flash will display a dashed, horizontal line as a guide when you have the new copy of the wheel at the same vertical position as the original wheel.

28. Click outside the wheel you just dragged to deselect it. Your finished truck should now look something like this:

29. Select File | Save and save your work.

Project Summary

In this project, you combined the use of several of the drawing tools to create an object that you could easily use in a movie. You learned that it is important to always check such details as the current color selections and the text size before you begin using the drawing tools so that you can get just the results you want. Finally, you saw that you can clone objects to ensure that copies look alike.

✔

Module 2 Mastery Check

1. The area of the Tools panel where you can choose settings for some of the drawing tools is the _____.

2. The _____ tool enables you to draw Bézier curves.

3. Once you have drawn a curved line, you can use the _____ tool to modify the shape of the curve.

4. To select objects by drawing a selection box, you use the _____ tool.

5. Which of the following is not one of the Pencil tool modes?

    A. Straighten

    B. Kink

    C. Smooth

    D. Ink

6. To select an irregular area, you use the _____ tool.

7. To draw a perfectly horizontal line, you hold down _____ as you draw the line.

8. You need to enter _____ as the value in the Rectangle Settings dialog box to create square corners.

9. To create a text box with a fixed width, _____ with the Text tool.

10. The _____ tool enables you to paint an area with a gradient fill.

11. To make objects automatically align with nearby objects as you draw them, you select the _____ icon in the Options pane.

12. To remove the fill from an object, select the _____ option before you click with the Eraser tool.

Project
2-1

Drawing a Truck and Adding Some Text

13. In addition to using the Properties panel, you can use the _____ menu to choose the font size.

14. If you want to continue the same gradient fill across multiple objects, you select the _____ option.

15. To duplicate an existing color, you can click that color with the _____ tool.

Module 3

Learning the Flash Panels

Virtually all the objects you create for your Flash movies have various optional settings. This wide variety of options wouldn't be very useful without a means of selecting and setting the options. In this module, you will learn how you do this in Flash—by using the panels.

CRITICAL SKILL
3.1 Understanding the Panels

Virtually all computer programs have some means for the user to interact with the program. Typically, these include such things as menus, toolbars, and dialog boxes. Depending on the program and the function it serves, these options are often sufficient to fulfill the user's needs. Sometimes, however, these tools simply are inadequate for the task at hand and something else is needed. In Flash, that something else is the *panel,* the subject of this module.

What Are Panels?

You're probably wondering just what a panel is, anyway. In effect, a panel is what is known as a *nonmodal* dialog box. That is, a panel can be thought of as a dialog box that does not need to be closed in order for you to continue working. When you make changes in one of the Flash panels, those changes are applied immediately without closing the panel.

TIP

Sometimes it is necessary to press ENTER to apply changes that you just made in a panel.

Because the panels will often remain open while you are working, Flash makes it very easy for you to access the panels. You can open any of the panels by selecting the Window menu and then choosing the panel that you want from the menu, as shown here. Notice that the Window menu has several submenus and that you will find groups of related panels on some of those submenus.

As the illustration shows, panels that are already open are shown with a check mark in the menu. In this case, Properties, Timeline, and Tools have check marks that indicate that they are open.

TIP

Notice that a number of the panels have keyboard shortcuts that are shown in the Window menu. By learning these shortcuts, you can quickly open any of these panels without going through the menus. These shortcuts are operating-system specific, however, so I am not indicating them in the text, to avoid confusion.

Locating the Correct Panel

The Flash panels are extremely useful, but only if you know which panel you need to use to accomplish your goal. To help you to know which panel to choose, I will now briefly introduce each of the panels. You will no doubt find that you use certain of the panels, such as the Properties panel, quite often. Other panels, such as the Strings panel, will probably have little value for you until you become considerably more advanced as a Flash movie developer.

NOTE

In most cases, you will find that the various options that are included in each of the panels are not labeled. This can make using the panels slightly more difficult when you are learning to use Flash. Fortunately, if you enable the tooltips in Flash, you will find that the panel options all show a tooltip if you briefly allow the mouse pointer to hover over the option. You can enable tooltips by using the Edit | Preferences command and then selecting the Show Tooltips option in the Preferences dialog box.

Properties Panel

The Properties panel, shown here, enables you to select the properties for whatever happens to be selected. Here the Text tool is selected, so the Properties panel enables you to select the properties for any text that you add to your movies. Many of the options that you see here are also available in the Text menu. For example, you can use either the Properties panel or the Text | Size menu to change the font size.

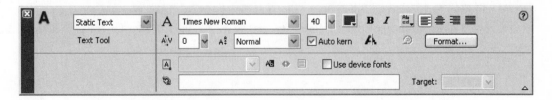

You can make selections in the Properties panel before you add text, or you can use this panel to modify existing text. If you want to modify the properties of existing text, you must select the text before making changes in the Properties panel.

When you first add a text box to your movie using the Text tool, Flash creates the text box as a *static* text box—one that holds unchanging text. If you want to be able to display the contents of a variable, such as a game score, you must change the text box to a *dynamic* text box. If, on the other hand, you want to obtain user input, you must change the text box into an input text box.

The Properties panel enables you to choose whether a text box displays static text, whether the text can change as your movie plays, or whether the box can be used to accept user input. You make this selection using the drop-down Text Type list box in the upper-left area of the Properties panel (this is the box that shows "Static Text" in the illustration). In addition, this panel enables you to assign variables to text boxes as well as to control the visual settings for text boxes.

Let's take a quick look at some of the other ways you can use the Properties panel by selecting different objects or tools. Notice that the options that are available in the Properties panel change as you select different types of objects or different drawing tools. That's one reason why you'll use the Properties panel so often—it is so versatile.

Modifying Instances   You can also use the Properties panel, shown here, to modify *symbol instances.* Symbols include objects such as buttons, movie clips, and imported graphics. Symbols are discussed in Module 8.

Symbols are an important feature in Flash movies. Symbols can be reused many times in a movie without saving individual copies of the symbol. This results in tremendous savings in the size of your published movie files, meaning that your movies will load faster than if you did not use symbol instances.

Modifying Strokes and Fills   The Properties panel can, as shown here, enable you to select the style, width, and color for lines (strokes) as well as the fill color for objects. Changes you make affect new lines that you draw or lines that are selected when you make changes in the panel.

By default, the stroke settings in the Properties panel are used for lines you draw with the Line tool and the Pen tool, as well as for the outlines of objects you create using the Oval tool and the Rectangle tool. Keep in mind, however, that the outlines for ovals and rectangles can be turned off by clicking the No Color button in the Colors area of the Flash Tools panel. This is one option that you cannot control using the Properties panel.

Modifying Frame Properties   You can also use the Properties panel, as shown here, to apply and modify *tweens*—animations—to frames in the timeline. This panel also enables you to add frame labels, which can be used along with ActionScript programming to control the flow in your movies, and comments, which can help you maintain your movies.

You can apply a shape tween only by using the Properties panel. Flash has a command on the Insert | Timeline menu for adding a motion tween, but none for adding a shape tween. You will learn more about adding tweens to your movies in Module 6.

TIP

If you see a warning sign icon in the Properties panel, Flash is telling you that there is a problem with the current tween selection. Click the icon to see the error message so that you can determine what is wrong and how you can correct your error.

Ask the Expert

Q: How can I draw a line that is wider than what the Properties panel settings allow? It appears that 10 is the maximum width I can select.

A: Stroke widths can be set anywhere in the range between 0.25 point and 10 points in the Properties panel. It is possible, however, to create lines that are wider than the maximum stroke width of 10 points. To do so, you need to change the line to a fill using the Modify | Shape | Convert Lines To Fills command. Once you have done so, you can scale the converted line using the Modify | Transform | Scale command.

Q: Isn't there some way that I can use a gradient fill for my lines? The stroke color selector doesn't have a gradient option similar to the one that is available in the fill color selector.

A: Gradient fills can be used only on fills—not strokes. Therefore, the way to accomplish what you want is once again to use the Modify | Shape | Convert Lines To Fills command to change the stroke into a fill. Then you can use any type of fill you want.

Progress Check

1. Which panel would you use to increase the size of some text to 36 points?

2. Which panel do you need to open if you want to add a shape tween to your movie?

3. How can you change the width of lines?

4. How would you allow the user to input some text?

---

1. Properties panel
2. Properties panel
3. Change the stroke width in the Properties panel.
4. Change the text box type to Input.

CRITICAL SKILL

3.2 Choose the Correct Panel for Your Needs

The Properties panel, while very important, is not the only Flash panel that you will use. Let's take a look at some other panels you will find useful.

NOTE

Although some of the Flash MX 2004 panels appear as freestanding panels when you issue the command to display that particular panel, most of the panels automatically dock themselves along the right side or the bottom of the Flash window. If you only see the panel's name but not the full panel, click the triangle to the left of the panel name to display the full panel. You can also drag the panel to a new location or undock it using the two vertical columns of dots to the left of the triangle.

Align Panel

The Align panel, shown here, is used to control the size, distribution, alignment, and spacing of objects on the stage. This panel, like most Flash panels, affects only those objects that are selected when you click one of the buttons in the panel. You use the Window | Design Panels | Align command to display the Align panel.

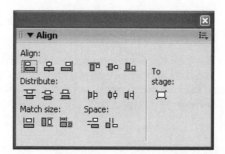

Each of the buttons in the Align panel has an associated tooltip. This means that you can easily determine the purpose of each button by allowing the mouse pointer to hover briefly over the button. The drawings on the face of each button also provide a visual clue to the purpose of each of the buttons.

TIP

When you want to use the stage as the determining factor in the alignment or spacing of objects, click the To Stage button before you click the other buttons in the Align panel. The To Stage button is a toggle, so it will remain selected while you use the other buttons. The To Stage button is the button off on its own at the right side of the Align panel.

Color Mixer Panel

You can use the Color Mixer panel, shown here, to create your own colors for use both in strokes and in fills. When you create a color in the Color Mixer panel, that color becomes the current selection in either the stroke color or fill color selector so that it will be used in new objects that you create. You use the Window | Design Panels | Color Mixer command to display the Color Mixer panel.

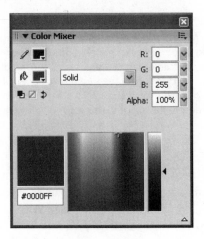

NOTE

You cannot use the Color Mixer panel to directly modify the color of an existing object. If you want to apply your custom color to an existing object, first create your custom color in the Mixer panel, and then use the Ink Bottle tool or the Paint Bucket tool to apply the new color to the stroke or fill—respectively.

Color Swatches Panel

The Color Swatches panel, shown here, enables you to select colors as well as to choose the color palette that will be used in your Flash movies. This panel is a near duplicate of the color selectors, but it also offers a number of menu selections that you can access by opening its menu. You use the Window | Design Panels | Color Swatches command to display the Color Swatches panel.

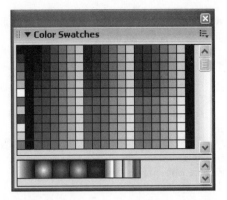

Once the Color Swatches panel is open, you can use the panel's menu (click the icon just below the panel's Close button to display the menu) to choose the color palette that you want to use. You can also duplicate existing color swatches so that you can modify them (to create your own custom gradient fill, for example).

NOTE

Using color on web sites can be somewhat problematic. Your carefully selected colors may not always render precisely on a visitor's monitor, so you may find that subtle color variations are not always very effective. There are many reasons for this, but ultimately they boil down to one thing—you should not depend on visitors being able to see colors accurately. For this reason, many Flash developers use fairly broad color changes between different objects in their movies. Highly contrasting colors offer a better chance of being easily seen on the broad range of devices that are used to browse the Internet.

Info Panel

The Info panel, shown here, provides you with information about a selected object. You can also use this panel to set an object's width, height, or position to precise values by entering those values directly into the text boxes in the Info panel. You use the Window | Design Panels | Info command to display the Info panel.

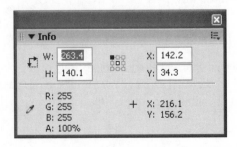

The size and position measurements that are used in the Info panel are in pixels. Position measurements are relative to the upper-left corner of the stage.

TIP

There are two ways to measure the position of an object. By default, Flash measures the position of the upper-left corner of the selected object. If you click the small white box in the middle of the grid to the left of the position measurements in the Info panel, Flash measures the position of the center of the object. Click the upper-left box to return to using the upper-left corner of the object for position measurements.

Scene Panel

The Scene panel, shown here, helps you work with multiple scenes in a movie. Using this panel, you can select the scene you want as active, add new scenes, or delete scenes you no longer need. You use the Window | Design Panels | Scene command to display the Scene panel.

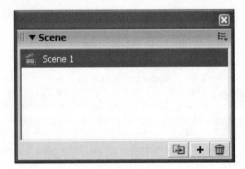

There are many different ways to organize Flash movies. Some Flash developers prefer to work with a single timeline (or scene), while others prefer to break the action down into multiple scenes to help organize their workflow. The method you choose is primarily a matter of personal preference and work style. Once you publish your movie, Flash flattens the movie into a one-layer, single-scene production, so the end result that is seen by anyone watching your movie is the same either way.

Transform Panel

The Transform panel, shown here, enables you to precisely scale, rotate, or skew an object. The object must be selected before you can enter any settings in this panel. You use the Window | Design Panels | Transform command to display the Transform panel.

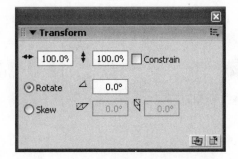

It is possible to both scale and rotate objects without using the Transform panel. You can right-click (or Command-click on a Mac) an object and select Free Transform from the pop-up menu, or you can use the Modify | Transform menu options. In either case, Flash displays a series of handles around the object that you can drag with the mouse. You have, however, an advantage in using the Transform panel. When you use the Transform panel, you can specify precise values that you want to use. It is much harder to make these transformations with precision when you are dragging the handles with the mouse.

Progress Check

1. Which panel would you use if you want to space a series of objects evenly across the stage?

2. Which panel would you use to create a customized color?

3. Which panel enables you to rotate an object by exactly 27 degrees clockwise?

Actions Panel

The Actions panel, shown here, is used for adding *ActionScript* code to frames in the timeline or to objects. ActionScript is the programming language that you use to automate actions within Flash. You will learn more about ActionScript programming beginning in Module 12. You use the Window | Development Panels | Actions command to display the Actions panel. The Actions panel, along with the Properties panel and the Help panel, is normally docked

---

1. Align panel
2. Color Mixer panel
3. Transform panel

along the lower edge of the Flash MX 2004 window, so you may not need to use the command to display the Actions panel.

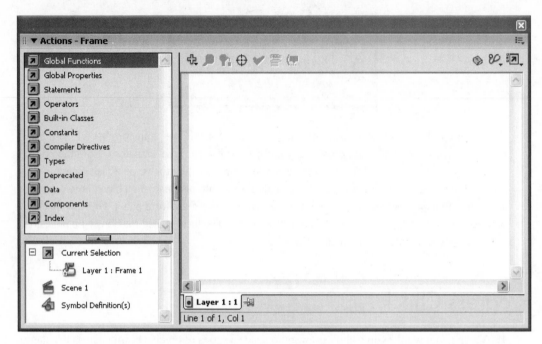

The Actions panel has two different modes. If a keyframe in the timeline is selected, the Actions panel title is "Actions - Frame." If an object that can have ActionScript code attached is selected, the Actions panel title is "Actions - Object." When you are using the Actions panel, it is often important to make note of which Actions panel mode is active. This can prevent you from accidentally attempting to add your ActionScript code to the wrong place.

Behaviors Panel

The Behaviors panel, shown next, is used to add predefined behaviors to objects in your movies. This makes it possible for you to add interactivity and other types of actions to objects without adding ActionScript code manually. You use the Window | Development Panels | Behaviors command to display the Behaviors panel.

Behaviors are ActionScript code that you add to an object such as a button simply by choosing options from a menu. You can use behaviors to do things like control the playback of a movie clip. You will learn more about using behaviors in Module 8.

Components Panel

The Components panel, shown here, includes a number of user interface elements that you can add to your movies and control with a small amount of ActionScript programming. The components each have a number of very sophisticated capabilities built in so that it is far easier to create highly interactive Flash movies. You use the Window | Development Panels | Components command to display the Components panel.

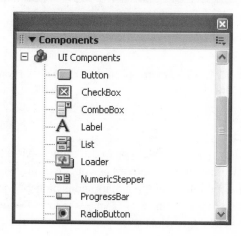

Component Inspector Panel

Closely related to the Components panel is the Component Inspector panel, shown here. This panel enables you to set various properties of components you have added to your movies. You use the Window | Development Panels | Component Inspector command to display the Component Inspector panel.

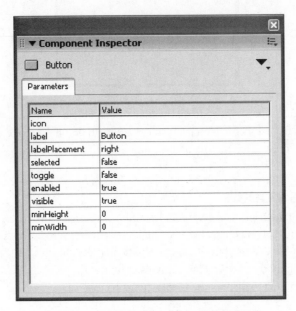

TIP

The Properties panel actually provides more options for working with components than the Component Inspector panel does.

Debugger Panel

The Debugger Panel, shown here, enables you to determine what is happening to the variables, properties, and other elements in your movies as you are testing your movie. This panel is primarily of interest to ActionScript programmers and is probably not going to be very useful to you as you are learning to use Flash. You use the Window | Development Panels | Debugger command to display the Debugger panel.

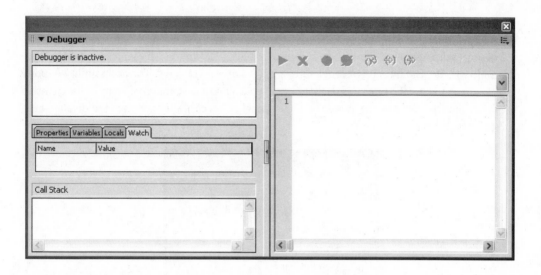

Output Panel

The Output panel, shown here, is a window you can choose to display when you are testing a Flash movie to determine how various elements of an ActionScript program are functioning. The Output panel typically is used during testing to display error messages or to display messages using the ActionScript trace command. You use the Window | Development Panels | Output command to display the Output panel.

Accessibility Panel

The Accessibility panel, shown here, enables you to make your Flash movies accessible to people who depend on screen reader software to navigate web sites. The accessibility options make it possible for the screen reader software to read aloud a description of many of the elements of your movies. You use the Window | Other Panels | Accessibility command to display the Accessibility panel.

History Panel

The History panel, shown here, records your actions as you work in the Flash MX 2004 development environment. You can then use the History panel menu to save a series of steps as a command or to replay a set of actions. This makes it possible for you to create your own custom commands that will appear on the Flash MX 2004 Commands menu. You use the Window | Other Panels | History command to display the History panel.

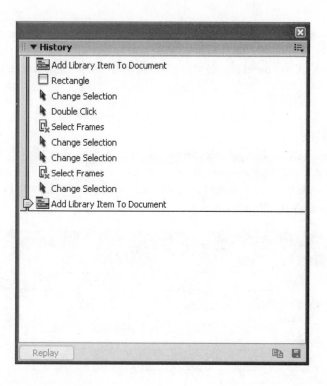

Movie Explorer Panel

The Movie Explorer panel, shown here, enables you to view the properties and relationships between the different elements in your movie. Using this panel, you can see which objects are contained within other objects, and you can see any ActionScript code that is attached to any of the objects or frames.

You are most likely to use the Movie Explorer panel once you have created a large and complex movie. It can be difficult to remember how everything in a large project fits together, and the Movie Explorer panel provides you with a method of examining all of the relationships visually.

Strings Panel

The Strings panel, shown here, enables you to create multi-language Flash movies by associating various text fields with language-specific strings. You probably won't have a lot of use for the Strings panel while you are learning to use Flash. You use the Window | Other Panels | Strings command to display the Strings panel.

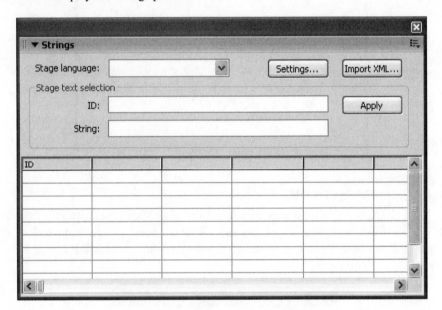

Help Panel

The Help panel, shown next, provides access to the Flash MX 2004 help content. You will likely find the Help panel to be an invaluable tool. You can use the Help | Help command to display the Help panel if it is not already docked along the bottom edge of the Flash window.

Progress Check

1. Which panel would you use to see how the objects in your movie are related?

2. How could you make certain that your Flash movies were accessible to users who depend on screen readers?

3. What do you use to add ActionScript statements to your movies?

4. Which panel would you use to create a custom command?

---

1. Movie Explorer panel
2. Use the Accessibility panel options.
3. Actions panel
4. History panel

CRITICAL SKILL
3.3 # Make Changes Using the Panels

Now that you have a good idea about which of the Flash panels you need to use in any situation, you need to understand a little more about how the panels actually work.

The Flash panels are typically quite easy to use. Actually, they do work much like dialog boxes. That is, when you open a panel, you will see familiar objects such as text boxes, list boxes, and option buttons. All of these function nearly identically to the way they function in a standard dialog box.

One of the important differences between the Flash panels and dialog boxes is that you can leave the panels open while you continue to work on your movie. This makes it easy for you to use the same panel again. You don't constantly have to return to the Flash menu in order to reopen a panel. Rather, you use the panel to make some changes, and then let it sit in an out-of-the-way place on the screen.

Selecting in Panels

Because the panels can remain open on your desktop, you need to be aware of what is selected before you make any changes in the panels. Remember, objects that are selected can be affected by those changes.

TIP

If the options in a panel are all grayed out, this generally means that you do not have an appropriate object selected. Once you select an appropriate object, the options in the panel will become available.

The Flash panels are intended for use with your mouse. Some of the standard keyboard actions that you use with dialog boxes simply won't work in the panels. For example, if you attempt to use the TAB key to move between options in a panel, you will find that pressing TAB selects a different object in the Flash workspace rather than moving within the panel.

Therefore, to make a selection in a panel, you click that selection with your mouse. Some options have a down arrow at the right edge of the option. If the option is a list box, clicking this down arrow displays a list of items from which you can choose. If the option is a text box, clicking the down arrow displays a slider that you can drag up or down to enter values in the text box.

Of course, sometimes when you select one option, this affects which options are available in the panel. For example, in the Properties panel with a text box selected, choosing the type of text box determines which other options appear in the panel. For this reason, the panels may not always appear identical to the illustrations that you have seen in this module.

Applying Panel Selections

When you want to use one of the Flash panels to make changes to an object, it is important that you understand how those selections are applied. Consider these rules:

- If no objects are selected, and you are able to make changes within a panel, your new selections will apply to future objects that you create. For example, if you change the stroke height in the Properties panel and then draw a box using the Rectangle tool, the new line width will be used for the outline of that box.

- If an object is selected, any changes you make within the panel typically will be applied to that object. Sometimes, however, the changes are applied only after you press ENTER.

- If no objects are selected, and you are unable to make changes within the panel, you must select an object before you will be allowed to make any changes.

TIP

It is always wise to quickly check to see which object is selected before you make any changes in the Flash panels. Otherwise, you will soon discover that it is very easy to make changes to an object accidentally. If you do make a change accidentally, use the Edit | Undo command immediately to reverse that change.

CRITICAL SKILL
3.4 Create and Save Custom Panels

The Flash panels are intended to make your development work much easier. But not everyone works quite the same way. Therefore, Macromedia accommodates different work styles by allowing you to customize the panels. Customizing the panels means creating sets of panels that are laid out the way you want.

NOTE

Although you can change the groupings of the panels, you cannot modify the layout of any particular panel. The reason for this is simple: if you were to modify the layout of the panel, you might forget to include important options, or you might include invalid options.

Creating Panel Sets

As you develop Flash movies, you will no doubt find yourself using certain panels an awful lot. For example, you might use the Properties panel, the Align panel, and the Actions panel all the time. You could keep all three panels open, but this might eat up too much valuable space on your desktop. As an alternative, you might memorize the keyboard shortcuts to display certain panels.

A better choice may be to create your own panel set that includes the panels you use most often. Once you have done this, you will have just the panels you want.

Saving Panel Sets

You probably don't want to go to the work of re-creating your customized panel sets each time you use Flash. You can avoid this prospect by saving your panel sets for future use.

To save a custom panel set, use the Window | Save Panel Layout command to display the Save Panel Layout dialog box shown here. After you enter a name for your panel set and click OK, Flash saves your custom panels for later use.

TIP

If more than one person uses Flash on the same PC, it will be easier for everyone if any customized panel sets are saved using the person's name.

Displaying the Standard Panels

If you discover that you want to return to the standard Flash panel sets, you will find that it is very easy to do so. This can be especially handy if you share a PC with another Flash user, because your custom panel set may be a little confusing for someone who was not involved in creating it.

To return to the standard Flash panel layout, select the Window | Panel Sets command to display the menu shown next, where you can choose from several different options. When you do, you will also see that the Window | Panel Sets menu enables you to open any of the custom panel sets you have saved.

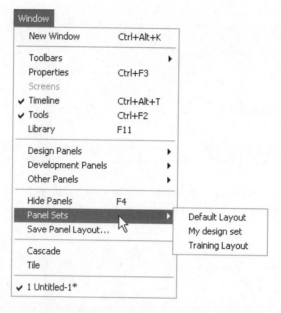

Project 3-1 Setting Properties with the Properties Panel

Now it is time to apply a little of what you have learned about the Flash panels. In this project, you will use the Properties panel to set a number of different properties for various types of objects in a Flash movie.

Step by Step

1. Open the Properties panel using the Window | Properties command.

2. If the Properties panel is docked along the bottom of the Flash window, move it by pointing to the two columns of dots near the upper-left corner of the panel (to the left of the triangle) and dragging it to a new location, as shown next. When a panel is undocked, you can place it wherever you want.

(continued)

3

Learning the Flash Panels

Project
3-1

Setting Properties with the Properties Panel

3. Click the Text tool to change the options available in the Properties panel, as shown here. When a text block or the Text tool is selected, you can make changes that will affect the text options.

4. Select different options in the Properties panel, and see how these affect text that you draw.

5. Click the Pen tool to change the options available in the Properties panel, as shown here. When a drawing tool or a drawn object is selected, you can make changes to properties such as the stroke color and width, and the fill color.

6. Select different colors and stroke widths, and then try drawing some objects to see how the changes affect your drawing.

7. Click frame 1 in the timeline to select it. This will change the Properties panel options so that you can add frame labels, apply a tween, add sounds, and so on.

8. Add a frame label and see how it appears in the timeline.

9. Drag the Properties panel back to the bottom of the Flash window until it docks in place below the stage. You may need to use the zoom control above the right side of the timeline or the options on the View | Magnification menu to once again see the entire stage.

Project Summary

In this project, you used the Properties panel to set a number of options. As you become more familiar with Flash, you will likely find that techniques like this make it easier for you to concentrate on developing your movies without spending so much time trying to remember which tools you need to use to accomplish your goals.

Module 3 Mastery Check

1. The Flash panels are similar to _____ in many other programs.

2. The _____ panel enables you to change the style of lines.

3. You use the _____ panel to view the help information for ActionScript statements.

4. When you drag a panel so that it is free floating, the panel is _____.

5. You can add a new scene to your movie by using the _____ panel.

6. To return the panels to their normal layout, you use the _____ command.

7. The panels appear on the _____ menu.

8. If you want to set an object to a very specific height and width, you can use the _____ panel.

9. To add a shape tween, you must open the _____ panel.

10. The _____ panel enables you to add ActionScript statements.

11. To replay a set of actions, you use the _____ panel.

12. Error messages are displayed during testing of a movie in the _____ panel.

13. You can add ActionScript code to objects automatically using the _____ panel.

14. You use the _____ panel to add labels and comments to timeline frames.

15. You use the _____ panel to make it possible for screen reader programs to describe objects in your movies.

Module 4

Using the Timeline and Layers

One of the primary purposes of Flash is to create animated movies. Any animation—no matter how it is produced—results from displaying a series of images that change with time. In Flash, you use the timeline to control when the images are displayed so that you can achieve the animation effects you want. In this module, you will learn how to make use of the timeline and the closely related timeline layers, which you use to help control the layout of objects and to allow objects to act independently of each other.

Understanding How the Timeline Works

As humans, we are used to thinking about where objects are in three dimensions. These geometric measurements are very useful for most purposes, but they fall short when you need an additional dimension—time. The time dimension becomes very important when you are creating animated movies in Flash, because you need the ability to place objects in different locations over time.

The Flash timeline gives you the ability to control objects in time. By using the timeline, you have the ability to use time the same way you use height, width, or depth. That is, you have an additional dimension that enables you to exercise precise control over the positioning of objects according to how much time has passed.

Although you were introduced to the timeline in Module 1, I'd like to take a moment to refresh your memory about the various parts of the timeline before we continue with the rest of this module.

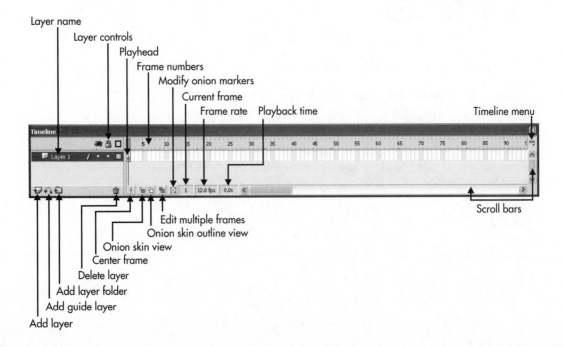

CRITICAL SKILL
4.2 Understanding Frames

Each frame in a Flash movie represents a view of the movie at a particular instant in time during the movie's playback. If you are using the default setting of 12 frames per second, then each frame would normally appear for 1/12th of a second before the movie moves on to the next frame.

By default, Flash movies run at 12 frames per second (fps). This means that during the playback of a Flash animation, 12 frame images are displayed every second. This playback rate is somewhat slower than the frame rate for motion pictures and television, but it is generally quite sufficient to produce a good effect in animated sequences. Although you can use a higher frame rate, doing so is not usually necessary and will greatly increase the size of your published movie file. Larger movie files take longer to download, and this can cause people to get tired of waiting. Unless you have some special requirements for a specific project, the default Flash frame rate will likely offer the best compromise between playback quality and file size. Of course, not everyone agrees that 12 fps is fast enough to produce smooth animation, so you'll have to decide what setting produces the best balance of smooth animation and reasonable file size for your projects.

NOTE

Playback can be stopped in several different ways as your movie plays. When playback is stopped, the current frame remains visible until the movie is advanced to another frame. Because of this, the frame rate actually specifies only the minimum time a frame may be visible—not the maximum time.

Even though each frame represents the view of your movie at one particular instant, this does not mean that you must create the content for each frame individually. Although you could do this, Flash offers some far more efficient alternatives:

- For static content—objects that remain in one position without any changes—Flash can simply display the object in a series of frames without any additional increase in the file size. You only need to add the object to the first frame where you want it to appear and then to tell Flash how long you want it to appear, and the rest is automatic. You do so simply by adding the correct number of frames for the length of time the object should appear.

- For objects that move from one place to another, you draw the object in the first frame where it appears in the movie. Then you specify the final frame for the object's movement and the object's position in that frame. Once you have done this, Flash takes over and displays the object in the intermediate frames without requiring you to draw the object in those frames. This is called a *motion tween*.

- For objects that change shape, you again draw the first shape in the first frame where the object appears. Then, in the final frame of the shape change, you draw the new shape. When this is complete, you instruct Flash to create a shape tween to automatically generate all of the intermediate shapes without any additional work on your part.

In reality, allowing Flash to do as much of the work in creating your movies as possible not only makes life easier for you, but it also greatly increases efficiency and allows for smaller file sizes.

Learning the Frame Types

Because frames are so important in Flash movies, you might expect that Flash has many different types of frames for different uses. Fortunately, this is untrue. Indeed, Flash has only two types of frames—ordinary frames and keyframes. The differences and similarities between the two types of frames are pretty easy to understand:

- During playback, all frames play for the same length of time (unless you have used some ActionScript code to modify the playback flow).

- You can add items to keyframes only. It doesn't matter what you want to add, you can do so only in a keyframe.

- Only Flash can add items to ordinary frames. You cannot do anything directly to a frame if it is not a keyframe.

What this all boils down to is that you do all of your work in keyframes, and Flash handles all of the other frames. As long as you remember this, working with the frames will be pretty straightforward.

This does not mean, however, that you have no control over frames that are not keyframes. Indeed, as you will learn in the next few sections, you can exercise considerable control over those frames—you just cannot work directly in them.

TIP

Keyframes always have a dot in the timeline. The dot is open if the keyframe is empty and filled if the keyframe contains some content.

Progress Check

1. What type of frame do you need when you want to add an object to the stage?

2. By default, how many frames play each second?

Selecting Frames

There are many different reasons why you select frames. Here are some of them:

- You select frames when you want to add a keyframe to the timeline.

- You select a keyframe to add to or modify the content of the keyframe.

- You select the frames between keyframes when you want to add or modify a tween.

- You select frames when you want to add, delete, or move frames.

It is important to make certain that you are selecting the correct frame. This is especially true when you start adding layers to the timeline, because frames are specific to their layer. For example, this shows a timeline that contains three layers. As the illustration shows, you can have keyframes in different places on different layers, and selecting frames on one layer has no effect on the other layers (although you can select frames on adjacent layers if you want to do so).

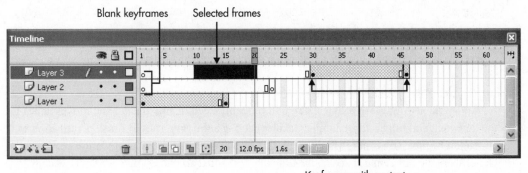

Blank keyframes   Selected frames

Keyframes with content

---

1. Keyframe

2. 12

In this case, frames 10–20 are selected in the topmost layer. The keyframes that contain content all have a black filled-in dot, while the blank keyframes do not.

When you select a frame in the timeline, you are actually selecting both the frame and the layer that contains the frame. For example, here I have selected frame 4 in Layer 2. When you select a frame, any changes you make are made only in the selected layer. So if I have selected frame 4 in Layer 2, any object I draw will reside on Layer 2 (and nowhere else).

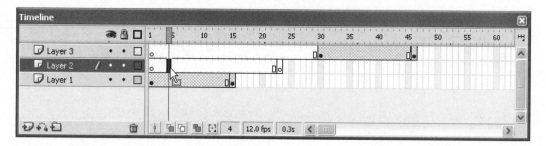

If you select a frame that is not a keyframe, it may seem as though you are being allowed to add content to an ordinary frame that is not a keyframe. In reality, though, when you do this, Flash will automatically place the objects in the previous keyframe. So in the case of the illustration where I have selected frame 4 (which is not a keyframe), Flash adds any objects I draw to frame 1.

TIP

Frame 1 is always considered to be a keyframe, so if you add objects to later frames without first creating a keyframe for them, Flash will place those objects in frame 1 (as long as there are no keyframes between the selected frame and frame 1).

Adding, Deleting, and Moving Frames

As you work on your Flash movies, you will probably need to add, delete, and move frames in the timeline. You might, for example, decide that one animation should finish before another animation begins. To accomplish this, you must make sure that the two animation sequences do not share the same time space on the timeline. If the first animation runs for three seconds—36 frames at the standard frame rate—you would have to start the second animation at some point after frame 36 to prevent overlap. Keep in mind, though, that if you do want animations to overlap, you can only do so if those animations are on different layers in the timeline.

The Insert | Timeline menu offers three commands that you can use to add the frames in the timeline. Table 4-1 describes these commands.

When you use any of the Insert | Timeline menu frame commands, be sure to select the appropriate frames before you issue the command. In particular, make certain that you have selected the correct layer. Remember, Flash will do what you tell it to do, even if that is not what you wanted it to do.

Command	Description
Frame	Adds one or more ordinary frames at the insertion point
Keyframe	Adds a keyframe that duplicates the contents of the previous keyframe
Blank Keyframe	Adds a keyframe that does not inherit the contents of the previous keyframe

Table 4-1 Insert | Timeline Menu Frame-Related Commands

The Edit | Timeline menu also offers several commands that you can use to modify the frames in the timeline. Table 4-2 describes these commands.

If you want to move frames in the timeline, you can drag the frames with the mouse. You can drag the beginning or the ending keyframe to change the length of an animation sequence. To move the entire sequence to a different point of the timeline, click the frames in between the keyframes and then drag the sequence.

TIP

It is always better to plan ahead so that you do not have to move frames to different locations in the timeline. Rather than creating a tween and then trying to move it to a different location, you will find that it is much easier to simply create it in the correct location in the first place.

One very common reason for adding or deleting frames from the timeline is to adjust the length of an animation. You might discover that an animation needs to run for more frames because it appears jerky. This can easily happen if you try to move an object too far in a given number of frames. By lengthening the time that an animation runs, you allow for smaller changes between the individual frames. Smaller changes between frames result in a smoother animation.

Command	Description
Cut Frames	Cuts the frames and moves them to the Clipboard
Copy Frames	Copies the frames to the Clipboard
Paste Frames	Pastes frames from the Clipboard
Clear Frames	Changes keyframes into ordinary frames
Remove Frames	Removes the selected frames and their content
Select All Frames	Selects all of the frames in the timeline

Table 4-2 Edit | Timeline Menu Frame-Related Commands

Using the Timeline and Layers

Ask the Expert

Q: When I try to add frames to the timeline, they are added to only one layer, and this messes up the relationships between my tweens. How can I add frames to all of the layers equally?

A: To add frames to all of the layers at once, you need to select the same frames in each layer at the same time. To do this, you must start by selecting empty frames in one of the layers and then dragging the mouse pointer across all of the layers. It may help to have an empty layer at the top or the bottom of the stack of layers so that you can select empty frames more easily. You don't have to have anything on this extra layer, but it really makes adding additional frames across all of the layers a lot easier.

Q: I wanted to add frames to an animation, but Flash replaced the solid arrow in the timeline with a dashed line. What does this mean?

A: If you do something that Flash thinks has destroyed a tween, the solid arrow that indicates a tween is replaced by a dashed line. Select Edit | Undo to undo the action immediately. Then try adding frames without selecting the keyframes—you will probably find that this does not destroy the tween.

Progress Check

1. When you look at the timeline, how can you tell if a frame is a keyframe?

2. How can you tell if a keyframe contains some content?

Commenting Your Work

Even if you never add any ActionScript programming to your Flash movies, those movies are still computer programs because they contain the instructions that tell computers how to do something. And, as with all computer programs, it can be difficult to understand what is happening in a Flash movie unless you get a bit of extra help. That is where *comments* come into play. Comments are notes that explain what is going on.

---

1. It has a dot.

2. It contains a solid black dot.

In a Flash movie, you add comments to frames in the timeline. When you have done so, the comments appear in the timeline. Your comments can be fairly simple, but they are still an important way to help make your movies easier to understand.

NOTE

Comments never appear when your movie plays. In fact, Flash does not include the comments when you publish your movie, so comments have no adverse effect on the size of the published movie file. Therefore, you can use comments freely without worrying about how they might affect your movie—they are simply an aid to helping you remember important things about your movies and how they operate.

To add comments to the timeline, follow these steps:

1. Select the keyframe where you want to add a comment. (Remember, you can add something only to a keyframe.)

2. Open the Properties panel using the Window | Properties command. If the Properties panel is docked at the bottom of the screen but you cannot see the contents of the panel, remember to click the triangle in the left of the panel's title bar to display the panel.

3. Type your comment in the Label text box (just below where you see "Frame" near the left side of the Properties panel), as shown here. (In this case, I have docked the Timeline and the Properties panel so that you can see how the comment appears in both places.) Be sure to place two forward slashes (//) at the beginning of the line to indicate that this is a comment.

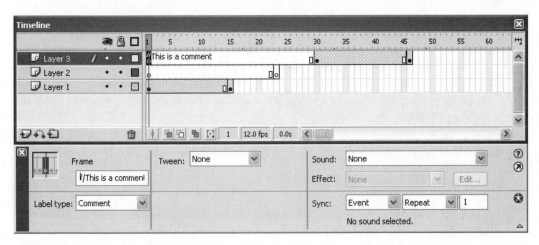

4. Press ENTER to apply the comment.

TIP

You may want to add a layer specifically for your comments so that they are more easily read and so that you have more flexibility in the placement of those comments. See "Adding Layers" later in this module for more information.

Comments can, of course, be added only to keyframes. In the timeline, comments will display in full unless another keyframe is encountered before the end of the comment. This is one of the reasons why a separate comment layer can be so useful—keyframes do not have to appear in the same frames on different layers, so you can adjust the keyframe placements in comment layers as needed.

Flash ignores the contents of comments. This means that you can use any characters or punctuation you want in your comments, as long as you begin any comments with the two forward slashes.

Adding Labels for Better Control

In addition to adding comments, you can also add labels to keyframes. Like comments, labels help to make your timelines easier to understand. But labels also serve another, more important purpose when you start adding ActionScript programming to your movies.

One of the most common ActionScript commands is the gotoAndPlay command. This command is used to control the flow of a movie by moving the playhead to a specific frame, and then playing the movie from that point onward. In its most simple form, the gotoAndPlay command accepts a frame number as an argument, as shown here:

```
gotoAndPlay(20);
```

In this case, the command moves the playhead to frame 20 and begins playing the movie from that frame forward. Consider what might happen, however, if you were to decide to lengthen an animation that appeared earlier in the timeline. If you added ten extra frames, the correct starting point for the gotoAndPlay command might be frame 30 rather than frame 20. Unfortunately, Flash would have no way to know this, so it might well try to move the playhead to the wrong frame.

The solution to this problem is to use frame labels rather than frame numbers. If you added the label "AnimationStart" to frame 20, your ActionScript command could look like this:

```
gotoAndPlay("AnimationStart");
```

The difference between these two methods of specifying a destination is an important one. If you add frames to the timeline, Flash will move the frame label along with the rest of the frames. Therefore, the AnimationStart label will continue to refer to the correct frame even after the timeline has been adjusted. Note that when you use a label in an ActionScript statement, you must enclose the label in quotes.

You add a frame label in much the same way as you do a comment. The only real difference is that you do not add the two slashes in the Label text box of the Frame panel when you are adding a frame label. You should avoid using spaces and punctuation in frame labels since these can cause problems when you want to use those labels in your ActionScript programming.

NOTE

When you add a label to a frame, you can also choose to select the Anchor option in the Label Type drop-down list box, which appears below the frame label text box. By doing so, you enable visitors to use the forward and back buttons in their browser to navigate in your movies.

Progress Check

1. What panel do you use to add comments and labels to the timeline?

2. How do you designate a comment?

3. What should you avoid in frame labels?

CRITICAL SKILL

4.3 Viewing Your Work with Onion Skins

When you are creating an animation in Flash, it can be difficult to visualize how objects will move between frames. You normally see only a single frame at a time, so you may find it hard to get a good picture of just where an object may go as it moves through the animation.

The solution to this problem is to use the *onion skin* view. This term comes from the traditional hand-drawn animation techniques where objects were drawn on transparent—

---

1. Properties panel
2. Add two forward slashes at the beginning of the comment.
3. Spaces and punctuation

or onion skin—paper, and it was possible to see different frames through the paper. Flash enables you to view the frames of your movie in a similar fashion, as shown here:

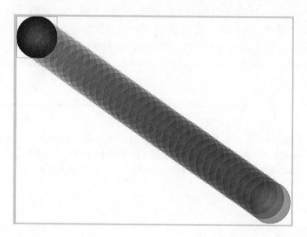

There actually are two onion skin modes. In addition to the standard onion skin view that shows progressively lighter images the further away you get from the current frame, you can also click the Onion Skin Outlines button to view objects as outlines only. You may find that you prefer one or the other of these two modes, but there is no real functional difference between them.

You will likely find it helpful to click the Modify Onion Markers button to display the menu shown here. You can use the options on this menu to control how the onion skin view functions. I suggest experimenting with these options to determine which settings work best for you.

Always Show Markers
Anchor Onion
Onion 2
Onion 5
Onion All

TIP

You can also drag the onion skin markers in the timeline to control the range of frames displayed in onion skin view. For example, you may want to see more frames before or after the current frame, and you can accomplish this by dragging the appropriate onion skin marker in the desired direction.

In addition to using the onion skin view, you may want to use the outline view for specific layers at times. The rightmost column in the layers area of the timeline has a box you can click to toggle between solid and outline view. Unlike when using the onion skin view, you can toggle outline view for specific layers. As this shows, you can then display one layer using the solid onion skin view and another layer using the onion skin outline view. Here I have the solid onion skin view selected for the ball and the outline view selected for the rectangle. (Outline view is the equivalent of the onion skin outline view.)

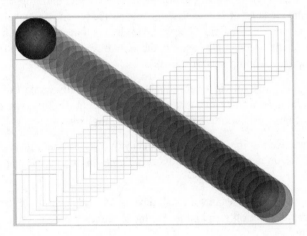

TIP

Outline view is also handy for viewing objects that do not move when you are working with multiple layers and need some visual alignment clues.

CRITICAL SKILL
4.4 Understanding Layers

Depending on the other drawing programs that you may have used, you may or may not be familiar with the concept of layers. *Layers* are an important part of the Flash development environment. In the following sections, we will look at why layers are important, and how you can make use of them as you create your Flash movies.

As you work with layers in Flash, it is important to remember one very significant fact. When you publish a Flash movie, any layers that you have created are flattened into a single layer. As a result, adding extra layers does not increase the size of your published Flash movie file. Therefore, you should feel free to use as many layers as necessary when you are creating a Flash movie.

The Purpose of Layers

One way to think of layers would be to think of clear plastic sheets where you can draw the objects that you will use in your movies. Each plastic sheet—layer—can act independently of all the others. If you have drawn objects on one layer and want to move them, you are free to do so without affecting the objects on other layers. But layers actually have a number of important uses:

- When you create a tween, all of the objects on the layer containing the tween must move together during the span of frames that encompass the tween. If you want to have stationary objects in your movie, they must be placed on layers that do not contain tweens. Also, if you have different tweens in the movie, these require separate layers (unless they occupy different, non-overlapping sets of frames).

- If you want to create a movie where objects are visible only on part of the stage, you need to use a special layer known as a *mask* layer. You might use this type of layer to create the effect of the character walking behind a window, for example.

- When you create a motion tween, the objects you were animating typically move in a straight line. If you want them to follow some other path, you use a special layer known as a *guide* layer.

- For organizational purposes, most Flash developers add separate layers for comments, for labels, and for any ActionScript code. Doing so makes it much easier to find specific items on the timeline.

- Sometimes, you may want it to appear as though one object were passing in front of another object. By using layers, you can easily achieve this effect.

You will learn more about the specifics of using the different types of layers as you continue through the rest of this module.

Progress Check

1. How many different tweens can you place on a layer?

2. How many layers do you need if you want some objects to remain in one place while others move?

3. How can you create animations that are independent of each other even though they occur at the same time during your movie?

---

1. As many as you want, as long as they do not have overlapping frames
2. At least two
3. Place them on separate timeline layers.

Adding Layers

You can add layers to the timeline at any time. There's no need for you to add every possible layer when you first begin creating your movie (unless you really want to, of course), since you can add them as the need arises.

You can use the Flash menu to add layers. The Insert | Timeline | Layer command adds a new layer immediately above the currently selected layer. You will probably find, however, that it is far easier to simply click the Insert Layer button at the lower-left edge of the timeline to add a new layer.

TIP

As you add layers to the timeline, get in the habit of checking to see which layer is selected before you make any changes on the stage. One of the most common errors that new Flash developers make is placing objects on the wrong layer. This is a very easy mistake to make, and one that can cause you to have to use the Edit | Undo command frequently.

Naming Layers

When you add layers to the timeline, Flash automatically names them using the not-very-descriptive names of Layer 1, Layer 2, and so on. Although there's no requirement for you to rename the layers, the default names certainly give no indication of the purpose of each layer. When you rename the layers, you can use descriptive names that clearly state the purpose of each layer. For example, you might name one layer "Background" to indicate that it is the background layer where you will draw objects that just sit there as the movie plays back. You might name another layer "Ball" to indicate that this is the layer where an animated ball will appear.

As I noted earlier, it is a good idea to also add layers for things like labels and ActionScript programming. When you do, you will probably want to name these layers with simple names like "Labels" and "Actions." Since the names are there for your benefit, you might as well make them something you will easily remember.

Understanding Layer Order Significance

As you start adding new layers to your movie, you need to understand how the layer order affects the visibility of objects. In this illustration, I have created a Flash movie that has two layers for the different objects in my movie. The layer in the front is named Car, while the layer in the back is named Background.

In the timeline, the layers look like the following. The Car layer is higher in the list than the Background layer, so everything on the Car layer appears to be in front of everything that is on the Background layer.

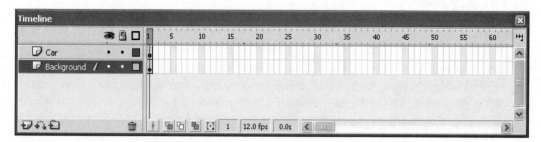

If I move the Background layer higher in the timeline than the Car layer, the objects that are in the Background layer now appear to be in front of the objects in the Car layer. The objects are all still in the same position on their own layers, but changing the order of the layers in the timeline affected their visibility.

Objects that are in layers higher in the timeline always appear to be in front of objects that are in layers lower in the timeline. You may need to rearrange the layers in order to make the objects appear in the correct order. You can do this by simply dragging a layer up or down in the layers area at the left side of the timeline list.

Progress Check

1. How many layers can you add to the timeline?

2. When you add objects to a new layer you just added, where will those objects appear in relationship to objects on the next layer down in the timeline?

CRITICAL SKILL

4.5 Use Layers Effectively

Adding Objects to Layers

Flash has three types of layers. Of these, the mask and guide layers have special purposes, but you can use normal layers for any other needs. That is, you can draw objects on any normal layer, you can add animations to normal layers, you can add ActionScript programming to any normal layer, and you can add labels or comments to normal layers.

Earlier in this module, you learned some of the reasons that you would want to use separate layers for different types of objects. You saw, for example, that you can use layers to separate stationary objects from those that move in an animation. You also learned that the order of the layers can be used to control the visibility of objects.

Using Drawing Layers

Drawings layers are simply normal layers. As you create your Flash movies, it makes sense to use separate layers for all objects that you might want to act independently of each other. That is, you may want to use more separate drawing layers than you first imagine.

---

1. As many as you want

2. In front of them

One reason for this is the way that Flash combines objects automatically. Consider the following illustration. In this case, I first drew a rectangle on the stage. Next, I selected a different fill color and drew the circle that overlaps the rectangle.

At this point, I decided that I didn't want the circle. I selected the circle and deleted it. As the following illustration shows, this also removed part of my rectangle because Flash automatically combined the rectangle and the circle when I drew them. Clearly, I didn't intend for the two objects to interact in that way.

If I had placed the two objects on different layers, deleting or moving the circle would not have affected the rectangle.

Flash does not treat grouped objects in quite the same way as it treats ungrouped objects. (All objects are ungrouped immediately after you have drawn them.) If I had used the Modify | Group command to convert the rectangle into a grouped object before adding the circle, it would have been unaffected when I deleted the circle. The reason for this is that Flash does not automatically combine grouped objects. Even so, it is generally better to use separate layers to hold objects that you do not want to interact with each other.

TIP

As a further hedge against accidentally modifying something that you have drawn, you can click in the Lock column for the layer (in the layers area at the left of the timeline) to prevent any changes to the objects on that layer. This also prevents you from drawing additional objects on that layer unless you first unlock the layer by clicking in the Lock column again.

Using Action Layers

I briefly mentioned ActionScript programming earlier. ActionScript is the programming language that you use when you need to add a little extra control to your Flash movies. For example, this shows a small ActionScript program that displays a message in a pop-up window when the movie is run:

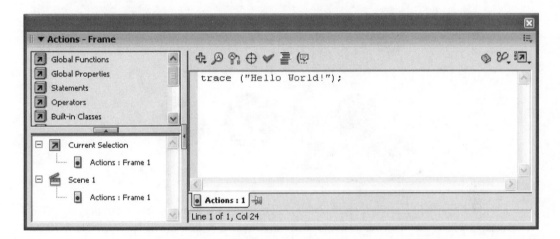

When you add ActionScript statements to the timeline, you can add them only to keyframes. By adding a separate layer for your ActionScript actions, you not only gain the flexibility of being able to place those keyframes anywhere in the timeline, but you also make it far easier to quickly locate the frames where you have added some code. You can add ActionScript code to any keyframe on any layer even if that layer is being used for some other type of content, but a separate layer for your ActionScript code is usually a much better idea.

TIP

Flash places a small letter *a* in keyframes that contain ActionScript statements.

You can, of course, use whatever name you prefer for the layer that contains your ActionScript statements. A convention that many Flash developers follow is to call this layer "Actions" to make it clear that the layer holds the ActionScript actions.

Mask Layers

Mask layers are one of the two special types of layers you can create in Flash. A mask layer acts as a window onto another layer. When your movie plays, the mask layer controls how much of the masked layer is visible.

To understand how a mask layer works, take a look at this illustration. Here I've added a number of colored balls to the stage.

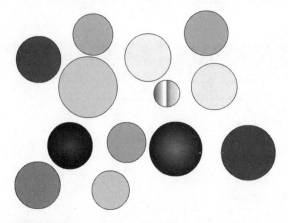

Now I have added a mask layer where I have drawn a rectangle over part of the stage. This rectangle will be the mask that controls what can be seen when the movie is played. Notice that several of the colored balls are outside of the area that is covered by the mask.

Finally, this shows how the stage will look during playback. The only portion of the masked layer that is visible is the area that was under the mask. Anything that was outside of the mask is invisible.

NOTE

Mask layers are discussed in detail in Module 7.

When you create a mask layer, the mask layer is associated with the layer immediately below it in the timeline. This is the masked layer—the one that is affected by the mask. The mask layer itself never appears when the movie is played. The objects on the mask layer simply act as though they were a window onto the masked layer.

TIP

You can use a tween to animate a mask. When your movie plays, this gives the effect of a moving window onto the masked layer. You can also use a tween to animate the masked layer. This is one way you can create scrolling banner text in Flash.

Guide Layers

Guide layers are the second of the two special layer types you will find in Flash. Guide layers are used to direct the path of a motion tween when you don't want the animation to follow a straight path. If you don't use a motion guide, the animation will always follow a direct, straight line from the object's position in the initial keyframe to the object's position in the final keyframe. Once you add a motion guide to your movie, this limitation no longer applies; the animation can follow the motion guide rather than a simple, straight path.

This shows an example of a guide layer. In this case, you can see that the ball starts moving at one of the upper corners of the stage and then follows a rather twisted path to the other upper corner of the stage. This sort of path is possible only when you use a motion guide.

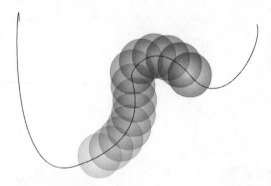

Like mask layers, guide layers (and their contents) do not appear in the published movie. You can use any sort of line as a motion guide.

TIP

You can use the same motion guide to direct more than one motion tween. This technique can be very handy when you want to move a number of objects along the same path. For example, you could create a motion guide to direct a number of buttons into place along a curved line.

To create a motion guide, you begin by creating a normal motion tween animation sequence. Then you add a motion guide layer and draw the motion guide path. Finally, you attach the tweened object to the motion guide, and the object will follow the path as it moves. Motion guides are covered in detail in Module 7.

Progress Check

1. How many types of layers does Flash have?

2. What type of layer controls the visibility of objects on another layer?

3. What type of layer enables a tween to follow a curved path?

---

1. Three
2. Mask layer
3. Guide layer

Project 4-1 Adding Some Layers and Frames to the Timeline

Now that you have had an introduction to frames and layers, it is time to put that knowledge into practice by adding several of these items to the timeline. This will be a relatively simple and straightforward project, yet it will lay the foundation for the Flash movies that you create in the future.

Step by Step

1. Open a new, blank Flash movie.

2. Select the Insert | Timeline | Layer command to add a new layer to the timeline. This new layer will be named Layer 2, and it will appear above Layer 1 in the timeline.

3. Click the Insert Layer button (at the lower-left edge of the timeline) to add another layer to the timeline. This layer will be named Layer 3, and it will appear just above Layer 2 in the timeline.

4. Right-click (Command-click on a Mac) the layer name area for Layer 3, and select Properties from the pop-up menu to display the Layer Properties dialog box shown here:

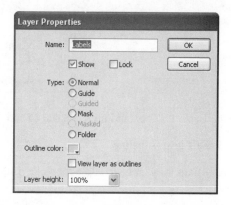

5. Type **Labels** in the Name text box to rename this layer.

6. Click OK to apply your changes.

7. Double-click the layer name for Layer 2, and type **Ball** as the new name for this layer.

8. Rename Layer 1 as **Background**.

9. Click frame 1 in the Ball layer timeline to select it.

(continued)

10. Use the Oval tool to draw a circle in frame 1 of the Ball layer.

11. Click frame 36 in the Ball layer timeline to select it.

12. Select Insert | Timeline | Keyframe from the Flash menu to add a keyframe to frame 36 of the Ball layer timeline.

13. Click frame 16 in the Labels layer timeline to select it.

14. Add a keyframe to frame 16 in the Labels layer timeline.

15. Click frame 10 in the Background layer timeline, and then drag the mouse pointer to frame 15. Continue holding down the mouse button while you drag the mouse pointer up to the Labels layer. When you release the mouse button, you should have frames 10 through 15 selected in all three layers.

16. Select Insert | Timeline | Frame to add the frames to all three layers.

17. Click frame 22 in the Labels layer timeline. This should be the keyframe you added in step 14. (The keyframe should have moved when you inserted the new frames.)

18. Use the Window | Properties command (or click the triangle left of the panel name) to open the Properties panel, as shown here:

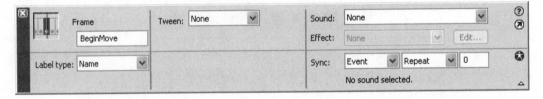

19. Type **BeginMove** in the Label text box and press ENTER to add the label to the frame.

20. Click frame 42 in the Labels layer timeline.

21. Select Insert | Timeline | Blank Keyframe to add a blank keyframe. Your timeline should now look like this:

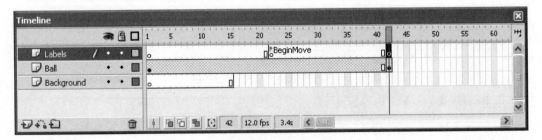

Project Summary

In this project, you added several layers to the timeline and then renamed them to make it easier for you to quickly recognize their purpose. Then you added keyframes and ordinary frames to the timeline layers. You saw that you did not have to add your keyframes to the same frames in each layer, so you have the flexibility to lay out the timeline as necessary. You also saw that when you add a new keyframe to a layer that contains objects, Flash copies the contents of the previous keyframe, duplicating both the objects and their positions. These will all be important points that you need to know as you draw objects and create animations for your Flash movies in later modules.

✔ # Module 4 Mastery Check

1. You can add objects only to _____ in the timeline.

2. To add labels and comments to a frame, you use the _____ panel.

3. If you want to add a comment rather than a label, you add _____ to the label.

4. To view several frames of an animation at the same time, you use _____ view.

5. When there are two or more layers in the timeline, the layer that is _____ in the timeline list appears in front of the other layer.

6. You can use a _____ layer to create a window onto another layer to control what will be seen as the movie plays.

7. _____ layers are used to direct a motion tween along a path.

8. Flash has _____ types of layers.

9. The different types of layers are _____.

10. Adding extra layers to your movie has which of the following effects?

    A. It increases the size of the published movie file.

    B. It decreases the size of the published movie file.

    C. It makes the movie run faster.

    D. It makes no difference to the size or speed.

11. When you add a motion guide to a Flash movie, that motion guide is _____ when the movie is played.

12. If you allow a Flash movie to play at normal speed, _____ frames will be needed for a ten-second movie.

13. If you want to prevent changes to a layer, you can click the _____ column.

14. To view just the strokes for the objects on a layer, you can click the _____ column.

15. Keyframes that contain content can easily be identified in the timeline because they contain a _____.

Module 5

Drawing Objects

Virtually all Flash movies include objects that are drawn. Learning how to use the drawing tools and to create objects for your Flash movies is a fundamental part of creating movies. In this module, you will learn to use those tools and to create objects. As you will see, creating objects that you can animate is not an overly difficult task, but you do have to understand certain concepts in order to be successful. For example, you will see that grouping objects is an important step both in making objects act independently of each other, and in being able to animate them.

CRITICAL SKILLS
5.1 Drawing Lines and Fills

On the surface, drawing objects in Flash is not a whole lot different than drawing objects in many other graphics programs. That is, you select the appropriate drawing tool and then draw objects on the stage. Still, Flash does have some important differences from most other drawing programs. For one thing, the objects that you draw in Flash are vector-based rather than being bitmap images (also true of certain other programs, of course).

Unlike bitmap images, vector graphics are really made up of mathematical descriptions of an object. In contrast, bitmap images are made up of thousands of data points. As a result, vector graphics can easily be scaled to different sizes without affecting the image quality. This is not true of bitmap images, since changing the image size requires interpolating missing or overlapping data points.

One of the consequences of the fact that Flash uses vector graphics is that you end up dealing with lines and fills as complete entities. This is very different from the way that you work in a bitmap graphic editing program. There, it is typically very difficult to modify an entire line or fill because these are not considered to be individual objects. Don't worry if this seems a little confusing at this point; you will quickly become quite comfortable with the way you work with objects in Flash.

Selecting Different Strokes

Flash uses the term *stroke* for what you probably call a line. We will use the two terms interchangeably. Whenever you use the Line tool, the Pen tool, or the Pencil tool, you always create a line. In most cases, you also create a line to outline the object that you are drawing when you use the Oval tool or the Rectangle tool.

TIP

To draw an oval or rectangle without an outline, click the stroke color selector and then the No Color button. This will add a diagonal red slash across the stroke color selector to indicate that no stroke will be drawn. Click the No Color button again to remove the diagonal red slash when you want to resume adding the outline to objects that you draw.

No matter which drawing tool you use to draw a line, Flash uses the current selections in the Properties panel to draw that line. Therefore, the Properties panel is the place to begin when you want to draw different types of lines. To make these selections, follow these steps:

1. Open the Properties panel as shown here using the Window | Properties command (or by clicking the triangle to the left of the panel's name if the panel is visible but collapsed at the bottom of the Flash window).

2. Select one of the tools (such as the Line tool) that draw lines so that the Properties panel will display the stroke options.

3. Click the down arrow at the right side of the Stroke Style list box to display all of the available stroke styles, as shown here:

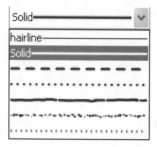

4. Click the style that you want to use. Any selections you make will appear in the Stroke Style list box. If you want to create a line that is as thin as possible and never scales up, choose hairline.

5. To change the line width, drag the Stroke Height slider up or down as shown here. You can also enter a value directly into the Stroke Height text box. The value for the line width must be between 0.25 and 10 points.

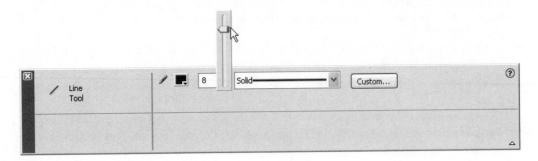

6. If you want to change the color, you can click the stroke color selector.

Once you have made your selections, any new lines that you draw will reflect those changes. It is not necessary for you to close the Properties panel unless you find that you need more room on your screen.

TIP

You can collapse any docked panel so that only its title bar is showing by clicking the downward-pointing triangle to the left of the panel name. The panel will reappear when you click the right-pointing triangle that replaces the down arrow when the panel is collapsed. You can collapse a free-floating panel to the size of the blue bar by double-clicking the blue bar. Double-click again to display the entire panel.

You can also modify the style, width, and color of an existing line by selecting the line and then making changes in the Properties panel. The new settings that you choose will also apply to any new lines that you draw until you select a different set of options in the Properties panel.

Choosing Different Fills

Ovals, rectangles, and other closed objects can be filled with a solid color, a gradient, or even a bitmap fill. Typically, you use the fill color selector to choose the fill for closed objects. However, you can also use the Color Mixer panel as shown here. To open the Color Mixer panel, use the Window | Design Panels | Color Mixer command.

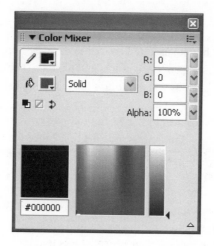

Generally speaking, you should choose the fill that you want to use before you begin drawing an object. If you want to change the fill in an existing object, you have a couple of choices. You can select the object and then use the Color Mixer panel to select a new fill. You also can use the Paint Bucket tool to add a different fill to objects.

TIP

To duplicate the fill of an existing object, click the Eyedropper tool in the Flash Tools panel, and then click the fill that you want to duplicate. This activates the Paint Bucket tool so that you can apply the selected fill to objects.

We will discuss gradient fills shortly. Bitmap fills are discussed in Module 9.

Progress Check

1. What is another term for stroke?

2. What types of objects can have a fill?

1. Line
2. Closed objects

Adding Complex Curves

In Module 2, you learned how to use the Pen tool to draw Bézier curves. These are curved lines that are defined by a series of click points and handles. The Pen tool is supplemented by the Subselect tool, which enables you to modify the curved lines after you have finished using the Pen tool.

The Pen tool and the Subselect tool are certainly powerful, but they can be somewhat tricky to use, and it can take a fair amount of time to achieve the results you want with them. Fortunately, these two tools are not the only options that you can use to create complex curved lines in your Flash drawings.

You can also use the Arrow tool to modify objects. With the Arrow tool, you can move corners as well as bend lines into quite complex curved shapes. As you will soon learn, the Arrow tool makes it very easy to make major modifications to the shape of drawn objects.

In addition to using the Subselect and Arrow tools to modify the shape of objects, you also have the option of using the Free Transform tool. Although quite similar to the Arrow tool, the Free Transform tool enables you to make a number of modifications with a single tool. You can, for example, scale, rotate, skew, and warp an object with the Free Transform tool. It is probably best, however, to learn the basics by using the Arrow tool first and then move on to the Free Transform tool once you are comfortable with those actions.

TIP

Before using the Arrow tool to modify a drawn object, make certain that you have used one of the drawing tools to create an object with at least as many corners as you will want in the finished shape. You can use the Arrow tool to remove unwanted corners, but you cannot use it to add extra corners to a shape that has already been drawn.

To use the Arrow tool to add complex curves to a drawn object, follow these steps:

1. Draw the object that you want to use as the basis for your new object. You will be able to make extensive modifications to the shape of the object, so the initial shape is not very critical.

2. Click the Arrow tool to select it.

3. To modify a corner, move the mouse pointer close to a corner so that the Arrow tool pointer shows a right-angle corner, as shown next.

4. Drag the corner to a new position, as shown here. If you drag an existing corner onto another corner, Flash will eliminate the corner you were dragging and connect the remaining corners.

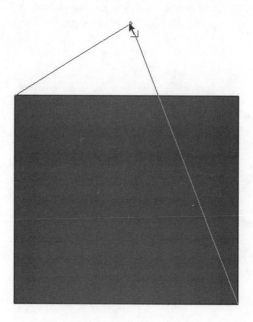

5. To change a line into a curved line, move the mouse pointer close to the line so that the Arrow tool has a curved line, as shown here:

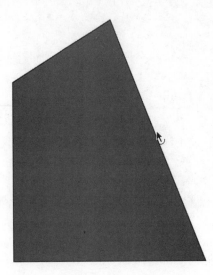

6. Drag the line into the curved shape you want, as shown here. Notice that you can modify the curve not only by dragging the line, but also by moving the mouse pointer toward or away from a corner.

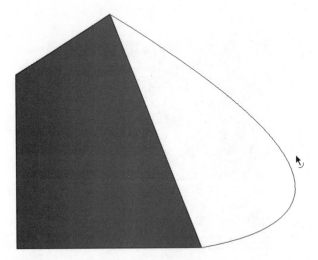

As you drag lines with the Arrow tool to reshape them, keep in mind that the corner points always remain anchored when you are dragging the middle of the line. However, if you drag a corner point, you will reshape both of the lines that are attached to the corner.

NOTE

You can also use the Subselect tool to reshape the lines of a drawn object. Unlike the Arrow tool, the Subselect tool can be used to bend a line into an S curve. Use caution when doing so, however, since this will add an oddly behaving corner where the line makes the transition from bending in one direction to bending in the other direction. Although the Arrow tool will treat this new corner as a corner, moving the new corner will not move the line segments in quite the fashion you might expect. In fact, you will probably find that once you have used the Subselect tool to modify the shape of an object, the Arrow tool will not produce very desirable results during further attempts to modify the object.

Progress Check

1. Can you change the number of corners in an object using the Arrow tool?

2. Which tool can change a line into an S curve?

CRITICAL SKILL
5.2 Using Colors

One of the things that people generally notice first when they visit a web site is the use of colors. Oh, they may not think too much about the colors they are seeing, but a colorful web site certainly does make an impression.

Actually, the use of color in animations is a very old concept. The Saturday morning cartoons that many of us grew up on certainly used a lot of bright colors to help make things interesting. That makes a lot of sense, really. No one would look at an animated cartoon (any more than they would look at a Flash movie) and mistake it for real life. Because of this, color can be used in an animation in ways it might not be used otherwise. Bright, bold colors can provide a lot of excitement and add to the overall experience.

You can choose colors for each line and fill that you add to a drawing. Flash has two color selectors—one for the stroke color and one for the fill color. In certain circumstances, you can also choose to not use a color:

- When you use the Oval tool or the Rectangle tool, you can click the No Color button when either the stroke color or the fill color selector is active. Doing so places a red slash across

---

1. You can subtract but not add corners with the Arrow tool.

2. The Subselect tool

the selected color selector to indicate that no color will be used. This effectively eliminates either the stroke or the fill when you then draw the object.

● When you use the Pen tool, you can click the No Color button only if the fill color selector is active. This prevents Flash from filling the object when you close the shape. You cannot use the No Color button to prevent the Pen tool from drawing the stroke.

● You cannot use the No Color button with the Line tool, the Pencil tool, or the Brush tool. These tools draw with only one color—the stroke color—and it cannot be turned off. These tools do not use the fill color because they do not automatically add a fill even if you use them to draw a closed object.

Choosing Colors

To choose a stroke or fill color, you begin by clicking the color selector you want in the Colors area of the Flash Tools panel. This displays the color selector pane, as shown here. In this case, I have opened the fill color selector, but the stroke color selector is nearly identical—except that you cannot choose a gradient fill for the stroke color.

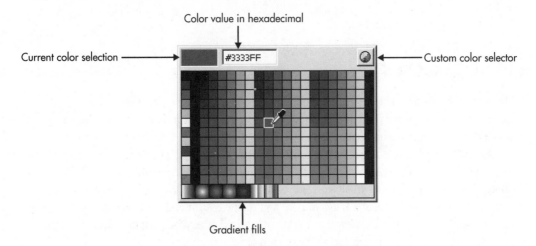

Color value in hexadecimal

Current color selection

#3333FF

Custom color selector

Gradient fills

When you open a color selector, the mouse pointer changes into an eyedropper. As you move the mouse around, the color that is under the tip of the eyedropper appears in the current color selection box. Also, the hexadecimal value of the current color selection appears in the box just to the right of the current color selection box. Although this value probably has little meaning to you right now, it will be important later when you want to control colors of objects using ActionScript programming.

You are not limited to selecting colors from the color selector pane. If you move the mouse pointer out of the color selector pane, you can select almost any color from any object on the screen. In fact, this is a good way to make sure that you match an existing color.

You also can use custom colors by clicking the custom color button in the upper-right corner of the color selector pane. This will display the Color dialog box, as shown here:

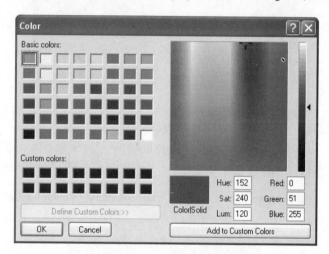

One advantage to using the Color dialog box is that you have the option of specifying an exact color using precise values. This might be very handy if you need to match a color such as the color of a corporate logo. After you select the custom color, click the Add To Custom Colors button to make that color the current color selection. When you close the Color dialog box, you can then use the custom color in your drawings.

Adding Gradients

Gradients are a special type of color fill that you can use. A *gradient* is a fill that blends two or more colors. A gradient always starts at one color and makes a smooth transition to another color.

There are two types of gradients:

- A *linear* gradient changes colors in a straight line from one side of the fill to the other side.

- A *radial* gradient changes colors as the distance changes from the center point of the fill.

You're free to use whichever type of gradient you prefer. That is, you do not have to use linear gradients in rectangular objects, nor do you have to use radial gradients in round objects.

Adding a gradient fill works just like adding a solid color fill. You simply choose the gradient fill you want to use, and Flash fills any new, closed objects with that gradient fill. This shows an example of using a gradient fill:

Creating Your Own Gradients

Using gradient fills is even more fun when you create your own gradients. You can create both linear and radial gradients to suit your needs. To create a custom gradient, follow these steps:

1. Use the Window | Design Panels | Color Mixer command to open the Color Mixer panel, as shown here:

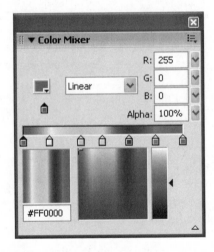

2. Select either Linear gradient or Radial gradient from the Fill Style list box.

3. Click one of the pointers below the Edit Gradient Range box to select it (this is the box that appears in the center of the panel when you select a gradient fill option). The selected pointer has a solid black triangle on top, while the other pointers show a gray triangle.

4. Click the gradient color selector to choose the color for the selected pointer.

5. To add a new pointer, click below the Edit Gradient Range box.

6. To move a color selection, drag it right or left as necessary.

7. To remove a pointer, drag it off the Color Mixer panel.

8. Click the menu icon in the upper-right corner of the Color Mixer panel (just below the Close button) to display the menu.

9. Select Add Swatch to save the custom gradient. This will place the new gradient as one of the selections in the fill color selector pane.

TIP

If you have selected one of the existing gradient fills as the fill color, you can then edit that gradient in the Color Mixer panel using the same procedure you just learned for creating a gradient fill.

Progress Check

1. Where can you use gradients?

2. What type of gradient fills outwards from a single point?

Warping and Bending Gradients

By default, gradient fills are centered in the object being filled, and the gradient is placed so that it sits at a normal horizontal orientation. There is no reason, however, why you cannot warp and bend the gradients to suit your needs. Often a gradient will produce a far better effect once it has been modified somewhat. For example, you might want to modify a gradient so that a set of pipes takes on a 3-D appearance.

Both linear and radial gradients can be modified. Radial gradients have one more adjustment than linear gradients, but otherwise the procedure is identical. To modify a gradient fill that you have applied to an object, follow these steps:

1. Select the Fill Transform tool from the Flash Tools panel.

1. As a fill

2. Radial gradients

2. Click the filled object that you want to modify to display the transform fill handles, as shown here:

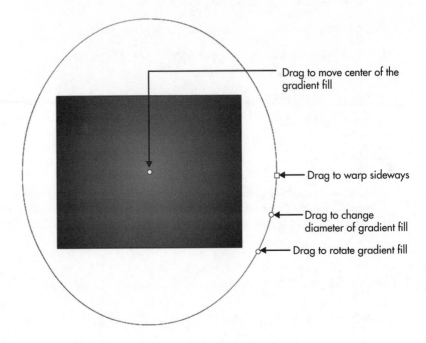

Drag to move center of the gradient fill

Drag to warp sideways

Drag to change diameter of gradient fill

Drag to rotate gradient fill

3. To move the center of the fill, drag the handle in the center of the circle.

4. To warp the fill in a horizontal direction, drag the square handle.

5. To change the overall diameter of the gradient fill, drag the middle handle. (This handle is missing when you are modifying a linear gradient.)

6. To rotate the fill, drag the rotation handle.

The next example shows how the gradient fill might appear after you have made a number of modifications using the various handles to warp and bend the fill.

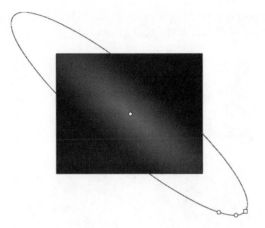

Controlling Alpha Settings

The *alpha* setting isn't strictly a color setting, but it is somewhat related. Alpha is the transparency property for an object. An object that has an alpha setting of 100 is completely opaque, while an alpha setting of 0 makes the object totally transparent (and therefore invisible). Settings between 0 and 100 result in partial transparency, as shown in this example, where the four boxes are set at 100 percent, 75 percent, 50 percent, and 25 percent, respectively. The text

Ask the Expert

Q: When I warp a gradient fill, the edges of the filled area take on a solid color rather than showing a gradient the way the center does. What's wrong?

A: When you change the width of a gradient fill, you need to watch the outlines that contain the transform fill handles. Anything that is outside the circular outline for a radial fill or the two parallel lines for a linear fill will be filled with the solid colors that are at the ends of the gradient fill pattern.

Q: I just want to change the center point of the fill. Do I need to mess with the transform fill handles for something so simple?

A: No, you can move the center point by clicking with the Paint Bucket tool. This method applies the gradient without any distortions, but it will replace any warping you may have done with the transform fill handles, so make certain you do not use this shortcut method if you want to keep any customizations that you may have applied.

that shows the alpha setting is on a separate layer behind the boxes. Notice that you cannot even see the text behind the box with a 100 percent alpha setting.

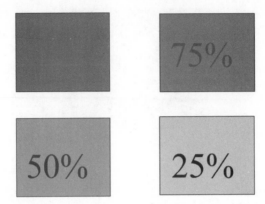

To set an object's alpha value, follow these steps:

1. Click the Arrow tool in the Flash Tools panel to select it.

2. Click the object whose alpha setting you want to adjust so that the object is selected.

3. Open the Color Mixer panel as shown here by using the Window | Design Panels | Color Mixer command:

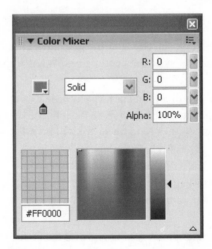

4. Enter a value in the Alpha box, or drag the slider to the correct value.

5. To adjust the alpha setting for additional objects, repeat steps 2–4 as necessary.

You can also adjust an object's alpha property using ActionScript statements or as a part of a tween. You could, for example, make an object fade into the background or make an object slowly come into view. This latter option can be used to create a very interesting effect when you want a set of buttons to appear on the stage.

Progress Check

1. What setting will make an object invisible?

2. What tool enables you to warp a gradient?

CRITICAL SKILL

5.3 Rotating, Skewing, and Scaling

So far, you have learned several ways to modify objects. Now we will have a look at some ways to modify objects while retaining their basic shape. Objects that you rotate, skew, or scale may not look as though they still have the same basic shape, but to Flash they do. This is an important point, since you can apply these effects as a part of a motion tween. If the basic shape were changed, you would not be able to use a motion tween to animate the objects.

You can rotate, skew, or scale pretty much any type of object that you create in Flash. Of course, some types of objects are better candidates for these actions. For example, it would be very easy to tell whether a rectangle was rotated, and almost impossible to tell if a circle had been rotated. Therefore, I will use rectangles in these examples simply so that it will be easier for you to see the effects of each action.

TIP

Before you begin trying to rotate, skew, or scale any objects, make certain that you have properly selected the objects that you want to modify. A little later in this module, we will discuss grouping objects to make certain that complete objects are selected. Until then, pay special attention to what you have selected before making any modifications.

---

1. Changing alpha to zero
2. Fill Transform tool

Rotating Objects

Rotating an object is the act of turning the object around its center point—in much the same way that the hands on a clock rotate around the center of the clock. When you rotate an object, the object maintains the same dimensions and angles that it had before it was rotated.

You can rotate an object using your mouse. To do so, follow these steps:

1. Click the Arrow tool in the Tools panel to select it.

2. Double-click the object that you want to rotate so that you select both the stroke and the fill. You can also draw a selection box using the Arrow tool if you prefer that method of selecting.

3. Select the Modify | Transform | Rotate And Skew command to add the rotation handles to the object, as shown here:

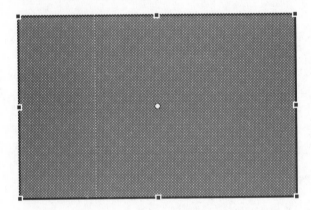

4. Use one of the corner handles to rotate the object by dragging, as shown here:

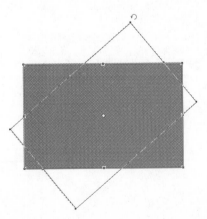

NOTE

When you are rotating an object, do not attempt to use the handles along the sides of the object because this will skew the object.

Skewing Objects

Skewing an object is a process that moves the sides of the object so that the sides remain parallel, but the angles of the corners are modified. You can skew an object by up to 45 degrees in either direction.

To skew an object, follow these steps:

1. First, make certain that you have selected the entire object, including the stroke and the fill.

2. Select the Modify | Transform | Rotate And Skew command.

3. Drag one of the side handles, as shown here. As you drag a side, that side will remain parallel to the opposite side of the object.

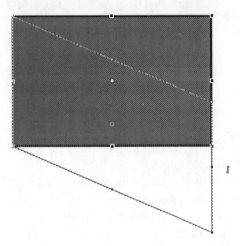

TIP

As you have seen in this example, Flash does not offer a separate command that you use to skew an object. You simply have to remember that skewing is related to rotating.

Scaling Objects

Scaling an object modifies the height or width of the object. You use scaling to make an object shrink or grow.

To scale an object by dragging, follow these steps:

1. Begin by selecting the entire object that you want to scale.

2. Select the Modify | Transform | Scale command.

3. Drag one of the handles, as shown here. If you drag one of the side handles, you will scale the object in just one direction. If you drag one of the corner handles, you will scale the object in two dimensions at the same time.

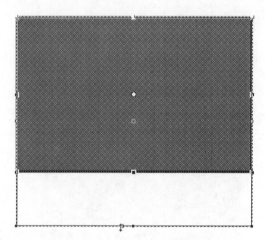

Rotating, Skewing, and Scaling Using the Transform Panel

One of the problems with rotating and scaling objects by dragging them is that this method is not very precise. It is difficult, for example, to rotate an object to a specific angle by dragging. Fortunately, Flash offers a different method that is more precise.

For the most precise control over all aspects of rotating, skewing, and scaling objects, you should use the Transform panel. This panel enables you to enter exact values, so you can get exactly the results you want.

To modify an object using the Transform panel, follow these steps:

1. Select the object that you want to modify.

2. Open the Transform panel as shown here using the Window | Design Panels | Transform command:

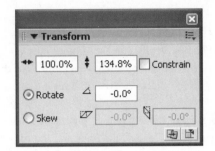

3. Enter the values that you wish to apply to the object.

4. If you want the object to scale equally in the vertical and horizontal dimensions, make certain that you select the Constrain check box.

5. If you decide that you should not have modified the object, click the Reset button in the lower-right corner of the Transform panel.

Progress Check

1. What will happen if you drag one of the side handles when the rotate handles surround an object?

2. Which handle should you drag to scale an object proportionally in both dimensions?

CRITICAL SKILL
5.4 Grouping and Ungrouping Objects

If you have tried drawing and animating objects in Flash, you may have experienced a certain amount of frustration. Although the process is fairly simple, some basic requirements can trip you up if you are unaware of them. In the following sections, we will discuss a very important topic that can have a profound effect on your ability to successfully draw and animate objects: grouping.

---

1. You will skew the object.

2. A corner handle

Understanding Ungrouped Objects

Objects that you draw in Flash typically consist of more than one part. Unless you draw a simple, straight line, almost all drawn objects have a number of different pieces that make up the object. At a minimum, filled objects consist of at least two pieces—the outline stroke and the internal fill.

Of course, many objects have more than two pieces. A square-cornered rectangle has five different elements when you count each of the lines and the fill. Rectangles with rounded corners have even more individual pieces. To see an example of this, draw a rectangle object with rounded corners. Then click different parts of the outline (hold down SHIFT if you want to add additional pieces to the selection). Once you have selected several elements, drag several of them away from the rectangle, as shown here:

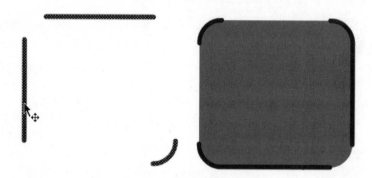

This example clearly demonstrates that Flash treats each element of a drawn object as a separate object. This has several important implications:

- You cannot apply a motion tween to drawn objects without first grouping them.

- You can apply shape tweens only to ungrouped objects.

- Ungrouped objects that are on the same layer will automatically combine if they are overlaying each other. If you attempt to move an object that is on top of another object, the part of the lower object that was under the top object will disappear.

- It is very easy to accidentally modify part of an ungrouped object without modifying the entire object. For example, if you click once inside a rectangle and then rotate the rectangle, you will leave the outline where it was and only move the fill.

Understanding Grouped Objects

Grouped objects are objects where all of the parts of the object have been joined together so that they function as a single entity. If you move or modify a grouped object, you affect all parts of the object.

Here are some important facts you need to know about grouped objects:

- You can apply a motion tween to a grouped object.

- You cannot apply a shape tween to a grouped object.

- Grouped objects do not affect other objects even if they are on the same layer. If you drop a grouped object onto another object, you can move the grouped object without removing any of the lower object.

- Grouped objects always act as if they were a single object, so modifications you make to a grouped object are applied to the complete object.

Progress Check

1. Can you animate ungrouped objects?

2. What happens when ungrouped objects overlap on a layer?

Simple Grouping Examples

By now, it should be fairly clear why you will often need to group the objects that you draw in Flash. Not only does this enable you to apply motion tweens to the objects, but grouping them also allows them to act independently so that you don't inadvertently wipe out part of an object by placing another object over it.

Okay, so now that you have a basic understanding of why you might need to group objects, it's time to see how you do so. Follow these steps:

1. Use the drawing tools to create an object on the stage.

2. Click the Arrow tool to select it.

3. Draw a selection box around the object to select it completely. If no other objects exist on the current layer, you can also use the Edit | Select All command to select everything on the layer.

---

1. Yes, with a shape tween.
2. They combine.

4. Select the Modify | Group command to group the selected object. As this shows, Flash then places a bounding box around the grouped object.

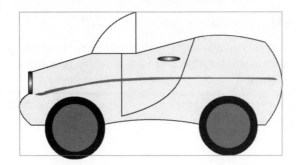

5. Click outside the object to remove the bounding box selection.

6. With the object unselected, drag it to a different location on the stage. Notice that even though it is not selected, the object moves as a single unit.

Although this example showed a fairly complex object, you can also group very simple objects. Try the example again using a circle that you have drawn with the Oval tool (holding down SHIFT to create a perfect circle). This time, use the double-click method to select the object for grouping. That is, rather than drawing a selection box, simply double-click the drawn object.

TIP

Double-clicking works to select a simple object that has a single fill area and an outline. More complex objects must be selected using a selection box or by SHIFT-clicking each element of the object.

Now that you have created a grouped object, try modifying that object to see how the various elements are affected. For example, here is our sports car after it has been scaled to make it longer and lower. Notice that every part of the grouped object was modified—even the wheels. Clearly, this is not quite the effect we want in this case. Next we'll look at how you can avoid this type of problem.

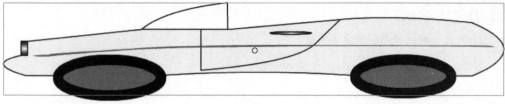

Ungrouping as Needed

As the last illustration showed, grouped objects act as a single entity, and this can cause problems in some cases. Indeed, you may find that you need to ungroup objects to make certain types of modifications.

To ungroup an object, you use the Modify | Ungroup command. This separates the object back into its individual components so that you can modify them individually.

Ungrouping objects brings back all of the shortcomings of ungrouped objects that were mentioned earlier. For example, any individual elements that overlap will once again interact. If you were to try to scale the automobile without changing the wheels, you would likely find that the effect would not be very satisfactory.

NOTE

Objects can also be made up of grouped objects. You can even group a collection of grouped objects. When you ungroup an object that contains groups, you do not ungroup the groups within the main object.

The Modify menu contains another command—the Break Apart command. This command is intended primarily for use with bitmap images (as you will learn in Module 9), but it also functions as a super ungroup command. That is, the Modify | Break Apart command destroys all grouping—even nested grouping—in the selected object. This command can make some very profound changes and deserves to be treated with extreme caution!

Project 5-1 Drawing a Button with a Gradient Fill

Now it is time to put together a number of the skills that you have learned in this module to create an object. In this case, you will create an artistic-looking button that you could use later as the basis for push buttons on your web site.

(continued)

Step by Step

1. Open a new, blank Flash movie.

2. Select the Rectangle tool in the Tools panel.

3. Use the Window | Properties command to open the Properties panel.

4. In the Stroke Style list box, choose the ragged line style.

5. Use the Stroke Height slider to set the line width to 5. The Properties panel should now look like this:

6. Use the Round Rectangle Radius option to set the corner rounding to 20 points.

7. Click the fill color selector.

8. Click a radial gradient, as shown here:

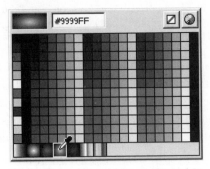

9. Draw a small rectangle on the stage.

10. Select the Fill Transform tool.

11. Click the rectangle you drew to select it.

12. Move the center of the fill to one corner of the rectangle, and then use the remaining handles to warp and rotate the fill, as shown next.

13. Click the Arrow tool.

14. Double-click the rectangle so that both the fill and the outline are selected. Alternatively, draw a selection box around the entire rectangle.

15. Select the Modify | Group command to group the rectangle.

16. Right-click the button and choose Scale from the pop-up menu. Alternatively, select Modify | Transform | Scale.

17. Drag one of the corner handles to reduce the size of the button to about one-half its current height and width. Choose a size that would make a reasonable size button for a web site.

18. Click outside the button to deselect it.

19. Use the File | Save command to save your work.

Project Summary

In this project, you created an object that you could use as a button. In doing so, you practiced many of the techniques that you learned in this module. You selected stroke options and a gradient fill to make the button more interesting. Then you adjusted the gradient fill to give the button a unique appearance. Next you grouped the object so that you could use it in an animation later if you like, and you scaled it to a size that would work well as a button.

Project
5-1

Drawing a Button with a Gradient Fill

Module 5 Mastery Check

1. You can use gradients for the _____ of an object.

2. If you want to use a _____ tween, you must group the object.

3. If you want to warp a gradient fill, you use the _____ tool.

4. To apply precise rotation, skew, or scale settings to an object, you would use the _____ panel.

5. To make an object partially transparent, you adjust the _____ property.

6. You can create your own gradient fills using the _____ panel.

7. Which of the following is not a fill style option?

   A. Solid

   B. Linear gradient

   C. Vector gradient

   D. Bitmap

8. Warping an object by dragging one of the side rotation handles is known as _____.

9. If you want to bend the side of an object using a single curve between two of the corners, you would use the _____ tool.

10. You can apply a new fill to an object by using the _____ tool.

11. Another name for a line is a _____.

12. To draw a rectangle without a fill, you click the fill color selector and then the _____ button.

13. A _____ gradient flows outwards from a central point.

14. To change the size of an object, you select the Modify | Transform | _____ command.

15. To rotate an object, you drag a _____ handle.

Module 6

Creating Animations

135

A nimation is certainly the most recognizable feature of Flash. If you took away the ability to create animations in Flash, you would still have a fairly competent vector drawing program, but it wouldn't be nearly as popular as it is without the animation capabilities. Quite honestly, animation is what makes Flash what it is.

Creating animations in Flash is pretty simple once you understand the basics. Still, there are some things that you need to know if you want to be as efficient as possible, and if you want to create the best possible Flash animations. In this module, you will learn those things, and when you finish the module, you will be able to work on creating your own Flash animations.

CRITICAL SKILL
6.1 How Animation Works

Animation—at least as far as Flash is concerned—is the process of making it appear as though objects were moving in a smooth, steady motion. This is accomplished by showing the viewer a series of still images where each image in the series varies only slightly from the previous image, and each image is shown very briefly. This whole process takes advantage of a characteristic of our vision that makes us perceive the independent images as continuous motion as long as the images are displayed quickly enough.

In reality, this method of producing the effect of continuous motion is exactly the same one that is used to produce motion pictures and television shows. It's true that these are typically done on a somewhat grander scale than the typical Flash movie, but the basic concept is identical.

Understanding Frame Rates

Once of the most important concepts you must grasp is what is known as the *frame rate*. This is the number of individual images that are displayed each second. Higher frame rates mean that each image is displayed for a briefer time, and that the changes between frames are smaller (since an animated sequence is typically defined by the length of time it plays rather than by the number of frames it occupies). This does not mean, however, that ramping up the frame rate is necessarily a good idea. Here are some of the important implications of higher frame rates:

- Higher frame rates mean that there are more frames per unit of playback time. More frames increase the size of the movie file, which results in longer download times.

- Beyond a certain point, higher frame rates do not noticeably increase the playback quality. Flash typically uses 12 frames per second, while motion pictures may use 25–30 frames per second. Human vision makes the images persist for a certain period, and a much higher frame rate does not modify this.

- It takes a certain amount of computing "horsepower" to display the vector graphics that make up a Flash movie. Frame rates that are too high can overwhelm older, underpowered computers—resulting in jerky, low-quality playback.

So, considering everything, it is probably best to simply use the default Flash frame rate of 12 frames per second—fps—in almost every instance. This frame rate represents a very good compromise between file size and playback quality for most uses.

NOTE

If you are using Flash to create animations for television or motion pictures, you will, of course, want to match the frame rate specified for the non-Flash portions of the production. These are special cases that do not apply to the vast majority of Flash developers.

Progress Check

1. How many frames appear in a second of typical Flash animation?

2. What is the main reason why higher frame rates are not a good idea?

How Flash Simplifies Animation

Okay, you understand that animation consists of displaying a series of images rapidly. The question is, how does this relate to Flash? When you create an animated sequence using Flash, you need to do only part of the work. The reason for this is that Flash acts as your assistant so that you need to create only the image at the start of the animation and the image at the end of the animation. Everything in between is created by Flash itself. That's where the term "tween" comes from—it refers to all of the in-between frames in the animation.

As you will recall from Module 4, any content that you add to a Flash movie must be added to a keyframe. When you create a tween, Flash handles all the frames between the keyframes. In traditional animation studios, a master artist drew all of the keyframes, and various other, lower-paid artists drew the in-between frames. You can see that in the Flash movie production model, you are the master artist, and Flash takes the place of your staff of artist assistants.

---

1. 12
2. They increase the file size.

For example, this shows a simple animated sequence that has a car on one layer and the background on another layer. To create this sequence, I drew the background in frame 1 of the background layer. I drew the car in frame 1 of the car layer. Then I added keyframes to both of the layers in frame 24. Then I moved the car to the position that I wanted it to occupy in frame 24 and added the motion tween. So, I drew content in two frames and positioned the existing content in another frame, and Flash took care of everything else. Keep in mind that even though you see the onion skin view of the car that shows how Flash created the in-between frames for the car layer, Flash also had to create all of the in-between frames for the background layer.

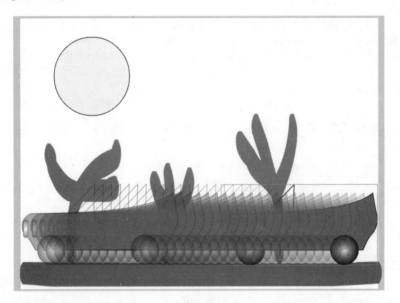

To get a real appreciation for how much of the work Flash is actually doing for you, consider that this simple example consists of two layers, each having 24 frames. So you could say that this movie has 48 frames. Of these, I drew two of them and Flash drew the rest. No matter how you look at it, Flash has greatly simplified the process of creating this animation. If I had to draw all 48 frames myself, it would take me far longer to produce even the simplest of animations.

Understanding the Timeline and Tweens

In Module 4, you learned about the Flash timeline, frames, and layers. Now let's take a closer look at how the timeline and tweens are related.

When you create a tween, you are creating an animation sequence that encompasses a series of frames on the timeline. Each of those frames represents one of the individual images that make up the animated sequence. At the standard frame rate, each frame is displayed for

1/12th of a second. If you want to create an animation that runs for a total of three seconds, you would therefore make certain that the animation included 36 frames.

In addition to simply specifying the length of an animated sequence, the timeline can be considered to be something of a clock. That is, suppose that you want to create several different animations that run at different times. You can use the timeline to control when each of the animations begins. To do so, you simply place the starting keyframe of an animation at the timeline frame that represents the point in time where you want the tween to begin. If you want an animation to begin ten seconds after the movie begins playing, then you would place the first keyframe of the animation somewhere around frame 120.

NOTE

As Flash movies become more complex, relying upon the timeline for precise control of events may not always be accurate. The reason is that you may add some ActionScript programming that controls the flow of the movie. In that case, the program flow may actually branch to a different frame at some point, thus rendering the timeline a poor indicator of what will actually be occurring at any point in time.

Progress Check

1. If a Flash movie just uses simple animation, how long will it take to reach frame 60 at the default frame rate?

2. Where do you add your drawings?

Learning About Tween Types

Flash has two types of tweens. Each can be used to create animations, of course, but each serves a slightly different purpose. Learning the differences between the two types of tweens is very important, and it is usually one of the most confusing aspects of learning to create Flash movies.

Unfortunately, motion tweens and shape tweens sometimes seem to overlap in certain areas. Fortunately, motion tweens are far more common than shape tweens, so if you are unsure of the type of tween that you need to use, you can guess at the motion tween and be correct most of the time. Let's take a look at the specifics of these two types of tweens.

1. Five seconds
2. To keyframes

Motion Tweens

Motion tweens are most commonly used to move objects from one place to another on the stage. But that's not all that you can do with a motion tween. You can use a motion tween to do the following:

- Change the position
- Modify the size
- Rotate objects
- Skew objects
- Change the color
- Control the alpha setting

Motion tweens can be applied only to specific types of objects. These are

- Grouped objects
- Symbol instances
- Text

NOTE To modify the color property of objects, you must first convert them into symbols as discussed in Module 8.

As you can see, a motion tween can make quite a few modifications to objects, and those modifications do not have to include changing the object's location. For example, you can use a motion tween to make an object appear or disappear without moving the object at all!

If you do use a motion tween to move an object, that motion is generally along a straight path from where the object was in the initial keyframe to where it ends up in the final keyframe of the animation. As you learned in Module 4, it is also possible to create a motion guide to move the object in a path that does not have to be straight. You will learn the specifics of creating and using motion guides in Module 7.

Shape Tweens

So far, all of the tweens that you have seen have been motion tweens. Flash can also produce another type of tween called the shape tween. In this type of animation, you change the shape of the object. For example, here I have used a shape tween to change a star into the shape of the state of Nevada:

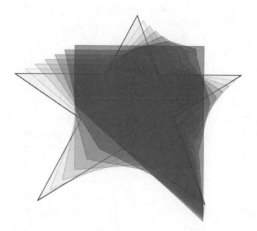

Ask the Expert

Q: When I try to create a tween, Flash places a dashed line in the timeline and my tween doesn't work. What's wrong?

A: When you create a tween, that same tween applies to all objects in the tween frame range on the layer where the tween is created. This means that all objects in those frames must be suitable for the type of tween that you are creating. If they are not, Flash will not create the tween, but rather will display a dashed line in the timeline where the tween arrow should be. In addition, because the tween applies to all objects in those frames, you cannot apply a tween to one object and leave another object untouched. This is one reason you use layers. Since a tween applies to a single layer, objects on different layers are unaffected by the tween.

Q: Does this mean I can have only one tween on a layer?

A: No, a tween is limited to the space from its beginning to its ending keyframes. Objects that appear on the same layer outside those keyframes are not affected by the tween. You can have as many tweens as you want on a layer as long as they do not overlap. Note, however, that a new tween can begin immediately after another tween so that the second tween's beginning keyframe is the first tween's ending keyframe.

As I mentioned earlier, there are a number of ways in which the two types of tweens overlap. This can best be seen by looking at what you can do with the shape tween:

- You can change the shape of objects.

- You can change the color of objects.

- Since the new object and the existing object do not have to be in the same location, you can change the position of objects.

Also like motion tweens, shape tweens are limited to specific types of objects. Basically, you cannot apply a shape tween to a grouped object, a symbol instance, a text block, or a bitmap image.

TIP

If you want to apply a shape tween to any of the objects that cannot normally have a shape tween applied, you can use the Modify | Break Apart command to break these objects down into simple forms. Once you have done this, you can then use a shape tween to morph the object.

You must use the Properties panel to apply a shape tween. Flash does not include a command on the main menu for applying shape tweens.

Choosing the Correct Tween

Since both types of tweens often overlap, choosing the correct type of tween can be a little confusing. As I mentioned earlier, when in doubt, you are usually safe if you choose the motion tween. Still, it is handy to know for certain which tween to choose.

Here are some guidelines you can use to help you choose the correct type of tween:

- If you want to morph the shape of an object, use a shape tween.

- If you want to move an object to a different position on the stage without affecting its shape, use a motion tween.

- If you want to move an object such as a button, which is a symbol instance, use a motion tween.

- If you want to change the color of an object, use a shape tween if you are modifying a simple object that can be broken apart. Otherwise, use a motion tween.

- If you want to change an object's visibility, use a motion tween.

- If you want to rotate or scale an object without changing its shape, use a motion tween.

Progress Check

1. What must you do before you can apply a shape tween to a grouped object?

2. Which type of tween can you use to change the color of an object?

3. Which type of tween can hide an object without moving it?

CRITICAL SKILL
6.3 # Creating Motion Tweens

Now that you have an understanding of the differences between motion tweens and shape tweens, let's step through the complete process of creating each type of tween. We will begin by creating a motion tween and then follow up a little later with a shape tween.

Drawing an Object for a Motion Tween

As you have already learned, you can apply motion tweens to several different types of objects. Most of these objects will be introduced in later modules, so we will start this example by using a simple grouped object.

Follow these steps to draw the object for your motion tween:

1. Open a new, blank Flash movie.

2. If you are going to have objects that will not be tweened, click the Insert Layer button to add a new layer to the timeline. Remember, all objects that appear on a layer within the frames of a tween must be a part of that tween.

3. Use your favorite drawing tools to draw the object. This object can be as simple or as complex as you want. Here is an example of an object that I am using:

---

1. Ungroup the object.
2. Either one, depending on your needs
3. A motion tween

TIP

If you are going to draw a lot of objects for your Flash movies, you may find a *graphics tablet* to be a worthwhile investment. For this illustration, I used a 4x5-inch Wacom tablet to quickly trace an image from a photograph. You can find out more about Wacom graphics tablets at www.wacom.com.

Getting the Object Ready for a Motion Tween

Next, you need to get the object ready for a motion tween. As you will recall from earlier in this module, you cannot apply a motion tween to an object that you have drawn until you combine all of the object's elements into a group.

To prepare the object for a motion tween, follow these steps:

1. Click the Arrow tool to select it.

2. Drag a selection box around the entire object so that it is completely selected. Remember that you can also double-click to select very simple objects such as an oval or a rectangle, but that objects you have drawn using more than one tool generally cannot be selected this way.

3. Select the Modify | Group command to group the selection. You should now see a bounding box around the object, as shown here:

TIP

If the bounding box does not encompass the entire object, you may need to try again using a larger selection box. Keep in mind, however, that if you have increased the stroke width, some of the stroke's width may extend past the edges of the bounding box even though the entire stroke is included in the grouped object.

Getting the Timeline Ready for a Motion Tween

Now that you have drawn the object and grouped it, you are ready to prepare the timeline for the motion tween. It is a good idea to try to have your objects drawn and grouped before you begin working with the timeline, because this simplifies your workflow and greatly reduces the chances for confusion.

To prepare the timeline for your motion tween, follow these steps:

1. Decide how long you want the animation to run. This will determine where you should place the second keyframe. For example, at the default frame rate, you would place the second keyframe at frame 36 for an animation that starts at the beginning of the movie and runs for three seconds.

2. Click the frame you have determined should be the ending keyframe for the motion tween.

3. Select the Insert | Timeline | Keyframe command to place a keyframe in the selected frame. Remember that you want to insert a regular keyframe rather than a blank keyframe to make certain that Flash copies the content from the previous keyframe. Your timeline should now look similar to this:

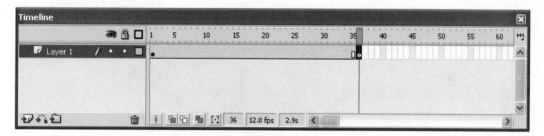

TIP

If you want to start an animation at some point later in the timeline, simply drag the starting keyframe to the correct frame. Remember that you will then have to adjust the position of the ending keyframe accordingly.

Applying the Motion Tween

Now that the timeline is ready, you are ready to apply the motion tween. To do so, you must first tell Flash what to do with the object during the animation, and then add the motion tween to the tween frame range.

To apply the motion tween, follow these steps:

1. With the final keyframe selected, move the object to the position you want it to occupy at the end of the animation.

2. If you want to apply any additional motion tween effects such as scaling or rotating, do so now. Remember that you can use the Modify | Transform command to select transformation effects. You can also use the Transform panel to modify the object.

3. Click the timeline frames between the beginning and ending keyframes to select the set of frames where the animation will appear.

4. Select the Insert | Timeline | Create Motion Tween command to add the motion tween to the timeline. This will add an arrow between the beginning and ending keyframes, as shown here:

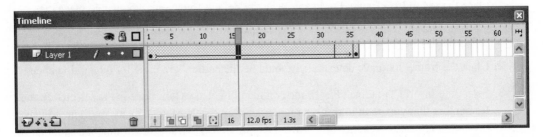

5. Select Control | Test Movie to test your movie. You can also view the animation frames using the onion skin view, as shown here:

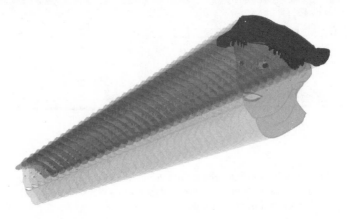

CAUTION

If you use Control | Test Movie to view your movie, you will see two Close buttons near the upper-right corner of the Flash window. Click the lower Close button to close the Flash Player and return to the development environment. Do not click the upper Close button because this will close Flash entirely.

You may also want to use the File | Save command to save a copy of your work. This will enable you to reopen the same file later if you want to make additional changes.

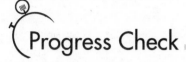

Progress Check

1. How many keyframes does each tween need?

2. After you draw an object, what command do you need to use before you can apply a motion tween?

CRITICAL SKILL

6.4 Creating Shape Tweens

Creating a shape tween is similar to creating a motion tween, but there are some important differences you need to be aware of. Let's take a step-by-step look at the shape tween process.

Drawing an Object for a Shape Tween

As with a motion tween, you begin your shape tween by drawing the object that you want to animate. As you do, remember that shape tweens morph objects from one shape into another. Because of this, it is generally best to keep the object fairly simple. Too many details can result in an animation that looks pretty confusing during the tween frames.

Shape tweens work only with ungrouped objects. When you are drawing an object specifically for use in a shape tween, this presents no problem, since all objects are ungrouped when they are first drawn. This does present a problem if you want to apply a shape tween to objects that have been grouped—whether you have done so explicitly or not. For example, bitmap images and text blocks are automatically grouped, and this makes it necessary for you to break them apart before you can shape tween them.

In some cases, though, you will need to use a little craftiness to accomplish your goals. One reason for this is that certain objects must be grouped in order to function properly in your Flash movies. For example, the buttons you use are an *instance* of a symbol, and this effectively means that they are grouped objects. As a result, you cannot apply a shape tween to a button. This does not mean, however, that you cannot create a visually identical effect. You could achieve the same visual result by creating a shape tween whose final keyframe has an object that is identical in size, shape, and position with the button you want to use. Then you could place the actual button in the next frame of the timeline. When the movie plays, viewers would have no way to determine that they were being deceived by a clever use of a shape tween and the timeline.

1. Two
2. Modify | Group

So, to create a shape tween, you need to begin with an ungrouped object. Here is the object I'm starting with:

TIP

When you draw an object for a shape tween, you may find it helpful to set the stroke color to none by clicking the No Color button while the Stroke Color selector is selected. That way, you won't have to deal with the object's outline as you apply the shape tween.

Getting the Timeline Ready for a Shape Tween

There isn't much difference between preparing the timeline for a motion tween or for a shape tween. In both cases, you begin by determining how long you want the animation to play, and then you add a keyframe to the timeline at the appropriate frame.

Shape tweens are a little different from motion tweens in one important area, however. Since the shape of the object is generally quite different at the end of a shape tween from the shape at the beginning of it, you may want to add a blank keyframe rather than an ordinary keyframe as the ending keyframe. Remember that an ordinary keyframe duplicates the contents of the previous keyframe, while a blank keyframe is simply empty. By adding a blank keyframe, you avoid having to select and delete an object you don't need, and you can begin creating the final shape on a clean stage.

To add the blank keyframe, use the Insert | Timeline | Blank Keyframe command. Be sure that you have selected the correct frame in the timeline before issuing the command. Once you have added your blank keyframe, go ahead and draw the shape that you want at the end of the shape tween. Here is the object I am using for the end of my shape tween:

Applying the Shape Tween

Now that you have your beginning and ending shapes, and you have added the necessary keyframes to the timeline, you can apply the shape tween. Here are the steps you need to follow to accomplish this:

1. Click the timeline within the tween frames. This will select the frames so that you can add your shape tween.

2. Use the Window | Properties command to open the Properties panel.

3. Select Shape from the drop-down Tween list box, as shown here. Since there is no menu command for applying a shape tween, you can apply one only by using the Properties panel.

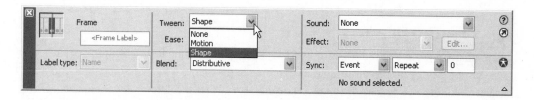

4. Use the Control | Test Movie command to test your movie. This shows an onion skin view of my shape tween. (Shape tweens are often somewhat difficult to view in onion

skin view, but it should be fairly clear that in this example, at least, the egg came before the chicken.)

Don't forget to use the File | Save command to save your work. Remember that you can close the Flash Player window by clicking the lower Close button. This will return you to the Flash development environment so that you can continue working.

Progress Check

1. What type of frame should you add at the end of a shape tween?

2. How can you apply a shape tween?

Using Easing

By default, all of the frames in an animation appear for the same length of time. As a result, the rate of change is constant from the beginning to the end of a tween. Sometimes you may want to modify this so that an animation begins slowly and accelerates toward the end. Or perhaps you might want the animation to slow down as it reaches the end. In either case, you can achieve this effect using *easing*.

The Easing control in the Properties panel (as shown here) has a text box and a slider. You can use the slider to enter values between –100 and +100. Positive values make the tween slow down as it plays, while negative values make the tween speed up as it plays. You can also enter values into the text box directly.

1. Keyframe
2. Use the Tween list box in the Properties panel.

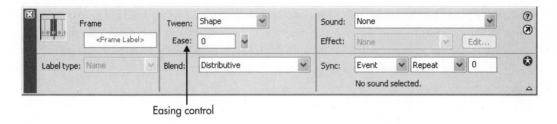

Easing control

TIP

Using easing does not affect the overall playback time required for a tween. It simply modifies the relationship between the display times for the individual frames in the animation. Your tween will play for the same length of time whether easing has been applied or not.

Easing can be used with both shape tweens and motion tweens. You will probably find that fairly large easing values are necessary to create a noticeable effect.

Using Shape Tween Hints

Shape tweens certainly create interesting effects. The ability to morph an object into something completely different can be a lot of fun. Sometimes, though, the effect that results from applying a shape tween is not quite what you expect.

When you apply a shape tween, Flash makes its best guess about how to create the images in the tween frames. Depending on the differences between the beginning and ending shapes, these interim images may represent a reasonable transition between the shapes, or they may end up being pretty strange—especially if the beginning and ending shapes are very different from each other.

Flash, of course, cannot actually recognize the objects you draw. To Flash, the objects you draw are meaningless shapes. When Flash creates the tween frames for a shape tween, it simply tries to find a logical way to convert between the two shapes as smoothly as possible. If the results aren't quite what you want, the solution is to give Flash a little extra help in the form of *shape hints*.

Shape hints are markers that you place on the beginning and ending shapes. These markers tell Flash to move the marked point on the beginning shape to the same marker on the ending shape. For example, if the first shape happens to be a head looking to the right and the ending shape is the head looking left, you might tell Flash to match up the two end-of-nose points.

To add shape hints, follow these steps:

1. Create your shape tween. You should have the entire shape tween completed before you begin adding shape hints.

2. Click the beginning keyframe of the shape tween.

3. Select the Modify | Shape | Add Shape Hint command to add a small red circle to the shape, as shown here. Each of the circles represents a shape hint point, and Flash sequentially labels the shape hint points starting with the letter *a*. In this case, I have already added several shape hints so that you can more easily visualize the process.

4. Drag the circle to the first point that you want to match to a point on the final shape.

5. Click the ending keyframe of the shape tween.

6. Drag the green circle (with the same letter) to the matching point on the final shape, as shown here. When Flash tweens the shape, it will move the points according to the matching shape hint points.

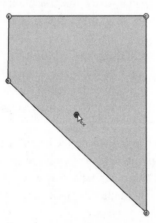

7. Continue adding shape hint points by repeating steps 2–6 until you have added all of the shape hints you want to use.

8. Select Control | Test Movie to test the new shape tween.

9. If necessary, move the shape hint points to fine-tune the shape tween. You can remove a shape hint by dragging it off the stage.

As you add shape hints and then test the results, you may realize that Flash probably didn't do too badly on its own without any shape hints. You will no doubt find that applying shape hints takes a fair amount of practice to achieve the results you really want. Remember that you can quickly remove all of your shape hints by using the Modify | Shape | Remove All Hints command. You must select the beginning keyframe of the shape tween in order to use this command.

Progress Check

1. How can you tell which shape hints are matching points?

2. What is the purpose of shape hints?

Project 6-1 Creating a Bouncing Ball Animation

Now that you have had an introduction to the concepts behind creating Flash animations, it is time to put all of it together and create an entire animated sequence. In this project, you will create a bouncing ball using two separate motion tweens. The first will show the ball dropping, and the second will make it bounce back to its original location.

Step by Step

1. Open a new, blank Flash movie.

2. Click the Oval tool to select it.

3. Choose the fill and stroke colors you want to use.

4. Draw a circle near the top of the stage. Remember to hold down SHIFT to draw a perfect circle.

(continued)

1. They have the same letter.

2. To specify how specific points of a shape tween should move

5. Click the Arrow tool to select it.

6. Double-click the circle so that both the fill and the stroke are selected.

7. Group the object using the Modify | Group command.

8. Select Edit | Copy to copy the ball for later use.

9. Click the timeline frame where you want the ball to be at the lowest point. In this case, click frame 24 to make the ball take two seconds to drop from the top to the bottom of the stage.

10. Select Insert | Timeline | Keyframe to add a keyframe to frame 24.

11. Hold down SHIFT as you drag the ball to the bottom of the stage. Holding down SHIFT will make the ball move in a completely vertical line.

12. Click the tween frames to select them.

13. Select Insert | Timeline | Create Motion Tween to add the motion tween to frames 1–24.

14. Select Window | Properties to open the Properties panel.

15. In the Easing box of the Properties panel, type **–100**, as shown here, and press ENTER. This will make the ball start dropping slowly and accelerate as it reaches the bottom of the stage.

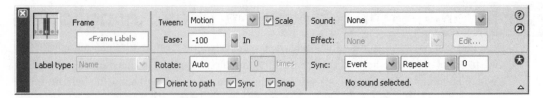

16. Click frame 48 in the timeline to select it.

17. Select Insert | Timeline | Blank Keyframe to add a blank keyframe.

18. Select Edit | Paste In Place to place a copy of the ball on the stage in the exact location it occupied in frame 1. This method is far more precise than attempting to drag the ball back to its original location.

19. Click the timeline between frames 24 and 48.

20. In the Properties panel, select Motion from the Tween box to add the motion tween to frames 24–48. Your timeline should now look something like this:

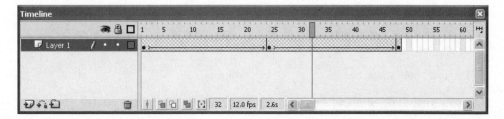

21. In the Easing box of the Properties panel, type **100** and press ENTER. This will make the ball start bouncing upward quickly and decelerate as it reaches the top of the stage.

22. Select File I Save and save your movie project.

23. Use the Control I Test Movie command to test your movie. The ball should drop from the top of the stage, accelerate until it reaches the bottom, and then bounce realistically back to the top of the stage. As this shows, the onion skin view clearly indicates that the ball moves less in each frame near the top of the stage than it does near the bottom. (Look at the bottom edge of each image of the ball to see this effect.)

Project Summary

In this project, you learned how to create a bouncing ball by placing two motion tweens sequentially on the timeline. You also learned how to make the ball's motion appear to be more realistic by applying easing to accelerate and decelerate the motion. This information is quite useful, since it allows you to create a Flash animation that adds an interesting touch to a web site in a very small file. In addition, the techniques you learned in this project can easily be adapted to even more complex animations in the future.

✓ Module 6 Mastery Check

1. You can apply shape tweens to _____ objects.

2. If you want an object to slow down as it reaches the end of a tween, you use _____.

3. To control the visibility of an object, you would use a _____ tween.

4. When you create a tween, you can use the _____ panel to control various aspects of the tween.

5. To help Flash create a better shape tween, you can add _____.

6. You can add a _____ tween using the Insert | Timeline menu.

7. By default, Flash displays _____ frames per second.

8. Timeline frames that have a tween applied are designated by an _____ in the timeline.

9. You can change the color of an object with:

   A. A shape tween

   B. A motion tween

   C. Both

   D. Neither

10. You can place a copy of an object that you have copied into the same location using the Edit | _____ command.

11. Flash animations actually consist of a series of _____ images.

12. The only type of tween you can apply to a symbol instance is a _____ tween.

13. When you add a shape tween to the timeline, the type of frame you will most likely want to add to the end of the tween is a _____.

14. If you use a negative easing value, the tween will _____ as it plays.

15. A dotted line in the timeline indicates a _____ tween.

Module 7

Using Guides
and Masks

Now that you have learned the basics of drawing and creating animations in Flash, we will turn our attention to some slightly more advanced topics. In this module, we will look at two special types of layers that you can use in your Flash movies. First mentioned in Module 4, guide layers and mask layers can really enhance the effects that you can create. Guides enable you to create motion tweens that follow a path that you draw rather than simply moving objects in a straight line. Masks act as a window onto the stage, enabling you to produce such special effects as scrolling banner text or moving spotlights. With these two tools, you will have the ability to really make your Flash movies stand out.

Both motion guides and masks are objects that you create on some of the special types of timeline layers that are available in Flash. In both cases, motion guides and masks add to the power of your Flash developer's toolbox. When you complete this module, you will have a better understanding of just how much power Flash places at your fingertips.

CRITICAL SKILL
7.1 Understanding Guides

When you create a motion tween in a Flash movie, the object that you are animating normally moves in a straight line from the first keyframe of the tween to the last keyframe in the tween. If, for example, you start a ball in the upper-left corner of the stage in the first keyframe, and you end with it in the lower-right corner of the stage in the final keyframe, the ball will follow a straight line that runs diagonally from that upper-left corner to the lower-right corner. For many types of animation, this straight-line path is perfectly acceptable.

Sometimes, however, an animation simply doesn't look very realistic if an object moves in a perfectly straight line. You might, for example, want a ball to follow a curved path so that it looks more like a real ball that someone has thrown. To create this curved path, you would use a motion guide.

A *motion guide* is a line that you draw on a guide layer. When a layer is designated as a guide layer, you can lock the path of an object to that line. Then, when the object moves, it follows the motion guide rather than moving in a straight line. The motion guide can follow any path you want, and it can even loop across itself.

How can you use a motion guide? Consider these possibilities:

- You can use a motion guide to make an object like a ball follow an arc as it is thrown across the stage.

- You could use a motion guide to make buttons follow the edge of a curved object to build a user interface with buttons that slide into place, one after the other.

- You can make an object turn a sharp corner—such as a 90-degree angle—as it moves across the stage.

- You could make an airplane do loops as it flies across the stage.

- You can make text swirl around and then line up for a corporate logo.

These, of course, are just a few of the possibilities. Motion guides make it possible for you to use your imagination rather than being limited to moving objects along a straight, boring line.

NOTE

Motion guides can be used to direct a motion tween only. You cannot use a motion guide to direct a shape tween.

One very important piece of information that you need to know about motion guides is that they are not visible when the movie is played. You can create a motion guide that exactly follows the edge of an object that exists on a different layer, but nothing that exists on a guide layer will ever be visible in the actual Flash movie.

Motion guides are also reusable. That is, a single motion guide can be used to guide more than one motion tween. Also, motion guides are quite flexible. You are not required to use the whole length of a motion guide. For example, here I have created a motion guide that displays three buttons at specific points along the edge of a curved object. Each of the buttons starts rolling down from the upper left and follows the curve. The first button moves almost to the bottom of the stage, the second button moves to the middle of the curve, and the final button moves just a short distance. When the animations are completed, I have a set of buttons spaced along the edge of the curve, ready for a user to click.

Although the motion guide in this example followed the edge of an existing object, there is no requirement that it do so. A motion guide is simply a line that is drawn on a guide layer, and it can be drawn wherever you want.

Actually, you can create a nonlinear path in a Flash animation using a totally different method that does not rely upon a motion guide. You can do *frame-by-frame* animation to move objects precisely where you want them. This manual animation method does come at a price, however. In frame-by-frame animations, you must create every frame of the animation without any help from Flash. That is, you would have to draw 12 frames manually for each second of animation you wanted to create. To add insult to injury, frame-by-frame animation also tends to result in larger file sizes for your published movies because Flash cannot optimize your drawings quite as well as it can a tweened animation.

Progress Check

1. What kind of tween can use a motion guide?

2. How many objects can follow a motion guide?

CRITICAL SKILL
7.2 Creating Guides

Motion guides are very easy to create. A motion guide is simply a line that exists on a guide layer. You can create that line using any of the drawing tools creates. This means that you can use the Line tool, the Pen tool, the Oval tool, the Pencil tool, the Rectangle tool, or the Brush tool to create a motion guide. To begin, though, you need to create the guide layer.

Creating the Guide Layer

A guide layer is one of the two special types of layers you can add to the timeline. You need to create a guide layer to hold the line that you will use as a motion guide. To create the guide layer, follow these steps:

1. Create the layers that you want to use for motion tweens that follow the motion guide. Remember, you will need one layer for each individual motion tween.

2. Click the topmost layer that you want as a guided layer.

3. Click the Add Motion Guide button near the lower-left edge of the timeline. Alternatively, use the Insert | Timeline | Motion Guide command to add the guide layer. When you add the guide layer, Flash indents the guided layer below it and names the guide layer by using the name "Guide" and the name of the guided layer, as shown here. (In this case, I'm showing the timeline from the earlier example where three different layers are all using the same motion guide.)

---

1. A motion tween
2. As many as you want

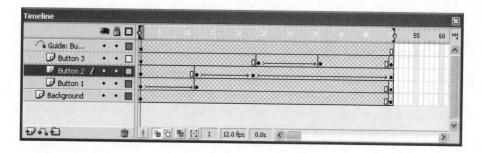

At this point, you have an empty guide layer. If you were now to create a motion tween, the object would follow the straight path it normally does from the beginning keyframe to the ending keyframe of the tween.

Drawing the Motion Guide

As I mentioned earlier, you can use any of the drawing tools to create a motion guide. The motion guide is a line that appears on the guide layer, but since it is invisible when your movie plays, there is no need to get fancy in creating the motion guide. Simply use whatever tool you prefer and draw your line.

In addition to drawing a line for a motion guide, there is another handy trick you can use if you want the motion guide to follow the edge of an existing object. Follow these steps to create a motion guide in this fashion:

1. On a layer other than the guide layer or any of the guided layers, draw the object that you want to use to guide the motion.

2. Click the stroke of the object to select it, as shown here. In this case, I hid all of the other layers by clicking in the column below the eye icon and then turned on outline view for the layer with the object I wanted to use as a guide to make the illustration a little easier to understand.

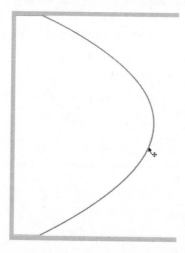

3. Select Edit | Copy to copy the line.

4. Click the guide layer to select it.

5. Select Edit | Paste In Place to paste a copy of the line onto the guide layer in the exact position it occupies on the layer where the object exists. That way, the objects that follow the motion guide will seem to be following the edge of a real object even though they are actually following the invisible (when the movie plays) motion guide.

TIP

Remember that you can quickly hide all of the layers by clicking the eye symbol above the timeline. Then, click in the column of a layer you want to view. Click the eye again to display all of the layers.

Progress Check

1. Which tools can you use to draw a motion guide?

2. Where do you draw a motion guide?

Locking Objects to the Guide

Once you have created your motion guide, you can lock objects to the guide so that they will follow it rather than moving along a straight path. This is very easy to do.

To attach objects to the motion guide, follow these steps:

1. Click the beginning keyframe of the guided layer to select that frame.

2. Drag the object so that the center point of the object is on the motion guide, as shown here. (Note that I have scrolled the view down slightly because the guide begins near the edge of the stage.) Place the object in the location where you want the motion to begin.

---

1. Any tool that draws an object
2. On a guide layer

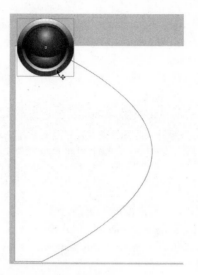

3. Click the ending keyframe of the guided layer.

4. Drag the object so that its center point is at the point on the motion guide where you want the object to stop.

5. Click the tween frames to select them.

6. Select the Insert | Timeline | Create Motion Tween command to add the motion tween to the selected frames.

7. Drag the playhead across the motion tween frames to verify that the object follows the motion guide properly, as shown here in onion skin view:

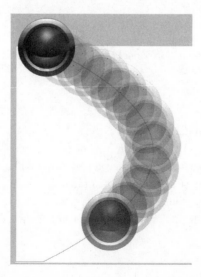

If you have problems getting the object to follow the motion guide, make certain that you are positioning it directly over the motion guide. You do not have to place the object at the end of the motion guide.

TIP

The beginning and ending points for the motion tween can be anywhere on the motion guide. If you want the object to stop short of the end of the motion guide, simply place the object at that position in the ending keyframe before you add the motion tween.

Extending a Guide Off the Stage

In real life, objects don't just suddenly appear and then start moving. If you want to create realistic-looking Flash animations, you probably don't always want objects to just suddenly appear on the stage, either.

One very effective way around this unnatural effect is to begin an animation with an object completely off the stage. That way, the object will move into view gradually as it moves onto the stage. Remember—objects that are off the Flash stage are not visible in the movie until they move onto the stage.

To create a guide that extends off the stage, you will probably need to use the scroll bars to display the part of the offstage workspace where you want to begin the guide. You may also need to use the View menu commands (or the zoom control) to display more of the Flash workspace. Once you can view the point where you want the motion guide to begin, simply draw the motion guide wherever you want it. At whatever point the guide crosses the stage, the object will be visible.

TIP

There is no reason why an animation cannot end at an offstage point, too. In addition, you can use offstage points to begin or end any type of tween—not just one that is guided by a motion guide.

Orienting the Motion

One of the main reasons for using a motion guide is to create more realistic-looking animations. Having an object follow a curved path often makes the object seem more real than if it simply followed a straight line. Unfortunately, as this animation clearly shows, simply following a motion guide does not always make for a believable effect. In this case, the airplane always remains perfectly level even when it should be banking up or down for a realistic-appearing loop.

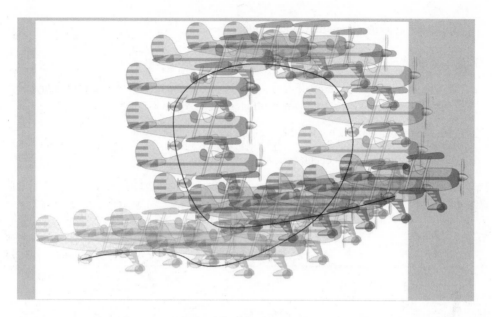

By default, the object maintains its orientation relative to the stage. It is possible to make the animation look a lot more realistic by orienting the object to the motion guide, as shown here. When you do this, the object maintains the same orientation relative to the motion guide throughout the tween. In this example, the airplane looks far more realistic because it is acting much more like a real airplane would when flying in a loop.

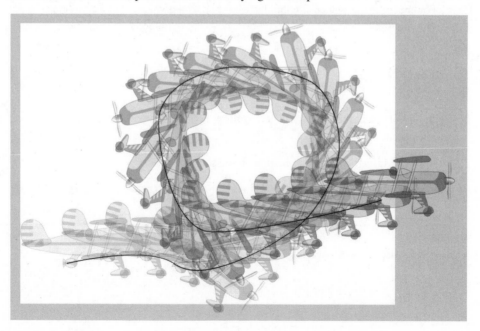

To set the object's orientation mode, follow these steps:

1. Create the motion tween and lock the object to the motion guide.

2. Click the beginning keyframe of the motion tween. Make certain you select the layer of the object that you want to orient to the motion guide.

3. Open the Properties panel using the Window | Properties command.

4. Select the Orient To Path check box, as shown here:

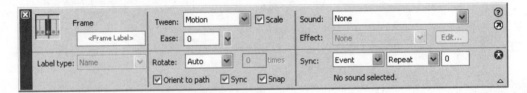

TIP

When you orient an object to a motion guide, the object maintains the same relationship to the motion guide throughout the motion tween that it had in the beginning keyframe of the tween. For the best effect, you will want to make certain that the motion guide has the correct orientation in that initial keyframe. For example, the motion guide should probably be essentially horizontal in the beginning keyframe for most animations. This will ensure that the object has the correct orientation to the motion in later frames.

Progress Check

1. If you do not select the Orient To Path option, how will the object move during the motion tween?

2. What happens if a motion guide begins on the stage?

---

1. It will remain level.

2. The object appears suddenly and starts moving.

Guiding More Than One Tween with the Same Guide

Motion guides can be used to control the motion tweens on more than one layer. This can be especially handy if you have several objects that you want to follow essentially the same path during their motion. Keep in mind that each of the motion tweens that you attach to a guide layer can begin and end at different points on the motion guide. In addition, there's no need for those motion tweens to occupy the same range of frames in the timeline. This gives you considerable flexibility in the use of the motion guide to control several motion tweens.

When you first create a motion guide, that motion guide is associated with a layer immediately below it in the timeline. You can also associate additional layers with the motion guide using any of several methods:

- You can select the guided layer and then insert a new layer using the Insert | Timeline | Layer command or by clicking the Insert Layer button. When you insert a new layer between a guided layer and its guide layer, the new layer automatically becomes a guided layer.

- If the layer that you want to make into a guided layer is below another guided layer, you can right-click (or Command-click on a Mac) the layer that you want to modify in the timeline, and select Properties from the pop-up menu.

- You can also select the Modify | Timeline | Layer Properties command from the Flash menu to display the Layer Properties dialog box shown here. Whichever method you choose to display this dialog box, click the Guided option button, and then click OK to make the layer a guided layer.

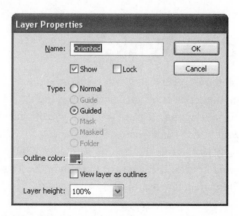

Guided layers must be below the guide layer in the timeline, and there can be no unguided layers between the guide layer and any guided layers.

Ask the Expert

Q: I can't seem to attach the object to the motion guide. What could be wrong?

A: You probably aren't getting the center point of the object close enough to the motion guide. Make certain that the Snap check box in the Properties panel is selected to make the object snap to the motion guide.

Q: I created a motion tween using a motion guide, but the animation just doesn't look right. Even when I select the Orient To Path option, I don't like the results. I tried modifying the motion guide, but that just messed up the motion tween further. Do I have to start all over to get the results I want?

A: No, you should be able to rescue what you already have by using any of several techniques. First, use the Layer Properties dialog box to change the guided layer into a normal layer. Next, you may want to use the Arrow tool or the Subselect tool to modify the motion guide. Finally, you can change the layer back into a guided layer and snap the object to the new motion guide. If you don't disassociate the guide layer from the guided layer before you modify the motion guide, you will have a very difficult time trying to modify the path.

CRITICAL SKILL
7.3 Understanding Masks

When you create a Flash movie, everything that is on the stage will normally be visible when the movie is played. Anything that is off the stage during the movie will not be seen as the movie is played. As you have already learned, you can use this fact to your advantage by creating tweens that begin or end somewhere off the stage.

A *mask* is another way to control what can be seen during the playback. Essentially, a mask creates a window onto one of the layers of the movie. You can use a mask for a number of different purposes. Here are a few useful ideas:

- You can use a mask to create a scrolling text banner. When you do this, you use a motion tween to move the text behind the mask.

- A mask can also be used to create a window effect in your movie. For example, you can create a mask that enables an object to be seen as it moves behind a window in a building or in a vehicle.

- You can apply a motion tween to a mask to make it move around as the movie plays. This can create a searchlight-type effect.

Whatever you would like to use a mask for, you must know certain essentials in order to use masks effectively, including these:

- The mask itself is never visible in the movie as the movie is played.

- Mask layers are one of the two special types of layers that you can add to the timeline.

- Each mask layer affects only the layers immediately below it in the timeline.

- Only the fill area of a mask is used to create the mask. Any outline is ignored.

- Although you can apply a tween to a mask, you cannot use a motion guide to move the mask.

NOTE

Although you cannot use a motion guide to move a mask directly, it is possible to create a movie clip instance that follows a motion guide. You can have the movie clip follow a motion guide, so this technique does enable you to move the mask as you like.

CRITICAL SKILL

7.4 Creating a Mask

Creating a mask uses a number of techniques that you already know. You can create a mask in several different ways. We will look at a couple of these next.

Adding a Graphic Mask

The simplest and most common mask that you will use is a filled object. This can be an object that you create using any of the drawing tools in the Flash Tools panel, but it must be a filled object. Flash ignores the type of fill that you use in a mask, so it is really up to you.

TIP

One of the most confusing things about using masks is that it is the solid part of the mask that is actually the window onto the masked layer. Although it would seem logical that the areas in the mask layer that are not covered would be where you could see the masked objects, this is actually the reverse of what happens.

You need at least two layers in your movie to create a mask effect. In most cases, however, you will probably want to use additional layers so that there are objects that are not affected by the mask. In this example, however, we will use only two layers so that the mask effect is more visible in the illustrations.

To add a graphic mask, follow these steps:

1. Begin by drawing the objects that you want to appear in the movie.

2. If you have not already done so, click the Insert Layer button to add a new layer above the current layer.

3. Right-click the new layer and select Mask from the pop-up menu to turn the layer into a mask layer. Alternatively, you can use the Modify | Timeline | Layer Properties command to display the Layer Properties dialog box, and select the Mask option button. Flash will indent the masked layer below the mask layer, as shown here:

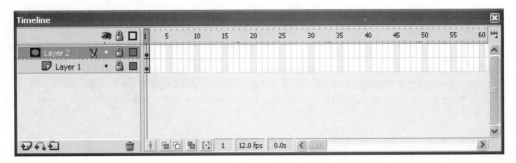

4. Click the lock column of the mask layer to unlock the layer—Flash automatically locks the layers when you convert a layer into a mask layer. You must unlock the layer before you can draw anything on the layer.

5. Draw the mask using your choice of the drawing tools. Remember that the object must be filled to act as a mask. Here I have drawn a circular mask near the center of the stage:

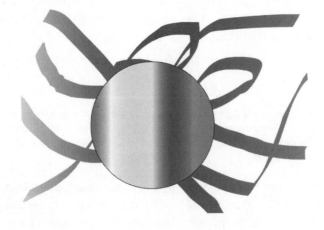

6. Click the Lock All icon to view the effect of the mask, as shown here. The mask effect can be seen only when the mask layer and the masked layer are locked.

TIP

The mask effect will always be visible when you play your movie, even if you forget to lock the layers.

Progress Check

1. How many layers can a mask affect?

2. What part of the mask becomes the window onto the masked layer?

Using Text as a Mask

One of the neatest ways to use a mask in Flash is to create a mask using text as the mask. When you do that, whatever is under the text mask shows through the text, and the effect is text that is filled with a gradient, a color, a bitmap image, or whatever else you have on the masked layer.

1. Only those immediately below it
2. The solid part of the mask

In some ways, using text as a mask imposes some extra requirements if you want to create a really interesting effect. Here are some important considerations you need to be aware of if you want to create a text mask that is effective:

- You need to use a very large font size.

- You should use a bold font that has wide strokes.

- The masked layer should be completely filled under the mask so that all parts of the letters are visible.

With these guidelines in mind, follow these steps to create a text mask:

1. Create the masked layer. An imported bitmap image (as shown here) can be very effective:

2. Click the Insert Layer button to add the mask layer.

3. Use the Text | Size command to display the text size menu. Select one of the very large sizes such as 96.

4. Select Text | Style | Bold to make the text bold.

5. You may also want to use the Text | Font command to select a font with large strokes. Remember, you can also use the Properties panel to set the text attributes.

6. Click the Text tool to select it, and then click where you want to add the mask.

7. Type the text that you want to use as a mask, as shown here:

8. Click outside the text box to deselect it.

9. Right-click the mask layer and choose Mask from the pop-up menu. You can also use the Layer Properties dialog box to set the mask property. The result should look something like this:

TIP

You may want to use the Control | Test Movie command to see the effect the way it will show up when the movie is played. Text masks can be difficult to view properly in the Flash development environment.

When you create a text mask, you will probably find that you need to make some additional adjustments to get just the effect that you want. Remember, you can use the Properties panel to change the alignment of the text and to modify most other text properties.

TIP

You can use the Modify | Break Apart command to convert your text into graphics. Once you have converted text into graphics, you can no longer edit it as text, but you can manipulate it as a graphic element. This means that you can, for example, scale the text horizontally to add a little extra width to the strokes.

Progress Check

1. Why is it important to use a bold font for a text mask?

2. What is the advantage of breaking apart the text used in a mask?

Modifying the Mask

After you have created your mask, you can modify it in the same way as any other object that you might create in a Flash movie. There is, however, just one small complication that you need to be aware of. As you will recall from earlier in this module, when you turn a layer into a mask layer, both the mask layer and the masked layer are locked automatically. If you want to make a modification, you must click in the lock column of the mask layer to unlock the layer. Once you have made your changes, you must then lock the mask layer again in order to see the effects of the mask while you are working on your movie.

Using a Mask in Animation

Even though the mask itself is not visible in the movie when it is played back, you can still create an animation sequence that involves the mask. You really have two options here. You can apply a tween to the mask itself, or you can apply that tween to the masked layer. It simply depends on the effect that you want to achieve.

There is one limitation that you need to be aware of. If you animate the mask itself, you cannot use a motion guide to direct the path of the mask. Other than that, you can apply a motion tween or a shape tween as needed to achieve the effect that you want.

---

1. So the image under the mask will be visible.
2. You have the ability to modify broken apart text as graphics.

Ask the Expert

Q: How can I create a mask that creates a spotlight effect? I want the objects to be dark but partially visible all the time, and then to light up as the light passes over them.

A: To create this effect, you need to make two layers that are exact duplicates and then modify the brightness of the objects on the masked layer to brighten them. To do this, begin by drawing the objects on the first layer. Once this layer is complete, use the Edit | Select All command to select everything on the layer. Use the Edit | Copy command to copy the selection. Then click the lock column so that this layer won't be affected by further changes. Add the new layer and use the Edit | Paste In Place command to add the objects. Select each object individually and click the fill color selector. When the fill color pane is open, click the color palette button in the upper-right corner to open the Color dialog box. To brighten the objects without changing the colors, increase the value in the Lum box. You may want to double whatever value is there. Click OK. When you have completed the modification of all of the objects, create your mask as usual, applying a motion tween to the mask. You will then have your spotlight effect.

Q: How can I create a text mask that moves?

A: Creating a text mask that moves is no different than creating any other moving mask. You simply apply a motion tween to the text box. Keep in mind, though, that a moving text mask may be a little hard to read—especially if it appears in front of a bitmap image. You will want to be especially careful to test the effect before you place this type of animation on a web site. You can also use a movie clip as a mask, but you will probably find that it is better to become completely comfortable using the other types of masks before you try this rather advanced technique.

TIP

If you really want to create a motion guide effect for a mask, you could simply do frame-by-frame animation or use a series of short, straight-line motion tweens to achieve a similar effect. Alternatively, you can create a movie clip that has a motion guide to move an object within the movie clip. Then you can use the movie clip instance as your mask. This will mean, of course, that you will have a considerably more complicated task of creating your movie and making certain that everything works as expected.

If you want to animate the mask, I suggest that you first create the object that you will use as the mask, and then apply whatever motion or shape tween you want to use. After you have tested your animation, turn the mask into a mask layer by right-clicking the layer and choosing Mask from the pop-up menu.

Creating Scrolling Text

A scrolling text banner is actually one of the better uses for masks. Flash makes it very easy for you to create a scrolling text banner in this fashion. Basically, you create a mask that shows several words in a row, and then you create a text block that moves under the mask using a motion tween.

There are two types of scrolling text banners. The most common one looks like a news ticker where the headlines scroll horizontally across the screen. You can also create a text banner where the text scrolls up one line at a time. This type of text banner is not as popular as the horizontally scrolling text banner, but you can use whichever suits your needs. Let's take a closer look at the basics behind these two options.

Scrolling Text Horizontally

Almost everyone is familiar with horizontally scrolling text banners. In this type of text banner, the text simply flows horizontally across a one-line box, usually displaying several words at a time.

Creating a horizontally scrolling text box is a fairly simple process. The effect is achieved through the use of a mask—generally a rectangle that is wide enough to display several words—and a one-line text box that scrolls horizontally underneath the mask using a motion tween. Here are some points you need to remember about creating this type of scrolling text banner:

- Make certain that the mask is tall enough and positioned properly so that the text is fully visible—including any uppercase characters.

- Make certain that the mask is wide enough so that the viewer will be able to easily read the text as it scrolls past.

- Create the text box by clicking once and adding the text on a single line. Make certain that you do not allow any carriage returns to drop text down to a second line—it won't be visible as the text scrolls.

- Keep the scrolling speed low enough so that the text can be easily read. It is a good idea to test this on someone who does not already know what is contained in the text.

- Avoid fancy text effects—they will limit readability.

TIP

If you want to add a lot of text, you may want to create it and proofread it in your word processor first. Then copy it and paste it into the text box. Make certain that you check for unwanted line breaks so that the text all remains on a single line!

Scrolling Text Vertically

You can also scroll text vertically. This type of scrolling text box is not nearly as popular as the horizontally scrolling text banner, primarily because vertically scrolling text banners take more space and can be harder to read.

Creating a vertically scrolling text banner is similar to creating a horizontally scrolling one, but there are some unique considerations you need to be aware of. Here are some important things to remember:

- The mask must be as wide as the entire text box. Otherwise, the ends of long lines of text will be cut off.

- The mask must be high enough to display more than one line of text. This enables the reader to see an entire line at once. (If the mask was exactly the height of the text, the whole line would only be visible for a very brief time because during most of the scrolling either the top or the bottom of the text would be cut off.)

- The text box must scroll upward at a fairly slow rate. Remember, people may need more time because they will need to comprehend an entire line of text before it scrolls out of view.

- You may want to add extra blank lines between paragraphs to improve readability.

A vertically scrolling text banner is probably superior to a horizontally scrolling one for displaying large amounts of text. You may want to consider making the mask tall enough that readers can see several lines of text at once as they would when reading text from a book.

Progress Check

1. When you create a scrolling text banner, which element has the motion tween applied to it?

2. How many lines should a horizontally scrolling text banner contain?

---

1. The text box
2. One

Project 7-1 Using a Mask to Create Banner Text

Now it is time to apply the information that you have learned in this module. For this project, you will create a horizontally scrolling text banner that you can use on your web site. Since this type of banner can be created as a very small Flash movie file, you will find this project useful for many different purposes, because it allows you to add a scrolling text banner to a web site with almost no effect on the amount of time it takes to load the page.

Step by Step

1. Open a new, blank Flash movie.

2. Click the Text tool to select it.

3. Optionally, use the Text menu commands (or the Properties panel) to select the font, size, and style for the text. You will want to make certain that the text is easily readable as it scrolls.

4. Click once to create a one-line text box that can expand horizontally to fit the text. Remember, all of the text must be on a single line.

5. Type the text that you want in the text box. For my banner, I entered the following text from one of Aesop's fables: **The Fox and the Mask   A Fox had by some means got into the store-room of a theatre. Suddenly he observed a face glaring down on him and began to be very frightened; but looking more closely he found it was only a Mask such as actors use to put over their face. "Ah," said the Fox, "you look very fine; it is a pity you have not got any brains." Outside show is a poor substitute for inner worth.**

TIP

You can copy the text from another document and paste it into the text box.

6. If necessary, drag the text box so that the first part of the text appears onstage, as shown here. (Notice that the text box extends well off the right side of the stage.)

The Fox and the Mask

7. Click the timeline frame that represents a reasonable period of time for someone to read the text. For example, if the text will take about 15 seconds to read, click frame 180. Depending on the frame you choose, you may need to scroll the timeline to see the frame you want to select.

8. Select Insert | Timeline | Keyframe to add a keyframe at the selected frame.

9. Click the Arrow tool to select it.

10. Hold down SHIFT and drag the text box to the left until the end of the text is visible, as shown here. (Holding down the SHIFT key ensures that you will move the text box horizontally.) Remember, you can drag the text box when the mouse pointer is a four-headed arrow.

11. Click the tween frames to select them.

12. Use the Insert | Timeline | Create Motion Tween command to add a motion tween to the text box. Your text box should now move horizontally as you drag the playhead back and forth across the timeline.

13. Click the Insert Layer button to add a new layer above the layer with the text box.

14. Click frame 1 of the new layer.

15. Click the Rectangle tool to select it.

16. Draw a rectangle so that it covers the text, as shown here:

17. Select the same frame in the new layer that you chose for the ending keyframe on the text box layer.

18. Select Insert | Timeline | Keyframe to add a keyframe to the rectangle layer in that frame. This will make the rectangle visible during the entire tween.

(continued)

7

Using Guides and Masks

Project
7-1

Using a Mask to Create Banner Text

19. Right-click (or Command-click on a Mac) the rectangle layer and choose Mask from the pop-up menu.

20. Use the File | Save command to save your work.

21. Test your movie using the Control | Test Movie command. The text banner should scroll across the stage, as shown here:

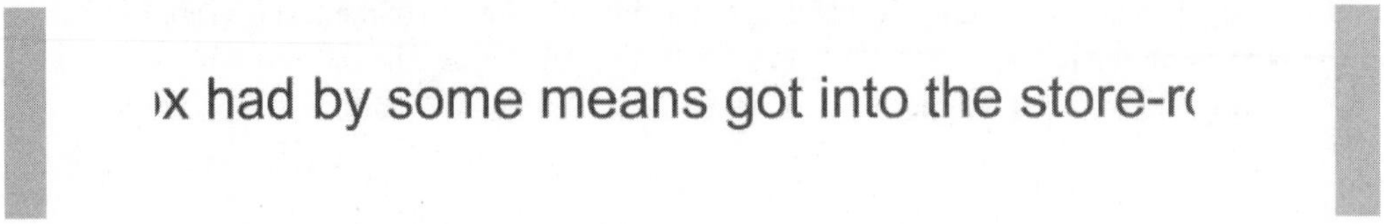

ıx had by some means got into the store-rı

22. If necessary, add additional frames to lengthen the tween and the mask.

Project Summary

In this project, you learned how to create a scrolling text banner. You saw that it was necessary to create a single-line text box and to animate it using a motion tween that moved the box horizontally. You probably also learned an important lesson about how slowly you need to scroll text in order for it to be fully readable. A scrolling text banner is a very useful addition to almost any web site, and one that you can now easily create on your own.

✓ Module 7 Mastery Check

1. You use a _____ to make a motion tween follow a curved path.

2. A _____ serves as a window onto a masked layer.

3. A guide layer appears _____ the guided layer in the timeline.

4. If you want the object being guided to rotate so that it stays perpendicular to the motion guide, you select the _____ option.

5. To create a scrolling text banner, you apply a motion tween to the _____.

6. When you use a mask, you can apply a tween to:

   A. The mask

   B. The masked layer

C. Neither

D. Both

7. Which of the following cannot be used as a mask?

   A. Text

   B. A rectangle

   C. A line

   D. A circle

8. When you create a mask, the _____ in the mask serves as the window onto the masked layer.

9. To view the mask effect in Flash, you must _____ the mask layer.

10. How many different motion tweens can use the same motion guide?

   A. Only one

   B. Two

   C. As many as you want

11. In addition to using a motion guide, it is possible to make a tween follow a curved path using _____ animation.

12. The mask is _____ when the movie is played.

13. To create a horizontally scrolling text banner, the mask must be at least as _____ as the text box.

14. To modify a mask, you must first _____ the mask layer.

15. To create a news-ticker effect, you use _____ scrolling text.

Module 8

Creating Symbols and Using the Library

Flash movies are popular for a number of reasons, but one of the most important is that you can pack so much into a very small file. This means that you can add quite a bit of interest to a web site without creating a download nightmare. In this module, you will learn about some of the Flash elements that contribute considerably to this great efficiency. You will learn about *symbols* and *libraries*—two pieces of the Flash development environment that are very important both to cutting the size of Flash movies and to reducing your workload by enabling you to reuse objects that you have created.

As you will also learn in this module, Flash comes with a number of ready-built objects that you are free to use in your movies. You can take advantage of these objects to add elements to your movies without always starting from scratch. As a Flash developer, you can use these tools to leverage your efforts so that you can focus on creating your movies rather than building every piece from the ground up.

Learning About Symbols

Symbols are objects that you create for use in your Flash movies. They differ from the objects you have created so far in some very important ways:

- Symbols are reusable. This means that you can use *instances* of the symbols as many times as necessary in a movie.

- Only one copy of a symbol is stored in the published movie file. Any instances of that symbol refer to the stored copy of the symbol—greatly reducing the size of the published movie file.

- Changes you make to the stored copy of a symbol affect all instances of that symbol. Thus, you can make a change in one place and be sure that all instances of the symbol that you have used will reflect that change.

- Symbols can be saved in a library that can then be shared with other Flash movies you create. This means that you can develop a symbol once and use it in as many movies as you like.

There are three types of Flash symbols. Each serves a very useful purpose in your Flash movie development. Let's look at each type of symbol to see how you can use them.

Graphic Symbols

Graphic symbols are objects that are images you have created, imported bitmaps, or animations that are tied to the main timeline of the movie. These are objects that you might want to duplicate a number of times throughout a movie, such as the trees on a background layer.

TIP

You don't use graphic symbols for interactive objects. That is, a graphic symbol can be a part of an animation, but it won't interact with the user. For interaction, you use button symbols.

You may have the impression that using instances of a graphic symbol might lead to a boring movie due to repetition. This does not have to be the case, since various instances of a symbol can take on different characteristics that can change their appearance. For example, instances of the same symbol can be scaled differently or use different colors as shown in the following illustration. Even with these differences, Flash still needs to store only one copy of the symbol in the movie file. Each instance then needs only to record the variations from the library copy of the symbol, and this takes far less space than saving an entirely new object.

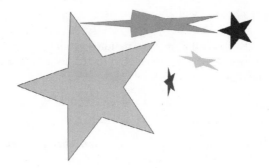

NOTE

Graphic symbol instances are a part of the main timeline of the movie. This means that they act according to the dictates of the main timeline, and that they can be used as a part of a main timeline animation.

Button Symbols

Button symbols are a special type of symbol that has built-in interactive capabilities. You use button symbol instances to create buttons that the user can click to interact with your movie. For example, you can use button symbol instances to provide Play, Rewind, and Stop controls for your movie.

TIP

Flash includes a number of prebuilt buttons that you are free to use in your movies, and this can save you the work of creating your own buttons from scratch. I discuss this option later in this module.

Button symbols have their own timeline with four frames as shown here:

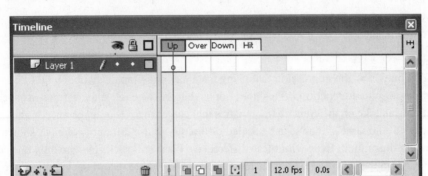

The four frames of a button symbol timeline are

- **Up**   This represents the condition of the button when it is up—that is, not interacting with the mouse. This is the default appearance of the button as it sits there in your movie waiting to interact with the user.

- **Over**   This represents the condition of the button when the mouse pointer is over the button but the mouse button has not been clicked.

- **Down**   This represents the condition of the button when the user is holding down the mouse button while the mouse pointer is over the button.

- **Hit**   This defines the area that is sensitive to a mouse click. Normally, this will be the same size as the other button states, but if you get fancy with the shapes in the other three button frames, you may need to set the hit area specifically so that mouse clicks are actually recorded.

TIP

When you draw the different frames for a button symbol, you can easily provide visual clues to let users know that they are interacting with the button. Typically, this is done by using different color fills in each of the frames, but you can also use different shapes if you want.

Button symbols provide some real hidden power for your Flash movies. You may not have given this aspect a lot of thought, but button symbols can save you an awful lot of grief, since they have the built-in ability to respond to mouse events. Imagine how difficult and complicated it would be if you had to create objects that could respond to the mouse from scratch! Needless to say, this is a huge time and work saver for every Flash developer.

When you create button symbols, you need to use ActionScript to make the buttons actually do something useful. This ActionScript code is attached to the individual button symbol instances rather than to the button symbol in the Flash library. This placement makes it possible for different instances of the button symbol to perform different actions.

NOTE

As you will learn later in this module, Flash MX 2004 offers an alternative to creating your own ActionScript code when you want to add interactivity to symbol instances such as buttons. This alternative is called *behaviors* and is actually a means of adding predefined ActionScript modules by making menu selections.

Movie Clips

Movie clip symbols are essentially movies within a movie. Movie clip symbols are typically small pieces of animation that can be placed within another movie to provide an independent piece of animation. For example, you might create a movie clip symbol that shows a rolling wheel. You could then use a couple of instances of this movie clip symbol to provide wheels for any vehicles in your main movie. That way, the wheels of the vehicle would turn as the vehicle moved, providing a much more realistic animation.

Movie clip symbols have their own timeline that is independent of the main timeline. You can control the movie clip's timeline from the main timeline, but the movie clip timeline is independent. (Don't worry if this seems a little confusing right now—it will all become clear once you start using movie clip symbol instances in your own movies.)

It is even possible for you to embed one type of symbol within another. For example, you can place a movie clip symbol inside a button symbol to create an animated button.

Understanding the Ripple Effect

Earlier I mentioned that one of the advantages of using symbol instances in your movies is that if you modify the master copy of the symbol, the changes will apply to all of the instances you have added to the movie. This has some very important implications. For example, consider these points:

- If you create a symbol that re-creates your company logo, you can update that logo wherever it might appear in your movie by simply modifying the copy that is contained within the library.

- If you were to create a rolling wheel movie clip, you could share that rolling wheel with different movies. To create a different type of wheel—a wagon wheel, for example— you would only have to modify the copy in the movie that needs a different wheel. Any instance of the wheel symbol in that movie would then take on the new appearance.

● If you created a button symbol for use in your movie and then decided you wanted to use a different color scheme, simply modifying the master button symbol in the library would change the color of all instances of the button throughout your movie.

Though there is a ripple effect that updates all instances of a symbol when you change the *master* copy in the library, you need to be aware that Flash does remember any specific changes you have made to a particular instance of the symbol. If, for example, you have created a graphic symbol that has a green fill and later change the master copy so that it has a red fill, that change will not be applied to an instance where you changed the fill to blue. On the other hand, if you decide to rotate the master copy of the symbol but have not rotated any of the instances, then the rotation will apply to all of the instances—even the one whose fill was not changed when the master copy's fill changed.

Progress Check

1. Which type of symbol has a special four-frame timeline?

2. Which type of symbol has an independent timeline?

CRITICAL SKILL
8.2 Creating Symbols

Creating new symbols is easy. Each type of symbol has its own requirements, of course, but you will primarily use techniques you have already learned in creating symbols.

In the following sections, you will learn how to create each type of symbol from scratch. Keep in mind, however, that you can also change existing objects into symbols. To do so, you use the Modify | Convert To Symbol command when the object is selected.

Creating Graphic Symbols

Graphic symbols are the simplest of all the symbol types. Creating a graphic symbol is also an easy task. Typically, graphic symbols are objects that you draw so that they can be used conveniently within your movie. You can create new symbols at any time, so you do not have to start with a new, blank stage.

---

1. A button symbol
2. A movie clip symbol

To create a new graphic symbol, follow these steps:

1. Select the Insert | New Symbol command to display the Create New Symbol dialog box, as shown here:

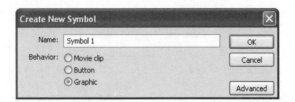

2. Select the Graphic option button.

3. Optionally, enter a name for the symbol in the Name text box. Although this step is optional, it is highly recommended—especially if you will be creating a number of symbols or if you want to reuse your symbols in other movies.

4. Click OK to enter the symbol editing mode. In this mode, Flash displays the name of the symbol ("Tree" in this example) above the timeline, as shown here:

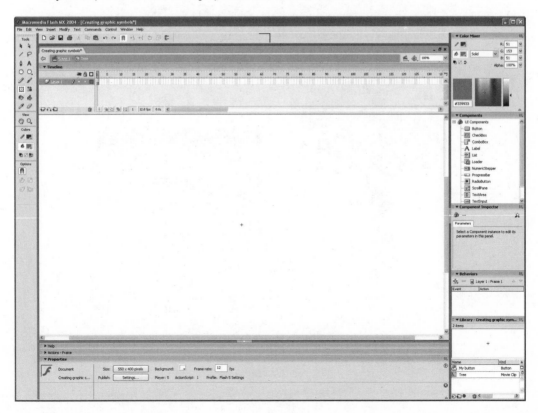

5. Use the drawing tools to draw the object that you want to use as a graphic symbol. As you draw the object, notice a couple of important points about the stage:

- First, the plus sign in the center of the stage is the *registration point* for the object—the point that Flash will use as the center of the object. You should center your object around this point as much as possible.

- Second, there is no workspace beyond the edge of the stage. Everything you draw will be a part of the symbol.

6. When you have finished drawing the object, click the Arrow tool to select it.

7. Draw a selection box around the entire object so that it is completely selected.

8. Select Window | Design Panels | Align to open the Align panel.

9. Click the To Stage button so that the alignment options you choose will control the object's alignment relative to the stage.

10. Click the Align Horizontal Center button. This is the second from the left in the top row of buttons. Clicking this button aligns the object horizontally so that it is in the center of the stage.

11. Click the Align Vertical Center button. This is the second from the right in the top row of buttons. Clicking this button aligns the object vertically so that it is in the center of the stage. Your stage should now look something like this:

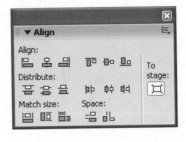

12. Close the Align panel by clicking its Close button.

13. Close the symbol editing mode by clicking Scene 1 above the timeline. Your symbol will disappear, but don't worry—it is safely saved in the movie's library. You will learn how to access the library shortly.

You can repeat the same steps to add additional graphic symbols to the library as necessary. Remember, though, that you can often use modified instances of the same symbol without creating new symbols. For example, we can use instances of our tree symbol that are scaled differently to create an entire forest of trees in a wide variety of sizes, and this will greatly reduce the size of our published movie file.

NOTE

Imported bitmap images are also a type of graphic symbol, but they cannot be created directly within Flash. Rather, they must be imported into the library from an existing graphic image file. You will learn more about using imported graphics in Module 9.

Progress Check

1. What does the plus sign in the symbol editing mode stage represent?

2. Which button do you click to align an object relative to the stage?

Creating Button Symbols

Button symbols are some of the most useful symbols you can create. If you want users to be able to interact with your movies, you will need to create button symbols. Remember, button symbols are a special type of symbol that already knows how to react to mouse events.

1. The registration point of the symbol
2. The To Stage button

To create a button symbol, follow these steps:

1. Select the Insert | New Symbol command to open the Create New Symbol dialog box.

2. Select the Button option button.

3. Enter a name for the button symbol in the Name text box.

4. Click OK to close the dialog box and enter symbol editing mode.

5. Use the drawing tools to create the image for the Up frame. Note: Do not add text to the button—you add text to individual instances after you have added them to your movie. This makes the button reusable for many different purposes.

6. Once you have drawn the button image for the Up frame, use the Arrow tool to select the entire button image.

7. Open the Align panel using the Window | Design Panels | Align command.

8. Use the To Stage, Align Horizontal Center, and Align Vertical Center buttons to make certain that the button is centered on the stage.

9. Click the Over frame in the timeline so that you can create the image that will appear when the mouse pointer is over the button.

10. Select Insert | Timeline | Keyframe to add a keyframe to the Over frame.

11. Use the fill color selector to choose a different color for the fill. This will make the button change color when the user moves the mouse pointer over the button.

12. Click the Down frame in the timeline.

13. Select Insert | Timeline | Keyframe to add a keyframe to the Down frame. Or, if you want to create a button that has a totally different appearance when it is depressed, use the Insert | Timeline | Blank Keyframe command to add a blank keyframe.

14. Select a new fill color or draw the image you want to use for the Down frame. This will be the image users see when they click the button.

15. Finally, add a keyframe to the Hit frame.

16. If you used the same image in all of the previous frames, you don't need to do anything else. If you used a different image for the Down frame, use the Edit | Copy command to copy the image from the Up frame, and then use Edit | Paste In Place to add the image to the Hit frame. The timeline and stage should now look something like the next image.

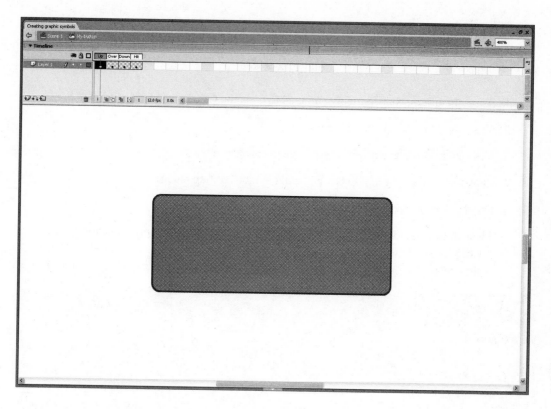

17. Click the Scene 1 name above the timeline to close the symbol editing mode and return to the main stage. Once again, your symbol will disappear, but will be automatically added to the library.

Progress Check

1. Why is it important not to add any text when you are creating a button symbol?

2. What do you need to draw in the Hit frame?

Creating Movie Clip Symbols

Movie clip symbols are some of the most fun symbols you can create. When you create a movie clip symbol, you are creating an independent piece of animation that you can

1. So that the button can be reused
2. Nothing, just add a keyframe.

use in your main movie to do things that would be very hard to accomplish in other ways. For example, you might create some animated legs to give a character the appearance of walking.

To create a movie clip symbol, follow these steps:

1. Select the Insert | New Symbol command to open the Create New Symbol dialog box.

2. Select the Movie Clip option button.

3. Enter a name for the button symbol in the Name text box.

4. Click OK to close the dialog box and enter symbol editing mode.

5. Use the drawing tools to create the object you want to animate.

6. Create the animation using the techniques you have learned in previous modules. For example, here I have created a flapping wing animation. (Notice that I created two tweens in the timeline so that the wing can flap down and then back up in a smooth motion.)

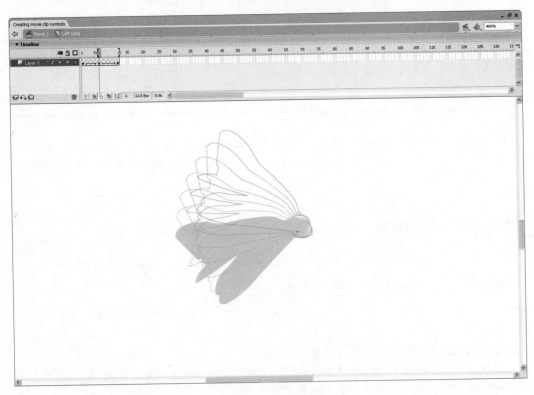

7. Click the Scene 1 name above the timeline to close symbol editing mode and return to the main stage.

Creating a movie clip symbol is essentially identical to creating an animation on the main stage. The primary difference is that the movie clip symbol can then be added as a separate animated element to an object you create on the main stage—or even to another movie clip symbol. In this way, you can create very complex animations without resorting to frame-by-frame animation techniques. As you can imagine, this also saves a huge amount of space in your final published movie file!

Progress Check

1. What happens to the symbol you were creating when you close the symbol editing mode?

2. How do you close symbol editing mode?

Opening Symbols for Editing

When you finish creating any type of symbol, you return to the Flash stage, where there is no indication that the symbol even exists. This can make it somewhat difficult for you to edit the symbols until you learn where to find them. Fortunately, Flash hasn't hidden them very deeply, and you'll easily be able to open them if you need to make some modifications.

To open symbols for editing, follow these steps:

1. Select Window | Library to open the Library panel, as shown here:

---

1. It is saved in the library.

2. Click the scene name above the timeline.

Ask the Expert

Q: I'm not sure what type of symbol I want to create. How can I choose the correct type?

A: Ask yourself the purpose of the symbol you want to create. If you want something that will interact with the user, you want to create a button symbol. If you want something that adds some animation that runs by itself, you want to create a movie clip symbol. If neither applies, you probably want to create a graphic symbol.

Q: My button symbols show the different frames when I roll the mouse over them or click them, but they don't make anything happen in my movie. What's wrong?

A: Actually, there is nothing wrong with your button symbols. You simply haven't added any ActionScript code to do any useful work to the buttons yet. You will learn to use ActionScript in Modules 12 through 14. You will also see how to add some interactivity using behaviors later in this module.

2. Click one of the symbols to view it in the upper pane of the Library panel.

3. To edit a symbol, double-click it in the list, or right-click it and choose Edit from the pop-up menu. This will open the same symbol editing mode window you used to create the symbol in the first place. You can also click the Library panel menu and choose Edit to open the symbol for editing.

4. Make any necessary modifications to the symbol.

5. Click the scene name above the timeline to close the symbol editing mode window.

NOTE

Make certain that you do not select Delete from the menus. Once you delete a symbol from the library, it is completely gone and cannot be recovered (unless you saved it in a separate library as discussed later in this module).

CRITICAL SKILL
8.3 Using Symbol Instances

The whole point of going to the trouble of creating symbols is to use instances of them in your movies. As you have already learned, using symbol instances offers many advantages including considerable savings in the size of your published movie files. In the following sections, we will look at how you can go about using the symbols you have created in your movies.

Adding Symbol Instances to Your Movie

All of the symbols that you create in a movie are automatically stored in the movie's library. To add an instance of a symbol to the stage so that it is a visible part of your movie, you must copy that instance from the library.

To add a symbol instance to the stage, follow these steps:

1. Use the Window | Library command to open the Library panel.

2. In the lower pane of the Library panel, select the symbol you want to add to the stage.

3. Drag a copy of the symbol onto the stage, as shown here. If you drag from the upper pane of the Library panel, you will be able to drag the registration point for more precise placement.

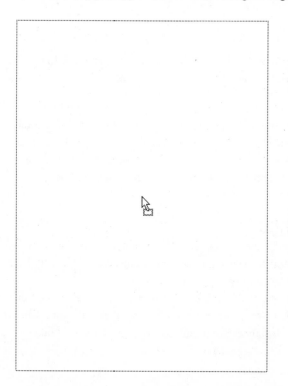

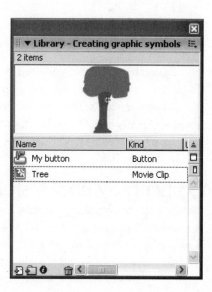

4. Continue dragging symbol instances onto the stage as needed.

5. If desired, close the Library panel to free up space for working.

Remember that you can use multiple instances of the same symbol with almost no adverse effect on the file size. This is in stark contrast to simply drawing and then copying an object, because the copied objects each must be stored separately in the movie file, while symbols are stored once, and the instances simply require a few bytes to record their positions and any special characteristics they may have.

Combining Symbols

Just as you can use symbol instances by dragging them onto the main stage, you can also use symbol instances as a part of another symbol. In fact, this is a very useful technique that can serve you quite well in a number of situations. For example:

- You can place a movie clip symbol instance onto the face of a button symbol to create an animated button.

- You can embed a movie clip symbol instance in a button symbol to create custom mouse pointers and to produce interactive games that allow the user to drag objects as your movie plays.

- You can use a graphic symbol instance to add a fancy appearance to buttons.

- You can create complex animations that combine several movie clip instances so that the motions of the various pieces of an object appear to be more realistic.

To combine symbols, you need to follow a general workflow pattern of creating the individual symbols first, and once you have built the pieces, you drag them from the Library panel while you are creating the combined symbol. Using a symbol instance inside of another symbol is really no different than using a symbol instance on the main stage. In both cases, you are simply adding a prebuilt object that makes your workload that much easier.

Modifying Symbol Instances

Just because you are using a symbol instance does not mean that you need to live with boring repetition. You can make quite a few modifications to those symbol instances with very little increase in the overall size of your published movie file.

Consider the following illustration. In this case, I have added three instances of the same graphic symbol to the stage. I then scaled two of the instances to make them take on different sizes and proportions. Because all three instances are produced from one symbol, it takes very little room to create an entire forest of differently sized and shaped trees.

In addition to such simple changes as scaling or rotating a symbol instance, you can make far more extensive changes, too. You can, for example, make changes such as these:

- Add text to individual button symbol instances. This can be used to let the user know the purpose of different buttons.

- Add ActionScript code to the button symbol instances so that each button performs a specific action when it is clicked.

- Change the alpha property of a symbol instance using the Properties panel, as shown here:

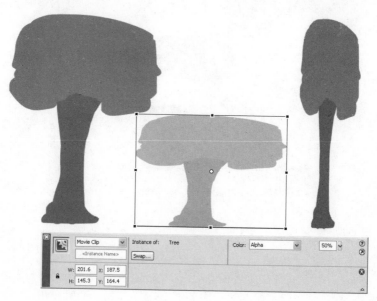

- Change the tint or brightness of a symbol instance using other options in the Properties panel.

- Change an instance into a different type of symbol using the Properties panel. This would enable you to play an animation in a graphic symbol independently of the main timeline, for example.

In addition to these instance-specific modifications, you may find that you want to modify the characteristics of the master symbol after you have added instances to the stage. While you can open the Library panel and then select your symbol for editing, Flash offers an easier way to edit the master symbol without ever leaving the main stage.

To edit the master symbol, all you need to do is to double-click an instance of the symbol. When you do, Flash opens the edit-in-place mode. In this mode, you can modify the selected symbol instance, but all other objects are grayed out and cannot be selected.

It is important that you realize what is happening when you are working in edit-in-place mode. Any changes you make apply to the master copy of the symbol and then ripple out to all instances of the symbol anywhere in the movie. For example, here I have put the tree symbol into edit-in-place mode. Then I selected the leaves at the top of the tree and moved them upward a little. Notice that the same change was also applied to the other two instances of the tree symbol.

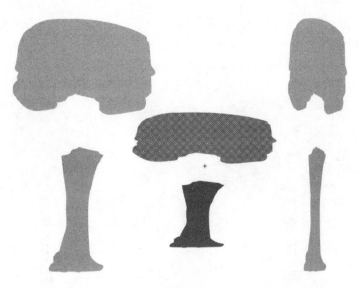

TIP

If you accidentally modify the master copy of a symbol, use the Edit | Undo command immediately to reverse the changes.

Progress Check

1. How many copies of the same symbol can you add to a movie?

2. What happens to instances of a symbol that are already on the stage when you make a change to the master copy of the symbol?

CRITICAL SKILL
8.4 Using Libraries

Earlier in this module, you learned that Flash automatically places any symbols that you create into a library. Libraries are an important item in helping you organize symbols that you create and in enabling you to reuse objects in more than one movie. In the following sections, you will learn what you need to know in order to most effectively use the Flash libraries.

Understanding Libraries

Each Flash movie has its own library. This library is a part of the movie project file—the file that is saved with an .fla extension whenever you choose File | Save, File | Save And Compact, or File | Save As from the Flash menu.

Libraries hold all of the symbols, imported bitmap images, and imported sound files that you use in a movie. When you use any of these items in the movie, Flash links to the library object. This means that multiple copies of the same object will all link to the same item in the library, thus reducing the amount of data that must be stored in the published movie file. The result, of course, is that your movies are smaller and download faster.

---

1. As many as you want
2. The modifications apply to all instances.

You open the movie's Library panel using the Window | Library command. When you open the Library panel, you will normally see a rather small window with just enough width to display the names of the objects that are contained in the library. As the following shows, however, you can drag the edges of the Library panel to reveal far more information about the objects in the library.

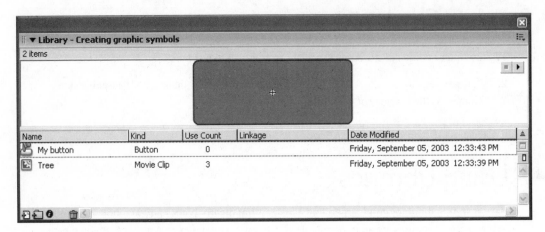

The Library panel has several columns:

- **Name** This is the name that you assigned to the object (or the default name Flash created for you).

- **Kind** This is the type of the object. You can also tell the object's type by looking at its icon to the left of the Name column.

- **Use Count** This tells you how many times the object has been used in the movie. Unfortunately, the count is often inaccurate, and you must use the Library panel Options menu Update Use Counts Now command to obtain the current use counts. (Avoid using the Keep Use Counts Updated command—it tends to put a rather severe strain on system performance.)

- **Linkage** This provides linkage information for objects that are used in *shared libraries*. These libraries are discussed a little later in this module.

- **Date Modified** This is the date and time information for when the object was last modified.

In most cases, you will probably want to keep the Library panel just large enough so that you can see the object names. The remaining information is typically not all that useful unless you are expending a lot of effort optimizing your movies to produce the smallest possible file size.

When you are working with the library, you will probably find the library menu (shown here) useful. As this shows, the library menu provides a number of commands that are handy for creating objects and for organizing the library.

```
New Symbol...
New Folder
New Font...
New Video
Rename
Move to New Folder...
Duplicate...
Delete
Edit
Edit with...
Properties...
Linkage...
Component Definition...
─────────────────────────
Select Unused Items
Update...
Play
─────────────────────────
Expand Folder
Collapse Folder
─────────────────────────
Expand All Folders
Collapse All Folders
─────────────────────────
Shared Library Properties...
─────────────────────────
Keep Use Counts Updated
Update Use Counts Now
─────────────────────────
Help
Maximize Panel
Close Panel
```

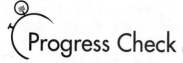

Progress Check

1. How do you open the Library panel?

2. What special command do you need to use to create a library?

───

1. Use the Window | Library command.
2. None, every movie project file automatically has a library.

Adding Your Objects to Libraries

Whenever you create a new symbol, that symbol is automatically added to the current movie's library. This is true whether you use the Insert | New Symbol command or whether you use the Modify | Convert To Symbol command. Both commands add a new symbol to the library.

In addition, you can add objects to the library by importing bitmap graphic image files or by importing sound files. In both cases, Flash places the objects into the library as soon as they are imported.

NOTE

The process of importing graphic image files may seem a little confusing at first. Unlike other objects that you place in the Flash library, Flash sometimes leaves a copy of the imported bitmap image on the stage when the file is imported. Don't worry—you can safely delete this copy since Flash automatically added a copy to the library as well. You will learn more about importing bitmap images files in Module 9.

You cannot arbitrarily add objects to the library. Except for imported bitmap graphic images and imported sound files, the only objects you can store in the library are symbols that you create (or symbols you borrow from another Flash movie). Flash also lists the tweens that make up movie clip symbols in the library, but these are not really objects that you can use independently.

Organizing Your Libraries

As you add more symbols and imported objects to the library, you may find that it becomes a little difficult to locate specific objects. One way around this is to add a little bit of organization. You do this by adding folders to the library and then using those folders to store related objects.

You add folders to the library by selecting the New Folder command from the library menu. When you do, Flash creates the folder with the default name "New Folder." You can immediately type a new name while the default name is selected, or you can double-click the folder name later and then rename it. Alternatively, you can select the folder and use the Rename command on the Options menu.

Once you have created folders, you can move items into those folders. You can do this using the drag-and-drop method, or by selecting the items you want to move and using the Move To New Folder command on the Options menu.

The precise organizational method you choose is really a matter of personal preference. I find that it makes a lot of sense to place any of the objects (such as tweens) that make up an object into a folder with a name that includes the name of the object. For example, if you have a movie clip named Wings, you might create a folder named Components of Wings. Another good organizational scheme would be to place related items—such as movie clips or imported bitmap images—together in a folder. Whichever method you choose, the goal is to try to make it easier to quickly find what you need.

Progress Check

1. In addition to symbols you have created, what other types of objects can you store in library folders?

2. How do you add an imported image to the library?

Using Standard Library Objects

One secret that new Flash developers are always pleased to learn is that Flash comes with a number of ready-made objects that you are free to use in your movies. These objects are stored in what are called *common libraries*. When you install Flash, these common libraries are also installed, giving you access to all of the objects that they contain.

To access the common libraries, you use the Window | Other Panels | Common Libraries command to display the menu shown here. Each of these libraries contains a number of objects that you can add to a Flash movie just the way you would add an instance from the movie's own library—by dragging and dropping.

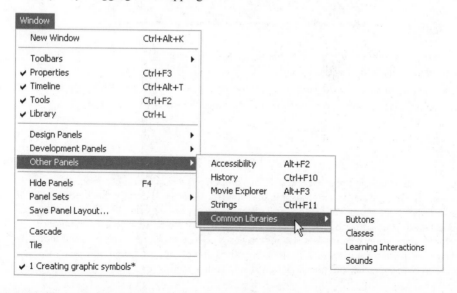

---

1. Imported images and sound files

2. Just import it and it is automatically added.

As an example, here is the common library that contains a large number of buttons that you can use by simply dragging them into your movie:

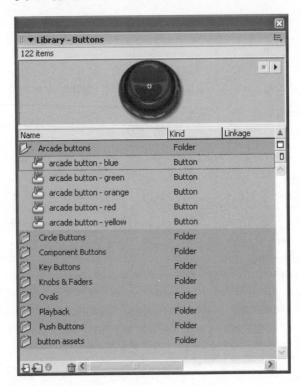

When you add an object from one of the common libraries to a Flash movie, that object is automatically added to the movie's library as well. This enables you to easily add more instances to your movie, and it gives you the ability to modify the imported symbol without worrying about messing up the original copy that remains in the common library.

NOTE

Flash has some additional objects known as *components* that you can use in your movies. These components are reusable user interface elements such as check boxes, radio buttons, list boxes, and so on. You access the components using the Components panel (which you open using the Window | Development Panels | Components command). Unfortunately, using components in your movies is considerably more complicated than using objects from the common libraries, because components are useful only with the addition of some rather advanced ActionScript programming.

Creating Reusable Libraries

The common libraries are really just Flash movie project files that are stored in a special location. If you have created a number of your own objects that you would like to be able to reuse in other movies, it is very easy for you to add your own common libraries.

TIP

When you create a Flash movie project file for use as a library, it's a good idea to delete everything else from that movie file before you save it. When a movie project file is opened as a library file, you won't be able to access anything that is not in the movie's library anyway, so deleting unneeded objects will reduce the amount of file space that is needed.

Once you have created the movie project file that you want to save as a common library, you can save it in the Libraries folder using the File | Save As command as shown here. The Libraries folder is located under the Flash program folder. On a Windows-based PC, this folder is typically named C:\Program Files\Macromedia\Flash MX 2004\en\First Run\Libraries.

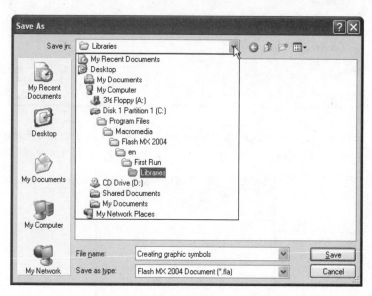

TIP

When you save a common library file, use a name that describes the contents of the library. Whatever name you use will be the same name that appears in the Window | Other Panels | Common Libraries menu.

Even if you don't save a Flash movie project file as a common library, you can still open it as a library so that you can use any objects that are contained in its library. To do so, follow these steps:

1. Select the File | Import | Open External Library command to display the Open As Library dialog box, as shown here:

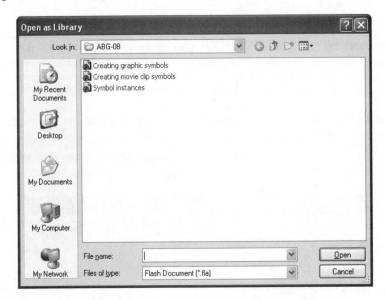

2. Select the movie project that you want to open, and then click the Open button. Flash opens a Library panel that has the name of the movie project file, as shown here:

3. Drag the objects you want to use onto the stage. As with the common libraries, this also places a copy of the borrowed object into the current movie's library.

4. Click the Close button for the foreign library file to close it.

Progress Check

1. What do you have to do to place objects from a common library into your movie's library?

2. How can you open a movie to use its library in your movie?

Using Shared Libraries

As I have tried to emphasize many times in the earlier modules, one of the real benefits of using Flash to create web site animation is the high level of efficiency of the Flash movie file format. As you develop your own Flash movies, you should constantly be on the lookout for ways to save a little space here and there to further reduce the size of your published movies. After all, smaller files download faster, and that encourages visitors to stick around for the show.

Flash offers another method of gaining efficiency that I'll just touch on briefly. _Shared library files_ are Flash movie files that you place on your web server. These shared library files contain objects such as sound files that you might want to use in more than one movie. Rather than containing the shared resource, your movie file contains a link to the shared library file, and the shared resource is downloaded from the shared library.

Creating the necessary links to shared library files can be rather complicated, and it is very easy to encounter errors if the shared library file cannot be opened for some reason. If an error occurs with the download from the shared library file, your movie won't play.

Despite the potential problems, there are still reasons why advanced Flash developers use shared library files. The primary advantage exists when you have multiple movies that all use the same shared resource. In some instances, the visitor's web browser is able to use the copy of the shared resource that was already downloaded when a later movie asks for the same file.

The best advice I can offer you about shared library files is to avoid them for now. If you become involved in developing a very large project, you may want to revisit the subject at a later date. Otherwise, you will likely find that shared library files are more trouble than they are worth for the average Flash developer.

---

1. Drag them into your movie, and they will be added to the library automatically.

2. Use the File | Import | Open External Library command.

CAUTION

The security model that is used to control which files a Flash movie can open have been considerably strengthened in Flash MX 2004. This can mean that Flash movies that were created in older versions of Flash and which used shared library files may no longer work if they are modified in Flash MX 2004.

Using Behaviors

Earlier in this module, I mentioned that you could create interactivity by adding ActionScript programming to objects such as button symbol instances. Although I won't be covering ActionScript programming until Module 12, I do want to take this opportunity to introduce you to another option that you can use to make objects interactive in Flash MX 2004.

Behaviors are prewritten ActionScript modules that you can add to symbol instances by making menu selections. By using behaviors, you can do many different things that in the past required learning ActionScript. Now you may even find that behaviors can handle everything that is necessary for you so that you don't have to learn any ActionScript programming.

Adding a behavior is a fairly simple and straightforward process. To do so, follow these steps:

1. Add a symbol instance to your movie. In this case, add one of the buttons from the Buttons common library so that you do not have to design your own button.

2. Open the Behaviors panel using the Window | Development Panels | Behaviors command.

3. With the button symbol instance selected, click the plus (+) icon near the upper-left corner of the Behaviors panel to display the menu, as shown here:

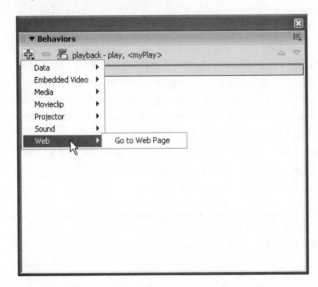

4. Select the action that you want the button to perform when it is clicked. In this case, select Web | Go To Web Page to display the Go To URL dialog box as shown here:

5. Enter the URL of the web page that you want the button to open.

6. If you want to specify the type of browser window to open, choose one of the options from the drop-down Open In list box.

7. Click OK to close the dialog box.

8. Save your movie and then select Control | Test Movie. When you click the button, your web browser should open the desired web page.

You may want to open the Actions panel as shown here so that you can see the ActionScript code that was added to your button symbol instance. This can be an excellent way to get your feet wet with ActionScript code, because when you add a behavior, you know what you want to happen when the button is clicked, and the Actions panel can show you one method of reaching that goal.

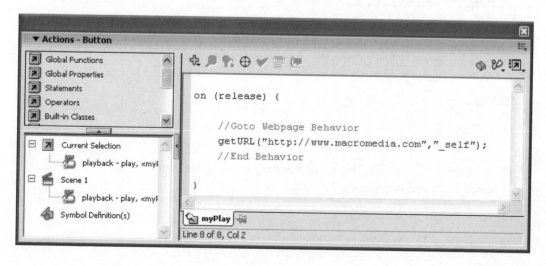

Project 8-1 Creating and Using a Rolling Wheel Movie Clip

Now it is time to apply the skills you learned in this module to create a movie clip symbol that you will be able to use in your movies. In this case, you will create a movie clip symbol that simulates a rolling wheel. Once you have created this basic movie clip, you will be able to add it to vehicles in your movies to provide a far more realistic-appearing animated effect when you move the vehicle across the stage.

Step by Step

1. Open a new, blank Flash movie.

2. Select the Insert | New Symbol command to open the Create New Symbol dialog box.

3. Enter **Rolling wheel** in the Name text box.

4. With the default Movie Clip option button selected, click the OK button to enter the symbol editing mode.

5. Click the Oval tool to select it.

6. Use the Window | Properties command to open the Properties panel so that you can set the drawing options for the tire and wheel.

7. Be sure that the line style is set to solid.

8. Make certain that the stroke color is set to black.

9. Drag the Stroke Height slider all the way to the top so that the stroke is set to the maximum width of 10 points.

10. Close the Properties panel or move it out of the way.

11. Click the fill color selector and then the No Color button. In this case, you want to create a wheel with spokes rather than a solid fill, so you don't want to use a fill.

12. Hold down SHIFT as you drag a circle near the center of the stage. Remember that holding down SHIFT will help you draw a perfect circle.

13. Click the Arrow tool to select it.

14. Draw a selection box around the circle.

15. Use the Window | Design Panels | Align command to open the Align panel.

16. Click the To Stage button in the Align panel so that the alignment commands will be relative to the stage.

17. Click the Align Horizontal Center button.

18. Click the Align Vertical Center button. Your stage should now look something like this:

 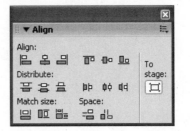

19. Close the Align panel.

20. Click outside the circle to deselect it.

21. Click the Line tool to select it so that you can draw the wheel's spokes.

22. Click the stroke color selector and choose brown.

23. Draw four spokes starting at the center point of the stage. These should extend just to the inner edge of the tire. It's okay if the spokes end up slightly short—you'll take care of that in a moment.

24. Click the Arrow tool to select it.

25. Click the circle to select it.

26. Use the Edit | Copy command to make a copy of the tire.

27. Use the Edit | Paste In Place command to add a new copy on top of the existing tire.

28. Select the Modify | Transform | Scale command.

29. Use the handles to shrink the new circle so that it is just inside the outer circle.

30. Click the fill color selector and choose brown to create a brown rim for the wheel.

31. Use the Arrow tool to select the completed wheel.

(continued)

32. Select Modify | Group to group the wheel. Your stage should now look something like this:

33. Click frame 12 in the timeline to select it.

34. Use the Insert | Timeline | Keyframe command to add a keyframe.

35. Right-click the wheel and choose Free Transform from the pop-up menu.

36. Drag the lower-right corner handle until it is on top of the lower-left corner handle.

37. Click the tween frames in the timeline to select them.

38. Select Insert | Timeline | Create Motion Tween to add the motion tween to the timeline.

39. Drag the playhead back and forth across the timeline to test your animation. Your wheel should rotate smoothly around the registration point.

40. Click the Scene name above the timeline to close the symbol editing mode.

41. Use the Window | Library command to open the Library panel.

42. Select your new Rolling Wheel movie clip symbol to display it in the top pane of the Library panel.

43. Click the Play button to see your movie clip symbol in action.

Project Summary

In this project, you created a movie clip symbol that you will find very useful in your movies. The rolling wheel movie clip symbol that you created can be added to vehicles to produce a far more realistic-appearing animated vehicle. Although this particular wheel rolls clockwise, you can easily create a counterclockwise rolling wheel following the same sequence of steps—just reverse the drag in step 36.

✓

Module 8 Mastery Check

1. When you create symbols, they are stored in the _____.

2. Which of the following is not one of the Flash symbol types?

   A. Movie clip

   B. ActionScript object

   C. Button

   D. Graphic

3. A _____ symbol has the built-in ability to react to mouse events.

4. When you place copies of symbols into your movie, those copies are called _____.

5. The button symbol has _____ frames in its timeline.

6. The _____ symbol uses the main movie timeline.

7. The _____ symbol has a timeline that is independent of the main timeline.

8. To use the prebuilt symbols that come with Flash, you open one of the _____.

9. Modifying a master copy of a symbol in the library affects which instances of the symbol?

   A. Ones you add to the stage after the modification

   B. Ones you have already added to the stage

   C. All instances no matter when they are added to the stage

   D. None of them

10. To use symbols from another movie, you can open that movie's library using the File | Import | _____ command.

11. You can add interactivity to a symbol instance using the _____ panel.

12. A button symbol instance needs some _____ code in order to do anything useful.

13. Using symbol instances rather than copies of ordinary objects _____ the size of the published Flash movie file.

14. You should add any text you want on a button to _____ of the button symbol.

15. The _____ frame of a button symbol defines the area a user can click.

Module 9

Using Imported Graphics

One of the common features of virtually all Flash movies is that they tend to be highly graphical. Although many Flash movies can do just fine with the relatively simple graphics that you can produce in Flash itself, it is often desirable to use images from other sources. For example, you might have an image from a digital camera that you want to add to a Flash movie. Or perhaps you want to use a vector drawing program such as FreeHand to produce effects that are not easily done within Flash. In this module, you will learn how to do these things as well as how you can convert text into graphics to produce some truly spectacular special effects.

As you follow through the subjects that are covered in this module, pay special attention to the details—especially regarding file size implications. One of the reasons that Flash movies tend to be very space efficient is the way Flash uses vector graphics. When you start importing graphics (and particularly bitmap images), it is easy to quickly bloat the size of your published movie files if you aren't careful about what you are doing. You can minimize the problems by being aware and making the proper choices. Just keep reminding yourself that smaller files produce far better download times and superior playback performance, and that these factors are at least as important as image quality in most Flash movies.

CRITICAL SKILL
9.1 Understanding Importing Graphics

As you already know, Flash uses vector graphics as its native image format. You may not, however, be fully aware of just what this means. Let's quickly review the subject and pin down the differences between image file formats.

Understanding Vector Graphics

Vector graphics are images that are defined by mathematical expressions. This means that in a vector image, each element in the image is defined something like this:

```
Start at point A and draw a straight line to point B
```

The actual definition of the line would be more complex, of course, but the idea remains the same. That is, the definition of the line does not say anything about specific pixels along the way, only where to begin and how to reach the destination. This approach has several important implications:

- The drawing object can be scaled up or down without affecting the quality of the image. The image does not deteriorate simply because the image is viewed at a different size than the one at which it was originally created.

- The object requires the same amount of file space no matter what its size, since the equation does not change when the object is scaled. This is one of the factors that results in vector graphic formats being so much more space efficient in the large image sizes.

- Vector graphic files can be read only by an application that understands the specific file format and mathematical equations that they contain. This means that vector image files typically are far less likely to be compatible with foreign applications.

- Lower-powered computers can have a difficult time rendering complex vector images simply because there are so many calculations that need to be performed. This is typically not much of a problem given the relative simplicity of most Flash graphics, but it can be a factor you need to consider if you import overly complex vector images from external sources.

Understanding Bitmap Graphics

In contrast to vector images, bitmap graphic images may be far easier for the average human to understand. In a bitmap image, each viewable bit—or pixel—in the image is defined using stored data. This data is *mapped* to specific bits, so reading the data is similar to opening a map and looking for the intersection of two map coordinates.

As with vector images, there are important factors you need to understand about bitmap images:

- Image quality in a bitmap image is defined by the number of pixels of data that are available. Scaling a bitmap image upward does not create additional data, so image quality suffers as the image is viewed at a larger size than the original image size. This is particularly true for diagonal or curved lines, since they tend to take on a jagged appearance when scaled up.

- Viewing a bitmap image at a smaller size than the original image size typically does not adversely affect the image quality, but since the file size depends on the amount of data in the bitmap image file, this can result in wasting a lot of disk space and creating longer download times. Also be aware that reducing the viewing size of a bitmap image can actually degrade the image quality in some cases due to problems such as the Moiré effect (an interference pattern that typically shows up as wavy lines in an image).

- Bitmap image formats tend to be more universal than vector image formats, making it far easier to open bitmap images in a wide range of applications.

- Bitmap images tend to have larger file sizes than vector images of the same size. This can be offset by using *compression* to reduce the file size of the bitmap image, but high levels of compression can result in unacceptable image quality compromises.

- Displaying bitmap images tends to be well within the capabilities of even quite low-powered computers.

Now that we have reviewed the two types of image formats that you can use in Flash, we will move on to the import process itself.

Progress Check

1. What type of graphics can be scaled without losing quality?

2. Which type of graphics tends to display jagged edges in diagonal lines?

CRITICAL SKILL
9.2 Importing Vector Graphics

Because vector graphic file formats are less universal than bitmap graphic file formats, you are somewhat restricted in the range of vector images that you can import. Still, there are a number of vector graphic file format options that you can use to import these types of images. These include:

● Macromedia FreeHand

● Adobe Illustrator

● AutoCAD DXF

● Flash Player

As you can probably guess, Macromedia recommends using FreeHand if you need a little more vector image creation power than you'll find in Flash. Therefore, we'll take a look at using FreeHand images in Flash next.

TIP

You may want to check the Macromedia web site at http://www.macromedia.com to learn about new file types that you can import by updating your copy of Flash.

Using FreeHand Graphics in Flash

Flash and FreeHand are often sold as a package, so you may already have a copy of FreeHand installed on your PC. FreeHand will seem quite familiar to anyone who has used Flash, since the appearance of the two programs is quite similar. Many of the tools in the FreeHand Tools panel are also found in the Flash Tools panel (although the FreeHand Tools panel has many options that are missing in Flash).

---

1. Vector graphics

2. Bitmap graphics

FreeHand is a fairly powerful vector drawing program whose main focus is producing printed output—as opposed to the web graphics and animations that are the primary focus in Flash. Because FreeHand has more drawing tools and options than Flash, it is far easier to create very complex images in FreeHand than in Flash. Fortunately, you can import most FreeHand effects into Flash directly without losing any of that complexity. (A few items such as gradients with more than eight colors are simplified when they are imported into Flash, but generally these few exceptions won't cause you any major problems.)

Setting the FreeHand Drawing Area

Because FreeHand is typically used for printed documents, the default size of the FreeHand drawing area is much larger than the Flash stage. You can avoid having to scale objects you import into Flash by setting the FreeHand drawing area to match the size of the Flash stage. By doing so, you will be far more likely to create objects that are already sized to the correct dimensions.

To set the size of the FreeHand drawing area to match the default size of the Flash stage, follow these steps:

1. In FreeHand, select Window | Document to display the Document tab of the Properties panel, as shown here:

2. From the drop-down Page Size list box, select Web (as shown in the illustration). This will automatically set the size of the drawing area to match the default Flash stage size of 550×400 pixels.

3. Select the View | Fit To Page command to zoom the view so that the drawing area essentially fills the drawing window, as shown here:

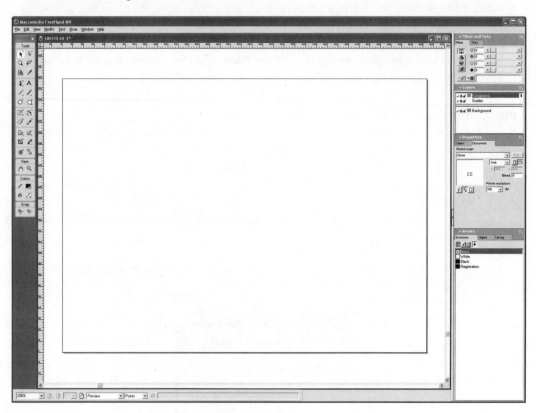

NOTE

In this illustration, I have also turned on the page rulers using the View | Page Rulers | Show command. The page rulers in FreeHand show the size of the drawing area in pixels, but there is an important difference between FreeHand and Flash on this point. In Flash, the upper-left corner of the stage is the measurement origin, whereas in FreeHand the lower-left corner is the origin. This will not really have any effect on your drawings, but you should be aware of the inconsistency between the two programs so that you are not confused when you view the FreeHand page rulers.

Drawing in FreeHand

Drawing objects in FreeHand is very similar to drawing in Flash (except for the greater array of drawing tools, of course). Basically, you select the drawing tool you want from the Tools panel and draw the objects you want.

TIP

Selecting tool options in FreeHand is a little different than the same process in Flash. Because the FreeHand Tools panel lacks the Options pane that you see in Flash, you access the FreeHand tool options by double-clicking on the tool whose options you want to set. When you do, FreeHand displays a dialog box that contains the options you can set. FreeHand drawing tools that have an options dialog box are indicated by a small marker in the upper-right corners of their Tools panel icons.

I don't have the room here to provide a tutorial on using all of the drawing tools in FreeHand. With a little practice, you will find that FreeHand is not too difficult. To provide a little inspiration, I offer the following illustration of a FreeHand image that was created for a web page logo:

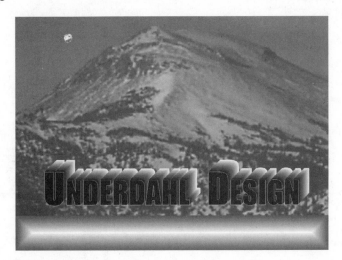

Saving Your FreeHand Drawing

When you have completed your drawing work in FreeHand, you need to save your creation so that it can be imported into Flash. This is one of the simpler parts of the whole project—you only need to use the FreeHand File | Save command and save your work as a FreeHand file. Flash already knows how to import a FreeHand file, and saving the file as a FreeHand file makes things much easier if you later decide to return to FreeHand to continue working.

TIP

If you want the option of saving your FreeHand drawing in an earlier version of the FreeHand file format, use the File | Export command and select the FreeHand version you want to use.

Importing Your FreeHand Drawing into Flash

To open your FreeHand drawing into Flash, you need to import the file. To do so, follow these steps:

1. Select the File | Import | Import To Stage command from the Flash menu to display the Import dialog box, as shown here:

2. Select the FreeHand option in the drop-down Files Of Type list box.

3. Select the FreeHand file that you wish to import.

4. Click the Open button to display the FreeHand Import dialog box, as shown here:

5. Choose the options you wish to use for importing the file. Generally, you will simply want to use the default settings.

NOTE

If you have used FreeHand features that are not supported in Flash, you may find that those features are changed into something that Flash does support. For example, if you create FreeHand gradient fills with more than the eight colors the Flash gradients can use, Flash will have to make some adjustments to the fill so that it can display the image.

Progress Check

1. What command do you need to use in Flash to open a FreeHand image file?

2. What type of graphics does FreeHand create?

Using Other Vector Graphics in Flash

Though it is very easy to use FreeHand graphics in Flash, you may prefer to use a different vector drawing program along with Flash. You might, for example, prefer something with a broader range of capabilities such as Canvas or Adobe Illustrator. If so, you are in luck, since Flash can easily import vector images from a number of different sources.

You may have noticed that the Flash Import dialog box does not list programs such as Canvas, and this may have you wondering just a little. If Flash doesn't list these other formats as an option, how can you import those files?

The answer is simple—you simply need to make certain that the source program you want to use can save files in Flash Player (SWF) format. Since Flash is so popular, many programs do indeed offer this as an option. Let's have a look at how you would go about the process in one of them—Canvas 9.

Creating a Canvas Drawing

Drawing in Canvas is generally similar to drawing in either Flash or FreeHand, although you will find that Canvas has many more options and is a far more powerful program than either of those applications. Still, you will find a pretty familiar toolbox and palettes in Canvas, so you shouldn't have too much trouble finding your way around.

---

1. File | Import | Import To Stage
2. Vector graphics

Just as with FreeHand, Canvas uses a default document size that is considerably larger than the Flash stage. This is easily adjusted using the Layout | Document Setup command to display the Configuration Center - Document Setup dialog box shown here:

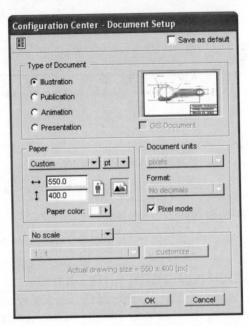

In the Document Setup dialog box, first choose Pixels from the Document Units drop-down list. Once you have done this, specify **550** in the width box and **400** in the height box. Click OK to close the Document Setup dialog box. When you do, Canvas automatically zooms in on the drawing area so that you do not need to use a separate zoom command.

When you use Canvas, there are a couple of important points to keep in mind:

- Double-clicking most items in the Tools panel will display an options dialog box for the selected tool.

- Holding down the mouse button while you are pointing at a tool icon will display a pop-out selection box that enables you to choose from a series of related tools.

- The tabs just above the drawing area represent docked palettes. You can open them in place or drag them into the workspace to keep them open as you work.

Here is an example of a web page logo I created in Canvas in just a few minutes:

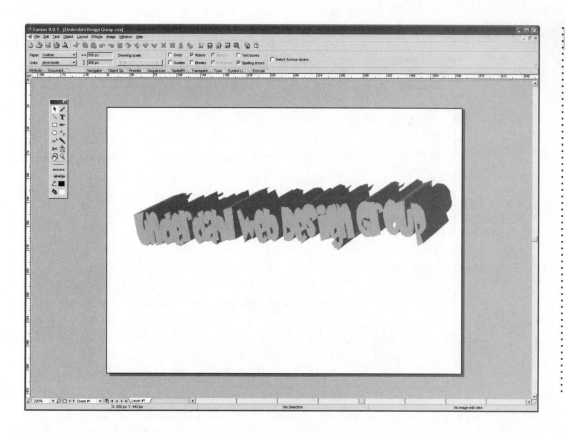

Saving Your Canvas Drawing for Flash

Canvas 9 has the capability to save images in Flash Player (SWF) format. This is the format of your Flash movies once they have been published—not the native Flash movie project file format (FLA). This limitation is not a serious problem because you can easily import Flash Player files back into Flash for additional development work.

NOTE

Flash Player format does have some minor limitations compared with Flash movie project file format, but Canvas provides you with methods of working around these limitations. For example, you can save layers in separate Flash Player files to work around the limitation of a single layer in a Flash Player file. Macromedia generally does not allow other software manufacturers to license the Flash movie project file format, so their only option is to use Flash Player format.

To save your Canvas drawing in a Flash Player format file, follow the steps on the next page.

1. Select File | Save As from the Canvas menu to display the Save As dialog box shown here:

2. From the drop-down Save As Type list box, choose SWF - Macromedia Flash. If you receive a warning about saving the file in Canvas format, acknowledge the warning and remember that you should also save your file in Canvas format so that you can further modify it if necessary.

3. Enter the name for your file in the File Name text box.

4. If you have created more than one layer, choose the area that you wish to save. (Or use Save Selection if you only want to save the currently selected objects.)

5. Click the Save button to display the Flash Options dialog box shown next.

6. From the Export Mode drop-down list, choose SWF Editors. This optimizes the file for importing it into Flash.

7. Click OK to save the file.

Importing the Canvas Drawing into Flash

Once you have saved your drawing in Flash Player format, you can import it into Flash for use in your movie. This is a simple process that takes almost no time at all and is identical no matter what application created the Flash Player file.

To import a drawing that is in Flash Player format, follow these steps:

1. Select File | Import | Import To Stage from the Flash menu to display the Import dialog box, as shown here:

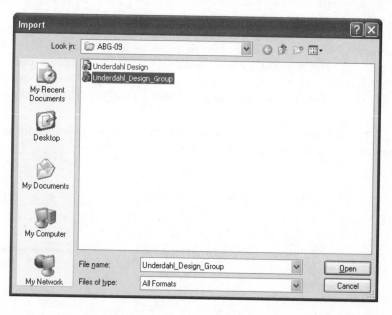

2. Choose the file you wish to import.

3. Click the Open button to import the file.

When you import a file into Flash, you add the imported images to the current movie. This enables you to import additional images into the same movie if necessary. For example, if you saved separate layers as separate Flash Player files in Canvas, you will want to import all of them into Flash layers. Make sure that you have added the necessary layers and that you have selected the correct layer before you import the file.

Progress Check

1. How many layers can you save in a Flash Player file?

2. How do you open a Flash Player file?

Ask the Expert

Q: I use a different drawing program to create vector drawings. How can I import those images into Flash?

A: As I mentioned earlier, vector graphic image file formats are not as universal as bitmap image file formats. If the Flash Import dialog box lacks a choice for your specific drawing program's native file format, your best bet is to try to save the image in Flash Player Movie format (assuming that is one of your options). Unfortunately, this may not be an option in your favorite program, so you may have to try saving or exporting the file in Adobe Illustrator or AutoCAD DXF format. Another option may be to use the Edit | Copy command in the source program and then to use the Edit | Paste In Center command in Flash. You may find, however, that this option does not always produce acceptable results.

Q: When I import my vector images into Flash, the text I added loses a lot of the fancy effects that I applied. What can I do?

(continued)

1. Only one
2. Use File | Import | Import To Stage.

A: That depends on the program you used to create the image, of course. Generally speaking, you will find that Flash does better with imported text effects if you convert the text to graphics in the source application before you save the file for use in Flash. Once the text has been converted into graphics, Flash should be able to display virtually any of the text effects. Remember, though, that Flash won't be able to edit the text as text—only as graphic objects.

CRITICAL SKILL
9.3 Importing Bitmap Graphics

Though bitmap image files tend to be larger than vector image files, sometimes only a bitmap image will do. For example, if you want a realistic-looking photograph, it would be hard to duplicate the quality of a bitmap image using vector drawings. In fact, all digital cameras produce bitmap images as opposed to vector graphics. Likewise, scanned images of photographs are bitmap images.

If you decide that you really must use a bitmap image in a Flash movie, there are certain things you should be aware of before you import the bitmap image file into Flash:

● Flash lacks the tools to do very much with bitmap images. If you need to edit the image, do so in your favorite bitmap image editor (such as Adobe Photoshop) before you import the file.

● Bitmap images are often much larger than necessary for use in a Flash movie. This added size simply wastes disk space and makes your Flash movie far larger than it should be. Use your bitmap image editor to crop or resize the image before you import it into Flash. Cutting the height and width of a bitmap image in half reduces its file size by a factor of four even if you make no other changes to the file. Scaling the image once it is in Flash does not reduce the file size.

● Bitmap images are generally stored in a compressed format to save space. If a bitmap image is recompressed, the quality suffers greatly. When you import compressed bitmap images—such as JPEG files—make certain that you tell Flash to use the imported image data rather than applying additional compression to the image.

TIP

You can display a thumbnail view of a bitmap image in your Flash movie but still allow your visitors to print a higher-quality copy of the image by importing the thumbnail-sized image and including a link to the larger image. That way, you won't be storing the larger image within your Flash movie file.

Importing the Bitmap Image

Once you have made any necessary modifications to the bitmap image in your bitmap image editing program, you are ready to import the image into Flash. To do so, follow these steps:

1. Select the File | Import | Import To Library command to display the Import dialog box.

2. Select the correct image format in the Files Of Type drop-down list box.

3. Choose the file that you wish to import.

4. Click Open to import the image into Flash.

Using the Imported Bitmap in Flash

After you have imported any bitmap images you want to use into Flash, you can then use those images in your movie. If you want to use the image as is, you can simply drag a copy from the library.

Imported bitmap images are not considered to be symbols even though they are stored in the library. You can convert bitmap images into symbols using the Modify | Convert To Symbol command. Converting an imported bitmap image into a symbol enables you to use the Properties panel to set the alpha property if you want to make the image partially transparent, for example. You can also apply a tween to the image.

Setting the Properties of an Imported Bitmap Image

Bitmap images can take a lot of space. To reduce the size of bitmap images, they generally are compressed. Flash uses the JPEG format for compressing images, and you have some level of control over how much compression is used. Remember, though, that applying additional compression to an image that is already compressed reduces the image quality—often to unacceptable levels.

NOTE

JPEG is a *lossy* image compression format. That is, JPEG compression actually discards image information. Unfortunately, once that information is discarded, there is no way to recover it. Therefore, it is best to choose the proper level of compression in the first place, since you will not be able to improve the quality later.

If you are using an imported bitmap image that was not compressed (or if you want to see what happens when you recompress a compressed image), you can adjust the way that Flash stores the imported bitmap. To do so, follow these steps:

1. Open the Library panel using the Window | Library command.

2. Select the image that you want to adjust.

3. Right-click the image and choose Properties from the pop-up menu. You can also choose Properties from the Options menu. Either method will display the Bitmap Properties dialog box shown here:

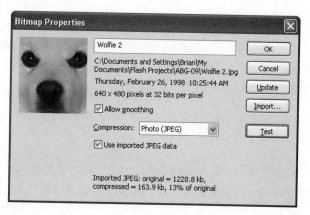

4. Click the Test button to see the current statistics for the image file.

5. To try a different compression setting, deselect the Use Imported JPEG Data check box. This will display the Quality text box, where you can enter a specific value. If you make any changes, click the Test button again to see the results. When you click the Test button, the sample window in the upper-left of the dialog box shows an example of the selected compression.

6. Click OK when you have completed any changes.

Even though you can make some changes to imported bitmaps inside Flash, I cannot emphasize this one point too strongly—it is far better to use your bitmap image editor to optimize the bitmap image file before you import it into Flash. By starting out with a bitmap image that has been resized to the absolute smallest size necessary for use in your movie, you will have a big head-start on minimizing the negative effects of using imported bitmap images in your Flash movies.

Progress Check

1. What happens if you recompress an imported bitmap image?

2. What happens if an imported bitmap image is larger than the stage?

---

1. The image quality is reduced.

2. It increases the size of the movie unnecessarily.

CRITICAL SKILL
9.4

Importing PDF Files

As a Flash designer you may sometimes find yourself being asked to make use of existing publications within your Flash movies. You might, for example, have a number of existing materials in the very popular Adobe Acrobat PDF file format. If so, you will be pleased to know that Flash MX 2004 can easily import these files so that you do not have to go to the effort of attempting to re-create them from scratch in Flash.

Importing a PDF file is quite similar to importing any other type of graphic file. To do so, you can use either the File | Import | Import To Stage or the File | Import | Import To Library command. This shows an example of a PDF file I imported into Flash:

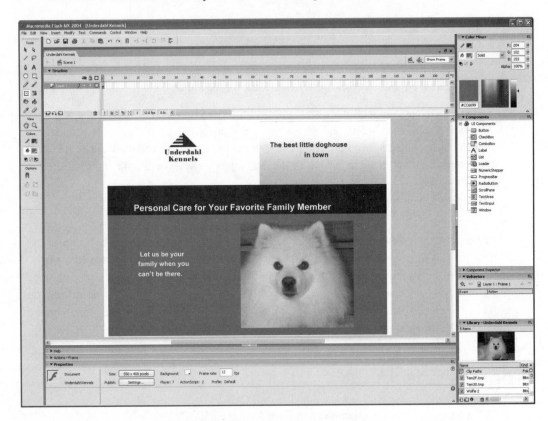

Converting Bitmaps into Vectors

Though you can use imported bitmap images in your Flash movies, Flash is a lot happier working with vector graphics than with bitmap graphics. Vector graphics generally take less space and are easier to use in tweens. In addition, you can use the Flash drawing tools to modify vector-based objects.

Fortunately, Flash provides a couple of different methods for converting bitmap images into vector-based objects. You can *trace* a bitmap to convert it into a vector-based drawing, or you can *break apart* a bitmap so that you can use it for a fill. In the next sections, we'll look at how you can use both of these options.

TIP

You can tell the difference between a bitmap image and one that has been traced or one that has been broken apart by clicking on the image. A bitmap image will show a selection border around the image, but you cannot select areas within the image itself. An image that has been traced or broken apart can be selected so that it shows the selection "dots" over the entire image.

Tracing a Bitmap

Tracing a bitmap image converts the image into a series of vector-based objects. Depending on the settings that you choose for the operation, the resulting image may look almost identical to the original bitmap image, or it may look quite different. In extreme cases, the effect appears to be very similar to the posterize filter in Photoshop—except that the Photoshop effect does not vectorize the image.

To trace a bitmap image so that it is converted into a vector-based drawing, follow these steps:

1. Import the image into Flash (using the process you learned a bit earlier in this module).

2. If the image is not already on the stage, open the Library panel using the Window | Library command.

3. Drag a copy of the image that you want to convert onto the stage.

4. With the image selected, use the Modify | Bitmap | Trace Bitmap command to display the Trace Bitmap dialog box, as shown here:

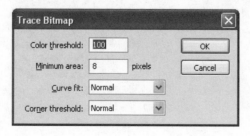

5. Enter a value in the Color Threshold text box. This value is the greatest difference between RGB color values that will be considered to be the same color. Smaller values will result in the image looking more realistic at the expense of file size. Larger values will posterize the image to a greater degree, since there will be fewer discrete colors in the final image.

6. Enter a value in the Minimum Area text box. This is the value for the number of pixels that will be used to set the color values. Again, smaller values will result in a larger file size and a more realistic appearance, while higher values will produce a more efficient result.

7. Choose a value from the drop-down Curve Fit list box. The options in this list box produce higher quality (and larger file size) images at the top of the list, and lower quality (but smaller file size) at the bottom of the list.

8. Choose an option from the drop-down Corner Threshold list box. Here, too, the quality and file size are reduced as you make choices further down the list.

9. Click OK to apply the selected options and trace the bitmap.

10. Click outside the image to deselect it so that you can view the results. This shows the results from the settings shown in the previous illustration:

11. If the results are not quite what you want, select Edit | Undo twice to return the image to a bitmap image. Then repeat steps 4–10 until you achieve the results you want.

When you trace a bitmap image to convert it into a vector-based drawing object, the new object is no longer associated with the bitmap image that is in the library. Depending on your needs, you may want to group the new object or convert it into a symbol. Remember, though, that if you want to use the object in a shape tween, you must leave the object ungrouped.

TIP

If you intend to experiment with the new vector-based image, you may want to create an extra offstage copy of the image on a new layer first. That way, you can easily revert to the original if you discover that your experiments are not working quite the way you had planned.

Breaking Up a Bitmap

You can also break a bitmap apart so that it can be used as a bitmap fill for objects. Breaking a bitmap apart converts the image into a vector-based drawing object, but it does so using the highest-quality settings possible. As a result, the broken-apart image looks virtually identical to the bitmap image. You can, however, use the drawing tools to modify the broken-apart image.

TIP

Unless you intend to use the bitmap image as a fill, it is generally better to trace the bitmap than to break it apart.

To break apart a bitmap image, follow these steps:

1. Drag a copy of the image onto the stage.

2. With the image selected, use the Modify | Break Apart command to break the image apart, as shown here:

To use the broken-apart bitmap as a fill, click the Eyedropper tool and then click on the broken-apart bitmap. The fill color selector will then display a miniature version of the bitmap, and Flash will automatically select the Paint Bucket tool. If you click a closed object, that object will then be filled with the bitmap. If you use the drawing tools to create a filled object, the bitmap fill will be used in that object, as shown here:

Once a bitmap image has been broken apart, you can also modify areas within the broken-apart image. For example, you can use the Lasso tool to change the color of a specific area within the broken-apart image.

Progress Check

1. What should you do to a bitmap image if you want to use it in a shape tween?

2. What should you do to a bitmap image if you want to use it as a fill?

Converting Text into Graphics

In Module 7, you learned how to use text along with a mask to create a scrolling text banner effect. To create that effect, you used ordinary text. Now we will look at some of the things you can do with text by converting that text into graphical objects.

Here are just a few ideas for ways that you can use text that has been converted into graphics:

- You can modify the shape of the characters after you convert text into graphics. For example, here I have modified a capital letter *B* that was originally in the formal-looking Times Roman font to produce a very different appearing letter:

- You can scale and rotate graphical text in ways that cannot be done when it is still ordinary text.

- You can apply a shape tween to broken-apart text so that letters appear to melt or so that they slowly form from shapeless lumps.

- You can apply a motion tween to individual characters to make them fly into place or to make words suddenly explode with letters scattering in many different directions.

---

1. Trace it.
2. Break it apart.

CAUTION

One thing that you cannot do with text after it has been broken apart and converted into graphics is to edit it as text. Make certain that your text is correct and does not contain any embarrassing typos before you convert the text into graphics!

Breaking Up Text

Breaking up text converts the text from editable text into graphical objects. These objects can then be manipulated just like any other graphical object.

NOTE

Although broken-apart text does make each character into a separate object, there is no requirement for you to start with a text string containing words or even multiple characters. You can, in fact, break apart a single character just as effectively as you can break apart strings of characters.

To break apart some text so that it is converted into graphical objects, follow these steps:

1. Use the Text tool to create the text that you want to use. Remember that you can use the Properties panel or the Text menu to set the characteristics of the text.

2. Click the Arrow tool to select it.

3. If the text block is not automatically selected, click it with the Arrow tool.

4. Select the Modify | Break Apart command to break apart the selection.

5. Click outside the text to deselect it.

Once the text has been broken apart, you can use any of the drawing tools to modify it—with the exception of the Text tool. Broken-apart text is no longer considered to be text.

Using Broken-Up Text

You can use broken-apart text just like any other object. In fact, once text has been broken apart, it is in the ideal condition for use in a shape tween. You must, however, group the broken-apart text if you want to apply a motion tween.

Once the text has been broken apart, you can modify the shapes of the characters, as shown next. In this case, I am using the Arrow tool to bend one side of a letter so that I can produce an interesting font for use as a web site logo. You can also use the Subselect tool to modify the curves and corners of the characters. Remember that the characters must not be selected if you want to modify their shapes. If they are selected, you will move the characters rather than modifying their shapes.

TIP

Because broken-apart text is a graphical object, you can change the fill using the Paint Bucket tool. This method enables you to easily apply a gradient fill to text, for example. You can also use a bitmap fill using the techniques you learned earlier in this module for breaking apart a bitmap image. In some cases, this might be superior to creating a text mask—especially if you want to apply a tween to the broken-apart text.

Progress Check

1. How can you edit broken-apart text?

2. What type of tween can you apply to broken-apart text immediately after it has been broken apart?

Project 9-1 Making Text Fly into Place to Assemble Words

Now it is time to apply some of the techniques that you learned in this module to create an effect that you will probably find useful in your movies. In this case, you will create a particularly interesting effect of text that flies into place to form words. To do so, you must first create text that is actually a graphical object. Then you must create the tween that will make the text move. One of the important points you will learn is that sometimes you must work backward from the result you want to achieve the effect you desire.

(continued)

1. As graphics only
2. A shape tween

Step by Step

1. Open a new, blank Flash movie.

2. Click frame 18 in the timeline to select it.

3. Select the Insert | Timeline | Keyframe command to insert a keyframe at frame 18. This will make the animation last for one and a half seconds.

4. Click the Text tool to select it.

5. Select Text | Size | 120 to set the size of the text to 120 points. For this effect to have an impact, it is important to make the text as large as possible.

6. Select Text | Style | Bold to make the text bold so that the characters will have broader strokes.

7. Click near the left edge of the stage just a little above the vertical center line of the stage to open a text box.

8. Type **Hello** into the text box. You are adding the text that you want to appear at the end of the tween.

9. Click the Arrow tool to close the text box. You should have a blue selection box around the text box. If the text box is not selected, click it once to select it.

10. Select the Modify | Break Apart command to convert the text into graphical objects. The stage should now look something like this:

Hello

11. Click frame 1 in the timeline so that it is selected.

12. Click the Oval tool to select it.

13. Near the bottom of the stage, draw five small circles. You will want one as the starting point for each of the letters.

14. Click the tween frames in the timeline to select them.

15. Use the Window | Properties command to open the Properties panel.

16. Select Shape from the drop-down Tweening list box. You can ignore the remaining options in the Properties panel for this project.

17. Click frame 48 in the timeline to select it.

18. Select Insert | Timeline | Keyframe to add a keyframe. This will make the letters remain stationary for a few seconds after the tween ends.

19. Select File | Save and then save your work.

20. Select Control | Test Movie to test your movie. This onion skin view shows an example of how your movie should look as the letters are forming.

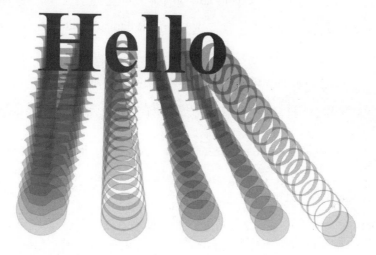

Project Summary

In this project, you learned how to create a shape tween that used broken-apart text as graphical objects. You saw that it is fairly simple to create a very advanced-appearing effect by treating text as graphics. You also learned that it is important to create the final text in the frame where you want the assembled word to appear so that the shape tween will end up with the desired result. It should be very easy for you to build upon this project to create your own morphing word animations. You might, for example, make words melt off the screen or make words change into different words.

Module 9 Mastery Check

1. The native graphic format for Flash is _____ graphics.

2. JPEG images are an example of _____ graphics.

3. You use the File | _____ command to bring in graphics from other sources.

4. To use text as graphics, you must first use the Modify | _____ command.

5. To turn a bitmap image into a vector-based graphic, you _____ the bitmap image.

6. To use a bitmap image as a fill, you _____ the bitmap image.

7. You use the _____ tool to select a bitmap as a fill.

8. _____ images can be scaled up without reducing their quality.

9. Reducing the size of a bitmap image by throwing away some of the detail is a process known as _____.

10. The _____ tool ceases to be effective on a block of text that has been broken apart.

11. Vector graphics are a type of image that can be scaled without losing quality because a vector image is defined by a _____ expression.

12. Macromedia _____ is a vector graphic editor that can create images that you can use in your Flash movies.

13. When you trace a bitmap, larger Color Threshold values will tend to _____ the resulting image.

14. If you choose a larger Minimum Area value when you are tracing a bitmap, the result will be a _____ file size.

15. You use the _____ dialog box to adjust the JPEG settings for an imported bitmap image.

Module 10

Adding Sounds to Your Movies

U p until now, all of your Flash movies have been largely silent. In this module, we'll look at adding sounds to make your movies even more interesting. With the addition of sound, your Flash movies can truly be called multimedia productions.

As exciting as sounds may be, it is even more important for you to be fully aware of all of the implications of adding sound to your movies, more so than of almost anything else that you might add. Not only are there serious file-size considerations, but there are also a number of usability considerations, too. In this module, you will learn about these factors and how they can affect you as a Flash movie developer.

Understanding the Sound Options

More than anything else you may do, adding sounds to your Flash movies can really have a huge impact on the file sizes—and therefore, the amount of time required to download your movies. If you want to make certain that your movies are compact and have the typical snappy Flash performance, you will really need to pay attention to the details.

Adding sounds to your Flash movies places them in an entirely different league as far as visitors to your web site are concerned. Instead of a quiet little movie they can watch without disturbing anyone else, visitors are now faced with sounds blasting from their speakers. If you don't provide a convenient option for muting the sounds, you may find that visitors quickly leave your web site and avoid returning. If you want to add sounds, you must keep in mind that many people work in environments where loud noises will disturb their neighbors, so web sites that insist on playing funky music won't be too popular. In addition, remember that musical tastes vary widely. The rap or country western sounds that you may like may sound like absolute garbage to many of the people you want to visit your site. It is far better to keep the sounds unobtrusive than to risk alienating your guests.

Computer-based sounds fall into two general categories. The most common are recorded sounds—such as *wave* sound files. Less common but still somewhat popular are *MIDI* (Musical Instrument Digital Interface) sound files—which are actually instructions that tell your computer how to produce sounds using its built-in synthesizer. You could think of recorded sound files as being functionally equivalent to bitmap image files and MIDI sounds as being the functional equivalent of vector graphics. Flash supports only recorded sounds and cannot use MIDI sound files at all.

A number of factors influence both the size and playback quality of recorded sound files. We will now look at some of the more important items that you need to consider.

Sampling Rates

On your computer, all recorded sound files are recorded digitally (as opposed to the analog recording method used for audio tape recordings). A digital recording *samples* the sounds at regular intervals and records a digital value that represents that particular instant in time. The number of these digital samples that occur each second is known as the *sampling rate*.

It is generally agreed that the sampling rate should be approximately twice the frequency of the highest frequency sound that you wish to record. Audio CDs, for example, use a sampling rate of 44,100 Hz (also written as 44.1 KHz). In theory, this allows an audio CD to accurately reproduce musical sounds up to about 22,050 Hz—generally considered at or above the upper end of the frequency range that most people can hear.

The sampling rate you choose has a direct effect on the size of the sound file that you record. At 44.1 KHz, you must store over 44,000 data samples each second. Cutting the sampling rate to 22.05 KHz cuts the number of data samples in half while limiting the theoretical upper frequency to around 11 KHz. Although this means that your sound files may be missing some of the higher frequency sounds, the difference probably won't be noticeable enough to adversely affect the typical Flash movie soundtrack.

TIP

Flash offers a number of sampling rate options, including several that are even lower than the 22.05 KHz rate just mentioned. You will probably be pleasantly surprised to learn that the lower rates will likely be more than adequate for most Flash movie sounds, and these lower sampling rates can really make a big difference in the size of your movie files. Don't automatically reject the lower sampling rates until you have tried them.

Bit Depths

The *bit depth* (also known as bit rate) is the number of bits of information that are recorded for each of the samples. Each bit can hold a single piece of on/off data. The bit rate is therefore directly related to the amount of data that can be recorded.

NOTE

The bit rate is the expression of a binary value. You can calculate how many discrete values can be recorded by raising the number 2 to the number of bits. So, for example, if you had 2 bits, you would have 2^2, or 4 possible values. If you had 4 bits, you would have 2^4, or 16 possible values.

Returning to the example of an audio CD, the bit rate that is used is 16 bits. This means that any of the digital sound samples can have any of 65,536 different values. Once again, this is far more than is necessary for most Flash movie applications. As with the sample rate, cutting the bit rate in half results in cutting the size of the sound file in half, too.

TIP

It's important to remember that your Flash movies are likely to be played on an awful lot of computers whose entire speaker system cost less than a fast-food lunch. No matter what settings you choose for the Flash sounds, most people who play your movies aren't really going to notice the quality very much unless you aim for the low end.

Stereo Versus Mono

Another very important factor in the size of your audio files is the choice between playing the sounds as stereo or mono. Stereo, of course, has two different sound channels, so the sounds that come from the speakers on either side of the monitor do not have to be identical. In a mono recording, the same signal is sent to both speakers. As you can imagine, a stereo recording takes exactly twice the disk space of a mono one.

Believe it or not, stereo sounds are largely wasted on the typical computer speaker setup. Even if they happen to have some fancy setup with a dozen speakers spread around their workspace, most people probably won't notice much difference between stereo and mono soundtracks in your Flash movies, so there's little reason to double the amount of disk space (and download time) just to add stereo sound.

TIP

Even if you use a mono soundtrack, that does not mean that you cannot achieve a moving-sound effect in your Flash movies. As you will learn later in this module, you can pan the sound from one side to the other even while you use a mono soundtrack.

Compression Method

By far the most important factor in determining the size of the sound files you use in your Flash movies is the compression method you choose. When you combine the proper settings with a really good compression method, it is possible to greatly minimize the adverse effects that adding sounds can have on the size of your Flash movie files.

Before Flash 5 came along, there weren't any really good compression options available. Once Macromedia included the option to use the MP3 sound file compression algorithm, however, things became a whole lot more reasonable for Flash developers who wanted to include sounds in their movies. For example, as the following illustration shows, by using MP3 compression, I was able to reduce the size of one of my sound files from 1703.7KB down to 38.6KB—2.3 percent of the original file size! Even if your results are far less dramatic than these, it is easy to see why MP3 compression is so important if you want to add a soundtrack to your movies.

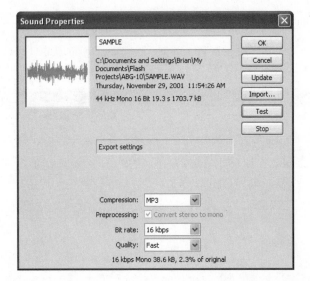

In addition to MP3, Flash offers three other sound file compression choices. Unless you need to maintain compatibility with Flash players prior to version 5, you should avoid using the other options, since they do not compress the sounds nearly as well as MP3.

Later in this module, in the section "Setting the Sound Output Options," you will learn how to set the various sound file properties. As you will see, you can set the options for the entire movie or for the individual sound files within a movie.

Progress Check

1. What value does the sampling rate measure?

2. How do stereo sound files compare to mono ones?

Importing Sounds

To use sounds in your Flash movies, you must import those sounds. You import sounds in much the same way that you import graphics.

---

1. The number of times per second that a sample of the sound is recorded
2. They are twice as large.

To import sound files into a Flash movie, follow these steps:

1. Select the File | Import | Import To Library command to open the Import To Library dialog box, as shown here:

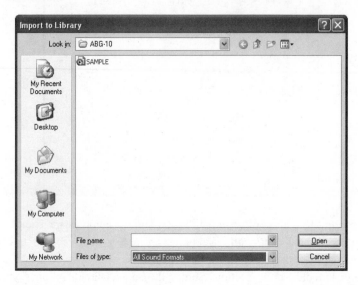

2. Select the sound file format you wish to import using the drop-down Files Of Type list box. If you aren't sure of the sound file format, choose the All Sound Formats option from the list box.

3. Choose the file that you wish to import.

4. Click the Open button to import the file.

When you import sound files into Flash, they are automatically placed directly into the movie's library. You can play the imported sound by selecting it and then clicking the Play button that appears in the upper pane of the Library panel as shown here when a sound file is selected:

Be very careful about the music that you choose to import for use in your Flash movies. The recent legal problems of file-sharing web sites (and their users) have highlighted one of the big hazards of importing sound files and using them in your Flash movies. Unless you have an explicit license to use a sound file, you could be opening yourself up for some major legal hassles by using copyrighted music on your web site. When in doubt, the safest course of action is to assume that you do not have the right to use music that you have downloaded from the Web or that you have copied from a music CD. It is possible to find royalty-free music that you can use in your Flash movies. Ignoring the copyright issues simply is not worth the huge potential headaches that you will encounter when some musician's lawyer contacts you regarding unauthorized use of that musician's work in your Flash movies.

When you choose sound files to import, you may want to keep the intended use of those sounds in mind. For example, if you simply want to add a little background music, you may want to consider importing a fairly short piece and then looping it several times rather than importing something that is long enough to play during the entire movie. By taking this approach, you may be able to further reduce the file size impact of adding sounds to your movies. You will learn more about looping later in this module in the section "Looping Sounds."

Progress Check

1. Where does Flash place the sounds that you import?

2. How do you import MIDI files?

Adding Sounds

Once you have successfully imported the sounds that you want to use in your movie, you need to add them either to the timeline or to a button so that they will play at the proper time. Sounds that you add to the timeline are played when the playhead reaches that point in the timeline. Sounds that you add to buttons are typically played when the user clicks the button.

Let's take a look at the process of adding sounds to the timeline or to buttons.

Adding Sounds to Frames

If you want sounds to begin playing at a specific point in the movie, you add them to frames in the timeline. That way, the sounds begin playing automatically when the playhead reaches that frame.

---

1. Into the library

2. You can't, because Flash can't use MIDI files.

It is generally best to add a layer to the timeline for each of the sounds that you want to add to the timeline. In that way, you are able to control each of the sounds independently of each other and of any other objects. All of the sounds are combined when your movie plays back, but separating the sounds on different layers does provide you with additional control over the playback.

To add sounds to a timeline layer, follow these steps:

1. First, import the sound into Flash.

2. Use the Insert | Timeline | Layer command or the Insert Layer button to add a new layer to the timeline for the sound.

3. Optionally, rename the sound layer so that it is easy to recognize in the timeline.

4. Select the Window | Library command to open the Library panel.

5. With the sound layer selected, drag the sound onto the stage. Flash adds the sound to the selected layer, as shown here. In this case, I added the sound to a keyframe that I added to the Sounds layer at frame 24.

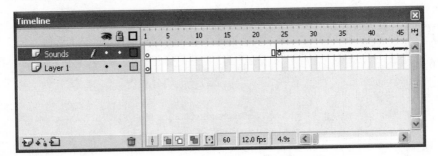

TIP

If you do not want the sound to begin playing immediately when the movie begins playing, add a keyframe to the sound layer where you want the sound to begin. Make certain that the keyframe is selected before you add the sound to the layer.

If you test your movie at this point, you may not be too pleased with the way that the sounds play. If so, don't worry, you will learn how to correct this shortly in the section entitled "Synchronizing Sounds."

Adding Sounds to Buttons

Even if you do not want to add a soundtrack to your movie, you may still want to add some audible feedback to let users know when they have clicked a button. This might be a simple click sound or something more outrageous, depending on the effect that you want to create.

TIP

Flash comes with a whole bunch of neat sounds that are perfect for adding to buttons. You can access these sounds using the Window | Other Panels | Common Libraries | Sounds command.

In Module 8, you learned that buttons are a special type of Flash symbol. They have the built-in capability to respond to mouse clicks, making it quite easy for you to create interactive buttons for your movies. You also learned that button symbols have a special four-frame timeline that corresponds to the different states of a button. When you add sounds to a button, you add those sounds to the appropriate button symbol timeline frame. For example, if you want a button to make a click sound when the user clicks the mouse pointer on the button, you would add the sound to the Down frame.

NOTE

It is generally not a good idea to add a sound to a button's Up frame. If you do add a sound to this frame, the sound probably won't play when you expect it to. You might think that a sound that is added to the Up frame would play whenever the button appeared on the stage, but that is not the case. Sounds added to button symbols are *event* sounds—which means that they need an event to occur before they will be triggered. A sound that you add to a button's Up frame will play *after* the button has been clicked and the mouse button has been released. In other words, the sound will be triggered by the event of the button returning to the up state after it has been clicked.

When you add sounds to a button, you add the sounds to the button symbol that is contained in the library rather than to an instance of the button that you have added to your movie. As a result, all instances of that button will play the same sounds. This also saves space in your movie file since Flash needs to store the sound file only once.

To add a sound to a button, follow these steps:

1. Create the button symbol that you want to use. Remember that you can use one of the pre-made button symbols from the Buttons common library, too.

2. Import the sound that you want to add. You can also use one of the sounds from the Sounds common library. Remember, button sounds are typically just a brief sound to let the user know that the button has responded to a mouse click.

3. Open the Library panel using the Window | Library command.

4. Right-click the button symbol and choose Edit from the pop-up menu. You can also use the Library panel menu Edit command to open the button symbol for editing.

5. Click the Insert Layer button (or use the Insert | Timeline | Layer command) to add a new layer to the button symbol's timeline for your sounds.

6. Optionally, double-click the sound layer name, and rename the layer with a descriptive name such as Sounds.

7. Click the Down frame in the Sounds layer.

8. Select Insert | Timeline | Keyframe to add a keyframe to the Down frame. This is where you will add your sound so that it plays when the button is clicked.

9. With the Down frame of the Sounds layer selected, drag the sound file that you want to add onto the stage. This will add the sound to the Down frame. The timeline should now look like the following illustration. Notice that in this case I am using a very complex button from the Button common library; as a result, the button symbol's timeline has quite a number of layers in addition to those shown in the illustration.

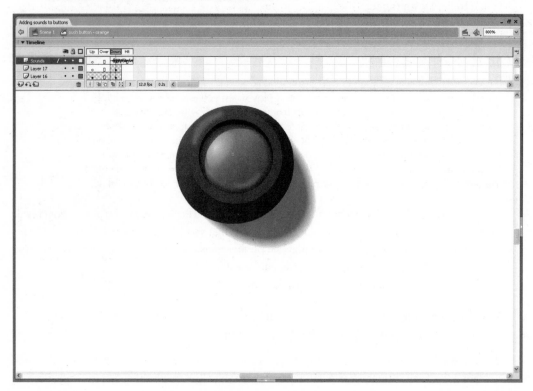

10. Click the scene name above the timeline to close the symbol editing mode and return to the main stage.

11. If you have not already done so, drag a copy of the button onto the stage.

12. Use the File | Save command to save your work.

13. Select Control | Test Movie to test the button. It should play the sound that you added when the button is clicked.

Because you added the sound to the master copy of the button symbol in the library, all instances of the button that you add to your movie will play the same sound when they are clicked.

Progress Check

1. Sounds that you add to a button symbol are examples of what type of sound?

2. To which button symbol timeline frame should you add sounds?

CRITICAL SKILL
10.4 Synchronizing Sounds

When you add sounds to a movie, you want those sounds to play at a certain time or when a specific event occurs. The process of specifying when sounds in your Flash movies will play is called *synchronizing* the sounds. This is just a fancy way of saying that the sounds should complement the action in your movie rather than simply playing randomly.

To control the synchronization options for sounds, you use the Properties panel, as shown here. You can display this panel using the Window | Properties command.

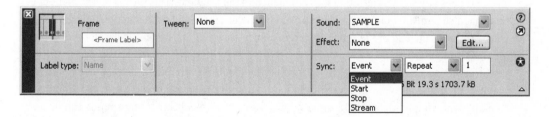

The synchronization options are set using the Sync drop-down list box, as shown in the illustration. The four options are

- Event

- Start

- Stop

- Stream

Next, we will take a closer look at each of these synchronization options.

---

1. Event sounds
2. The Down frame

Event Sounds

Event sounds are sounds that play when a specific event occurs. For example, the most common type of event sound is the one that is triggered when a user clicks a button instance. You can use a number of different types of events to trigger an event sound—in Module 13, you will learn about using *event handlers* in ActionScript to make Flash objects react to specific events.

Once an event sound starts playing, it continues until it has played completely through. This means that an event sound can actually keep on playing after your movie has stopped. It is good to keep this characteristic of event sounds in mind so that you make certain that the event sounds you add to your movies actually fit the action.

Start and Stop Options

The Start option works very much like an event sound, except that this option always starts a new instance of the sound.

The Stop option stops the sound from playing. It is a good idea to use the Stop option after you use the Start option so that the sound will stop playing when you want it to.

Streaming Sounds

Streaming sounds synchronize with the timeline so that the two work together. If the animation stops, so does any streaming sound that is attached to the timeline. This means that the length of time that a streaming sound plays is controlled by the timeline, and the sound will stop playing when it reaches the end of the frames that it occupies—even if the sound file has not played all the way through.

Streaming sounds place an extra burden on the Flash Player. When a streaming sound is playing, the Flash Player must attempt to keep up with the sound playback. If the frames cannot be drawn quickly enough, some frames may be skipped. Streaming sounds can be an especially big problem if the user is connected to the Internet via a slow dial-up connection or if the Internet is slow due to heavy traffic.

We will examine the remaining sound options in the following sections on editing sounds.

Progress Check

1. What type of sound always plays completely?

2. What type of sound is controlled by the timeline?

---

1. Event sounds
2. Streaming sounds

CRITICAL SKILL
10.5 Editing Sounds

Sometimes the sounds that you can import for use in your Flash movies need a little fine-tuning to make them just perfect. Although Flash does not have a full-fledged sound editing application, it does provide you with certain basic capabilities that may well serve your needs—at least as far as tweaking the sounds for use in your movies.

Let's take a look at the sound editing options that you can use in Flash.

Using Fades

Fades are sound effects that depend on changing the volume of the sound. Fades can be used to slowly ramp up a sound as it begins to play, or to slowly make the sound disappear as it ends its playback. Fades can also be used to simulate a stereo effect. By changing the relative volume level of the sound coming from each side of the monitor, you can make it seem as though the sound is moving across the stage.

Flash has a number of ready-to-use fades that you can select from the Effect drop-down list box in the Properties panel (as shown here):

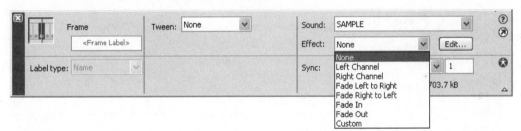

TIP

Using side-to-side fades is an excellent alternative to using a stereo soundtrack. Side-to-side fades can make a mono soundtrack seem to move from one side to the other, and a mono soundtrack is exactly half the size of a stereo soundtrack. Along with side-to-side fades, you can use one of the single-channel sound options (also in the Effect drop-down list box) to hold the sound to one side as needed.

In addition to using one of the fades that are available in the Effect drop-down list box, you can also create your own custom fades by manually editing the envelope (the volume profile). You will learn more about editing the sound envelope shortly.

Looping Sounds

Longer sounds require more disk space than shorter ones, of course. One way to save space in your Flash movies is to use a relatively short sound and *loop* it. Looping a sound means that you play the same sound more than once.

Often it is possible to create a relatively short sound—such as a piece of music—that can be played a number of times without seriously degrading the overall effect. Of course, this will probably work best with an instrumental piece, because most people would soon notice if a singer were repeating the same words over and over.

To make a sound file repeat, you use the Number Of Times To Loop text box in the Properties panel. Simply enter the number of times that you want the sound to play. Make certain that you have the Repeat option selected—if you select the Loop option, the sound will simply continue to loop indefinitely.

NOTE

Remember that an event sound will play until it is finished even if the movie has completed its playback. If you repeat an event sound too many times, the sound may continue to repeat long after the end of your movie. This would be a sure way to annoy and alienate visitors to your web site, so you would be wise to use some common sense in specifying the number of loops.

Progress Check

1. What type of sound effect can you use to simulate motion?

2. What option can you use to play the same sound several times?

Editing the Envelope

The *envelope* is the shape of the volume parameters for a sound file's waveform. You can edit this envelope to create your own custom fade effects. For example, you might want to:

- Make a soundtrack slowly fade away and then continue looping at a very soft level while the user is deciding which button to push.

- Make the sound bounce between the right and left speakers to give the audible impression of an object bouncing between the two sides of the stage.

- Start a sound at a very low level in one speaker and then pan it until it is very loud in the other speaker to produce the effect of an object zooming in from the back of the stage on the one side and flying out over the front of the other side of the stage.

1. A fade
2. Looping

NOTE

You can also produce a fade effect using ActionScript programming by setting the properties of the Sound object. This method offers the advantage of making the sound follow a moving object precisely; it is often used in programming interactive games in Flash. You will learn more about setting properties using ActionScript in Module 14.

Editing the sound envelope does not modify the pitch of the sound. The only characteristic that is changed is the volume. In fact, even if you were to drop the volume to a point halfway through the sound file, you would not really be shortening the length of the sound—you would simply be making it inaudible. This is an important point to remember because the sound editing capabilities in Flash are rather limited. If you want to make more comprehensive changes to the sound file, you will have to use a different sound editor to modify the sound before you import it into Flash.

When you edit the sound envelope in Flash, you are modifying an instance of the sound rather than the copy that is stored in the library. Therefore, you must select an instance that you have added to the timeline or to an object in order to make any changes.

To edit the sound envelope, follow these steps:

1. Select the object or frame that contains the instance of the sound that you want to modify.

2. Use the Window | Properties command to open the Properties panel.

3. Make certain that the name of the sound that you want to modify is showing in the Sound drop-down list box. If it is not, you either do not have the correct object selected, or the sound is not attached to the selected object.

4. Click the Edit button to display the Edit Envelope dialog box, as shown here:

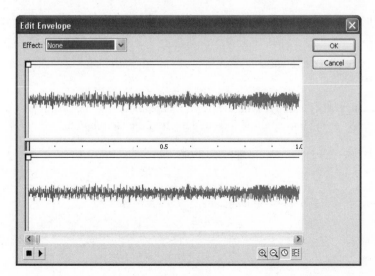

5. To use one of the existing fade effects, you can choose it from the drop-down Effect list box.

6. To modify the envelope manually, you drag the boxes that appear in the volume line (the line that starts with a single box at the top of each of the channel displays).

7. To add an additional box, click the volume line where you want to add the new box. When you add additional boxes to the volume line, you can then create a more complex fade effect by dragging the new boxes, as shown here. Note that when you add a box to either pane, Flash automatically adds a corresponding box to the other pane. The upper pane represents the left channel, and the lower pane represents the right channel.

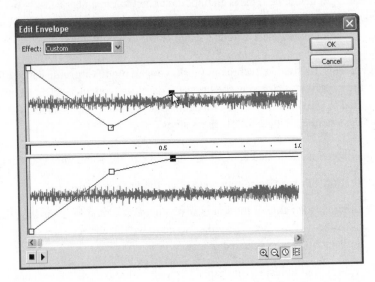

8. Click the Play button near the lower-left corner of the dialog box to hear the effects of your changes.

9. If necessary, you can click the zoom-in or zoom-out buttons for a closer look at any part of the envelope.

10. You can toggle between viewing the playing time and the frame position by clicking the clock button or the frame button (just to the left of the Help button).

11. When you have finished your changes, click the OK button to close the Edit Envelope dialog box.

Progress Check

1. When you edit the sound envelope, which property of the sound are you modifying?

2. Why does the Edit Envelope dialog box display separate panes for the right and left channels for mono sound files?

CRITICAL SKILL
10.6 Setting the Sound Output Options

Sound files can be a real problem for a Flash movie developer. You may have taken great care to ensure that all of the elements of your movie were as compact and efficient as possible, but when you add a sound file to your movie, the size of the published movie file can bloat to many times the size of the movie without any sounds. If you want to make certain that your movies download quickly and play back properly, you really do need to be concerned about the properties of any sound files that you have used.

Flash provides you with two different ways to set the sound file output options. You can specifically set the options for any particular sound file that you have used, and you can set global options that apply to any files that do not have individual settings. Let's take a look at these two methods.

Setting Individual Sound File Output Options

If you have added a very large sound file to your movie, or if how a particular sound file sounds when played back is quite important, you will want to set the properties of the file specifically. By setting the properties of individual sound files, you have the ability to preview the effects of any changes that you are making.

To set the properties for a specific sound file, follow these steps:

1. Import the sound file into Flash.

2. Open the Library panel using the Window | Library command.

---

1. The volume

2. So you can create fades

3. Right-click the sound file you want to modify and choose Properties from the pop-up menu to display the Sound Properties dialog box, as shown here. Alternatively, you can select the file and use the Options | Properties command to display the Sound Properties dialog box.

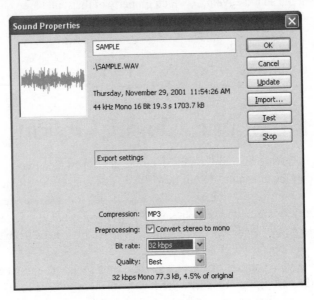

4. Select the compression method you wish to use from the drop-down Compression list box. Unless you have a specific need to use a different compression method, select MP3 for the most efficient compression.

5. After each new setting selection, click the Test button both to hear the results and to view the effect of the selected options in the status display at the bottom of the dialog box.

6. If the Convert Stereo To Mono check box is available, you will probably want to make certain it is checked. (Some compression options make this check box unavailable.)

7. Select the remaining options and test your selections. The available options will vary depending on the type of compression that you have selected.

8. Click OK when you have completed your selections.

Setting Global Sound File Output Options

It is a good idea to also set the global sound output options. These settings will apply to any imported sound files that you have not specifically configured using the Sound Properties dialog box. In this way, you can make certain that any sounds that you have added to your movie will have a minimal impact on the file size even if you don't want to bother setting their properties individually.

Because the global sound settings apply to the entire movie, you use a method of setting these options that you probably have not yet encountered. The global sound settings are accessed through the Publish Settings dialog box.

To set the global sound options, follow these steps:

1. Select File | Publish Settings from the main Flash menu to display the Publish Settings dialog box.

2. Click the Flash tab, as shown here:

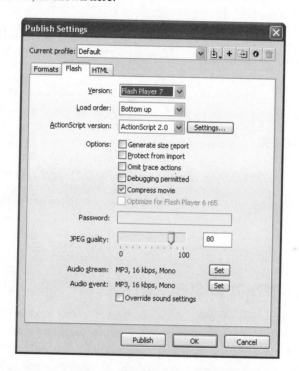

3. To set the global options for streaming sounds, click the Set button to the right of the Audio Stream option to display the Sound Settings dialog box shown here:

4. Choose the options you prefer. Remember, these settings will apply to all streaming sounds that have not been explicitly set to different settings using the Sound Properties dialog box.

5. Click OK to close the Sound Settings dialog box when you have finished selecting your preferred options for streaming sounds.

6. Click the Set button to the right of the Audio Event listing.

7. Choose the options you prefer for event sounds.

8. Click OK to close the Sound Settings dialog box.

9. Optionally, you can select the Override sound settings check box to make your selections apply to all sounds—even sounds that were set individually.

10. Click OK to close the Publish Settings dialog box.

Progress Check

1. Which sounds are affected by settings you choose in the Sound Properties dialog box?

2. Which sounds are affected by options you choose through the use of the Publish Settings dialog box?

Project 10-1   Compressing and Using a Soundtrack

Now it is time to put together the skills that you learned in this module to add a soundtrack to a Flash movie. In this project, you will see how the settings that you choose can make a big difference in the size of your published movie file, and you will learn that it is generally possible to come up with a compromise that produces acceptable sound quality without making your movie so large that it will be a burden to download.

NOTE

For this project, you will need a sound file that you can import into Flash. You will probably find that there are a number of suitable files that you can use for this project on your computer already—if not, you may need to find a sound file on the Internet.

---

1. Only the selected sounds
2. All sounds that were not individually set using the Sound Properties dialog box

Step by Step

1. Open a Flash movie to which you would like to add a soundtrack. Alternatively, create a new Flash movie and add an animated sequence to the movie.

2. Click the Insert Layer button to add a new layer for the sound that you will be adding to the movie.

3. Double-click the name of the new layer and rename it as **Sound**.

4. Select the File | Import | Import To Library command to open the Import To Library dialog box, as shown here:

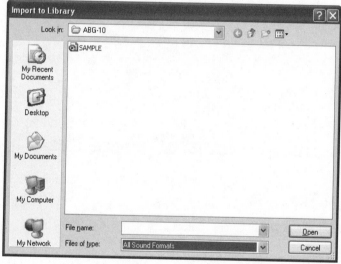

5. Select All Sound Formats from the drop-down Files Of Type list box.

6. Select the sound file you want to add to your movie.

7. Click Open to add the sound to the library.

8. Use the Window | Library command to open the Library panel.

9. Right-click the sound file in the Library panel and choose Properties from the pop-up menu to open the Sound Properties dialog box (or select Properties from the Library panel menu).

10. Choose MP3 from the drop-down Compression list box.

11. In the Bit Rate drop-down list box, select 16 kbps.

(continued)

12. In the Quality list box, select Fast.

13. Click the Test button to hear an example of the compressed file. Notice the compression statistics at the bottom of the Sound Properties dialog box, as shown here:

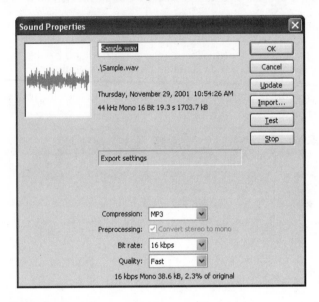

14. When you are satisfied with the sound quality and file size, click the OK button to close the Sound Properties dialog box.

15. Click frame 1 of the Sound layer to select it.

16. Drag the sound you just imported onto the stage. The sound waveform will now appear in the Sound layer in the timeline.

17. Open the Properties panel using the Window | Properties command. (If the sound options do not appear, make certain that you click frame 1 of the Sound layer.)

18. In the Sync list box, choose Stream so that the sound will play only for as long as the animation.

19. Use the Control | Test Movie command to test your movie.

20. When you have noted how the sound plays, close the test window to return to the Flash development environment.

21. Try the other sync options, and notice how they affect the playback when you test your movie. You may be especially interested in noting how quickly the Event option creates an awful cacophony as your movie loops several times.

22. Use the File | Save command to save the movie project file when you are happy with the results.

Project Summary

In this project, you stepped through the whole process of adding a simple soundtrack to a Flash movie and making certain that the added sound did not make the movie project file grow too large. In addition, you saw how the different sync options can affect the playback. You will be able to apply this information to your own movies when you want to add a soundtrack.

Module 10 Mastery Check

1. The _____ rate refers to the number of data points that are recorded each second.

2. The _____ file format typically offers the best compression ratio for sound files in Flash.

3. The process of adjusting volume levels to make it appear as though the sound were moving is known as _____.

4. _____ sounds play until they are finished, even if the movie has ended.

5. To make a sound play just as long as the animation, you set the sync option to _____.

6. To make a sound play more than once, you set the _____ option.

7. Selecting a lower bit rate _____ the size of your movie file.

8. The settings you make in the Properties panel apply to an _____ of the imported sound file.

9. The Edit Envelope dialog box enables you to adjust the _____ of a sound.

10. Sounds you add to button symbols are _____ sounds.

11. Stereo sounds take _____ the space of mono sounds.

12. You use the _____ panel to set most options for imported sounds.

13. You can use the options in the _____ dialog box to override the individual sound settings.

14. To make a button produce a sound when someone clicks the button, you add the sound to the _____ frame.

15. Adding a sound to the _____ frame of a button would play the sound after the mouse button was released.

Module 11

Publishing
Flash Movies

When you set out to learn how to use Flash, your primary goal was almost certainly to be able to create Flash movies for use on web sites. So far we have not really talked about the issues involved in placing a Flash movie onto a web site, because we have been concentrating on the basics of learning how to create Flash movies. In this module, we will finally look at what it takes to place your movies where more people will be able to see them—on your web site.

In reality, placing a Flash movie onto a web site is not a terribly difficult project, but it is one that you will want to do correctly to avoid problems. For example, the web page must have the right HTML statements so that your movie loads properly. In addition, you will want to avoid creating a movie that has severe performance bottlenecks that make it difficult to view over a standard dial-up connection. In this module, we will look at all of these issues as well as how you can create stand-alone Flash movies that can be run by themselves without first placing them on a web page.

CRITICAL SKILL
11.1 Getting Your Movie Ready to Publish

In previous modules, you learned the basics of creating a Flash movie. Still, it is worth taking a moment to review the process. Here are the concepts that you should have mastered to have a Flash movie that is ready to publish:

- You should start out with a plan for what you want your movie to do. The more complete the plan, the more likely that you will be satisfied with the final results.

- With your plan in hand, you can then add the layers and draw the objects that you want in your movie.

- Next, you add the motion tweens and shape tweens that create the animation sequences for your movie.

- Along the way, you may also create a number of symbols that you will use in your movie. Remember, using symbol instances rather than drawing separate objects greatly improves the efficiency of your movie.

- You may also need to add some motion guides or masks to create certain effects.

- Depending upon your movie, you may need to import and manipulate graphic images or sound files.

- When your movie is in reasonable shape, you will want to test it to make sure that things work as expected.

- Finally, at various points along the way, you will save your movie project file so that it is available for further editing.

If you have mastered all of these points, you are able to create basic Flash movies that are essentially ready to publish and place on your web site. Notice that there was no mention of any mastery of ActionScript programming in my list. This was an intentional omission. While it is true that some use of ActionScript commands can certainly enhance a Flash movie, it is also absolutely true that you can create quite impressive Flash movies without learning any ActionScript programming.

One of the very important things in the list is testing your movie as you go along. When you are developing a Flash movie, you are working in the Flash development environment. In this development environment, you can see how some things work, but you cannot get a true picture of how your movie will appear once it has been published. To see that, you need to use the Control | Test Movie command. When you test your movie using this command, Flash actually publishes your movie using the current default settings and then plays the movie in a version of the Flash Player. This gives you a fairly good feel for how your movie will look to visitors to your web site.

NOTE

Unfortunately, simply testing your movie without taking a closer look at how well the movie will download over a typical connection can be a little deceiving. Later in this module, we will look at the tools Flash provides to help you understand the download process a little better.

The final point in my list is also an important one. When you save your Flash movie project file, you name that file. This same name is also the name that Flash uses for the published movie file. The only difference between the name of your movie project file and your published movie file is the file extension. The movie project file uses .fla as its extension, and the published movie file uses .swf as its extension. Therefore, you should save your movie project using the name that you want to appear on your web site. It is possible to use a different name for the published movie file, but the default is to use the same name as your movie project file.

Progress Check

1. Which command do you use to test your movies?

2. How is the name of your published movie file determined?

---

1. Control | Test Movie

2. It uses the same name as the movie project file, but with .swf as its extension.

CRITICAL SKILL
11.2 # Optimizing Your Movies

When you publish a Flash movie, one of your goals should be to create the most efficient movie possible. This process is known as *optimization*. Optimizing a Flash movie means making the movie as small as possible without compromising the quality or effects that you have created. By keeping the movie as small as possible, you minimize the download time and maximize the playback performance.

You need to consider a number of factors in order to optimize your Flash movies. These include the following:

- You should use symbols whenever possible because multiple instances of the same symbol use far less room than multiple copies of ordinary drawn objects.

- Keep lines and curves as simple as possible. The more complex these are, the more room they will require in the movie file.

- If you use text in your movies, select one of the standard fonts that are installed on most PCs. That way, your movies can use the resident fonts rather than having to download the fonts along with the movie file.

- Although gradients look cool, they are less efficient than solid color fills. Try to limit the use of gradient fills to just those few places where they will have a major visual impact.

- Likewise, you may want to avoid using alpha effects any more than necessary. These also increase the size of your movie file.

- If you are including a soundtrack, always use the MP3 format, and be ruthless in selecting compression settings. Wherever possible, use a short, looped sound rather than a full-length music file.

- Remember that using bitmap images is generally not very efficient. Use the Flash drawing tools to create objects whenever possible.

- The tweened frames in an animation require far less space than keyframes. Try to lay out your animations so that Flash is doing as much of the drawing as possible.

- Use layers to separate animated objects from static objects.

- Grouped objects take less space than ungrouped objects.

No one expects that your first efforts will necessarily be as successful as the results you will obtain after you have created a number of Flash movies. You will certainly pick up a number of tricks along the way as you try out various options. Remember, even expert Flash developers were rank amateurs at one time.

Once you have done as much as possible to make your movies efficient, you may want to look at some more advanced techniques to make the download fast and the playback clean. Next, we will look at some of these.

Progress Check

1. What do you call the process of making certain that your Flash movies are as efficient as possible?

2. What type of sound file is the best for use in your Flash movies?

Understanding Bandwidth

Bandwidth can be thought of as the amount of data or information that can be passed through a connection in a specific period. When you have a higher-bandwidth connection, you can transmit or download more data in the same amount of time. Essentially, a higher-bandwidth connection is like a larger-diameter pipe—you can send more stuff through it at the same time.

Of course, one of the beauties of using Flash to create web site content is that Flash is pretty efficient. Flash movies tend to make good use of the available bandwidth.

In an ideal world, everyone would have an extremely high-speed Internet connection. You would be able to put pretty much anything on your web site without worrying that it would take too long to download. In the real world, most people do not have high-speed Internet connections. In fact, the vast majority of Internet users still connect to the Internet by way of the rather slow dial-up connection. If you are one of the fortunate few who has a high-speed connection, it may be harder for you to remember the importance of keeping your Flash movie files small and efficient.

Flash movies are an example of *streaming* content. This means that a Flash movie can begin playing before the entire movie has been downloaded. There are, of course, limitations on this. For example, if your movie includes a large bitmap image that is first displayed in frame 10, the movie may begin playing and then pause when it discovers that the image has not yet been completely downloaded at the point where the image should be displayed. This is where bandwidth considerations become very important. As you are aware, each Flash movie has a constant frame rate. By default, 12 frames of content are displayed each second. If someone is viewing your movie over a low-bandwidth connection, the content that is

---

1. Optimizing
2. MP3

contained in the later movie frames may take too long to download, resulting in the starting and stopping of the playback. This is one of the reasons why you want to keep your movie files as small as possible. By doing so, you give a viewer with a low-bandwidth connection more of a fighting chance to view your movie as you had intended.

Looking for Bottlenecks

When you're trying to optimize the downloading of a Flash movie, it helps to know where the problems exist. For example, as I mentioned earlier, you might have an object that appears in the timeline before the Flash Player is able to completely download the object. You could try to determine where the problems were through guesswork, but this is really not necessary, since Flash provides a tool specifically for this purpose. This tool is the bandwidth profiler.

The following illustration shows an example of using the bandwidth profiler to check out how well a particular Flash movie will download under certain conditions. In this instance, I used the View | Download Settings menu to set the bandwidth profiler to show the effect of a 14.4-Kbps (kilobits per second) connection—slower than most dial-up connections today, but the results are pretty interesting anyway. (Flash uses 1200 B/s (bytes per second) for a 14.4-Kbps connection.)

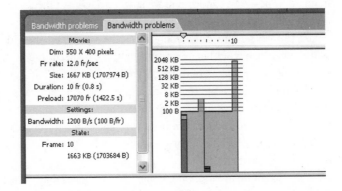

The graph on the right side of the illustration shows some very interesting information. Each bar in the graph represents the content that must be loaded before the frame that contains the content can be played. Notice that the bar in frame 1 sits just below the red line at the 100 B (bytes) mark. This line shows the amount of data that can be loaded during the time it takes to play the frame. As long as the bar is below this line, the Flash Player will be able to download data fast enough to keep on playing. Whenever the bar goes above the line, the Flash Player must wait for more data before continuing.

Notice that the first problem crops up in frame 4, and that a really big problem comes along in frame 10. In both cases, the bar goes above the red line, so the Flash Player would have to stop and wait for the data before continuing.

NOTE

It is important to notice that the increments above the red line are not linear. Each line's value is double the previous line's value (once you get above the bottom line, that is). As a result, the very tall bar in frame 10 represents a really big problem! As a matter of fact, the Preload value in the left pane shows just how big a problem we have. The movie will take 1422.5 seconds—the equivalent of 17,070 frames—to download enough content to be able to play the ten frames in the movie. I doubt that most web site visitors would be quite that patient.

Using the Bandwidth Profiler

As you have seen, the bandwidth profiler is a pretty handy tool for seeing how your movies will perform under real-life conditions. This tool is available when you are testing your movie in the special version of the Flash Player that appears when you use the Control | Test Movie command.

Once you have opened the Flash Player so that you can test your movie, follow these steps to use the bandwidth profiler:

1. Select View | Bandwidth Profiler to display the bandwidth profiler in the upper area of the Flash Player window.

2. Click the View | Download Settings menu to open it.

3. Choose the download speed that you would like to simulate.

4. Optionally, select View | Download Settings | Customize to display the Custom Download Settings dialog box shown here:

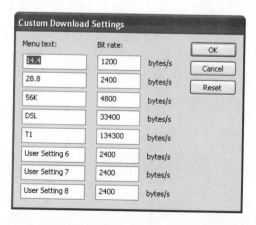

5. Enter any special settings you want to test and then click OK.

6. If you created a custom setting, choose it from the View | Download Settings menu.

TIP

Remember that the bit rate settings are estimates rather than guarantees. When Internet traffic is heavy, download performance may well be somewhat below the values shown on the menu.

It is a good idea to test your movies at several different download speeds. What may appear to be quite acceptable at 56 Kbps may turn out to be marginal at best at slower download speeds.

When you are using the bandwidth profiler, you can view the graph of the download statistics in two different ways:

- Choose View | Streaming Graph to see how the data that makes up your movie will be downloaded as the movie is streaming from the host computer. This option is generally the most useful, since it shows the overall picture of what will happen as your movie is downloading.

- Choose View | Frame By Frame Graph to see the individual frames but without seeing how the Flash Player will be downloading data for future frames.

Viewing the Streaming

In addition to showing you the statistics, the bandwidth profiler can actually simulate the download process at the selected download speed. This simulation is often the best way to visualize what your users will experience, since you will have the opportunity to see any pauses or skipped frames that would occur during actual playback.

To view the streaming simulation, select the View | Simulate Download command while the bandwidth profiler is active.

TIP

You can stop the streaming display by pressing ESC.

Progress Check

1. What does bandwidth represent?

2. What is the purpose of the red line in the bandwidth profiler graph?

3. What important setting do you find on the View | Download Settings menu?

Optimizing Movie Loading

Now that you have seen how the bandwidth profiler can show you where your movies may have some problems downloading properly, you are no doubt wondering how you can use that information. You can use the information about how your movie will download in a number of ways:

● If the bandwidth profiler shows that certain frames will go well above the red line that indicates the limit of what can be downloaded, you may want to add some very simple animation at the beginning of your movie. This will delay the point at which the heavy content is needed and will provide additional time during which that content can download.

● You can examine the contents of the movie frames that exceed the download capabilities to see if some items can be simplified or compressed so that they will not place such a heavy download burden on the Flash Player. For example, you might find that you inadvertently selected the wrong compression option for a sound file and that a better choice will eliminate the problem.

● You might want to rearrange your movie so that it consists of several movie clips rather than one long timeline. As you will see shortly, this would enable you to use the ActionScript loadMovie command to load movie clips into memory before they are needed and while some other parts of your movie are playing.

● You could also decide to create a *preloader* that displays a message such as "Loading, please wait" for a few seconds to give your movie a chance to load more of its content before the main part of the movie begins playing. We will look at this option shortly, too.

---

1. The amount of data in a given period that a connection can deliver
2. To show the maximum amount of data that can be downloaded in a frame
3. The download speed

The basic idea here is that once you are armed with the knowledge about how your movie will load, you can make some choices that will help optimize the download and playback process. No two Flash movies will be identical, and the best solution in one case may not work well in another.

Using the loadMovie Command

So far we have managed to avoid adding ActionScript code to our examples. ActionScript is the programming language that you use to exert some additional control over the playback of your movies. ActionScript is not a particularly difficult programming language to use, but you have seen that it is possible to do some pretty amazing things without ever resorting to ActionScript programming.

Now, however, it is necessary to look at a small amount of ActionScript programming— if for no better reason than to see what you can do with a very small amount of effort. This example does not attempt to teach you how to use ActionScript—we'll get into ActionScript programming starting in the next module. Rather, we will use this example to introduce a concept that you will likely find valuable at some point as you develop Flash movies.

Normally, Flash loads everything that is contained in your movie in a sequential order. That is, the content is loaded frame-by-frame from the first frame onward—a logical way to load the data in most cases.

Sometimes, however, it may be advantageous to modify the loading order. Imagine for a moment that your movie contains a large sound file that will be needed beginning in frame 36. But suppose the sound file was so large that it actually took ten seconds to load. If your movie were to begin playing as soon as it had enough data to play frames 1 through 35, the result would likely be that the movie would start playing, run for about three seconds, and then pause for around seven seconds. Needless to say, the effect would probably not be what you wanted.

Now consider what would happen if the first thing that the movie did was to load the sound file and then begin playing the animation. There would be a ten-second delay while the sound file was loading, but then the animation would play through smoothly, since there would be no need to pause to wait for more data. This is the basic idea behind using the loadMovie command—you gain the ability to exercise control over the loading order of the pieces that make up your movie.

The loadMovie command loads movie clips. As you learned in Module 8, movie clips are simply movies that play as a part of your movie. You could actually build a Flash movie that consisted entirely of movie clips that were played at specific times during the playback. This is, in fact, an excellent way to reuse animated bits that you have developed. You can simply string them together like building blocks.

Going back to our example, imagine that you have created a movie clip named Soundtrack.swf, which contains the sound file you want to load. You can use the loadMovie command as shown here to load the movie clip:

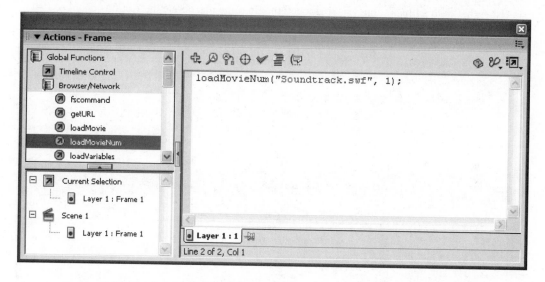

This illustration shows the Actions panel, which you can display using the Window | Development Panels | Actions command. In this case, the Actions panel shows the title "Actions - Frame" to indicate that we are adding our ActionScript code to a keyframe in the timeline. Don't worry if this seems a little confusing right now; you will learn more about using ActionScript in the next three modules.

Creating Preloaders

A *preloader* is another method for making certain that once your movie begins playing the main part of the movie, it will have enough data downloaded that the playback can proceed smoothly. A preloader works by checking to see how much of the movie has been downloaded, and waiting until a specified amount has been downloaded before moving on with the playback.

In most cases, Flash developers design preloaders so that some sort of simple animation plays during the preload sequence. This might be something as simple as just flashing a message like "Loading..." on and off, or it might be something more complex. Regardless, the idea is that you want to make certain that your movie will play without pausing once the main animation begins.

You also need to use a little ActionScript code to create a preloader. A number of different ActionScript statements can be used to create a preloader. The simplest option (although not necessarily the best in all circumstances) is to use the ifFrameLoaded statement, as shown here. (Note that in this illustration, I have docked the timeline just above the Actions panel so that you can see the labels in the timeline.)

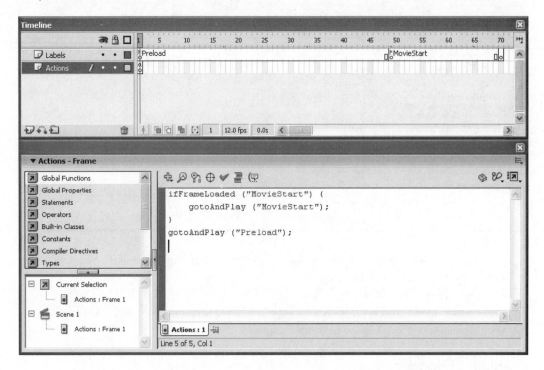

In this example, we are using the ifFrameLoaded statement to determine if a frame named MovieStart has been completely loaded. If it has, the gotoAndPlay command that follows makes the playhead move to that frame and begin playing the movie. If the frame has not been fully loaded, the first gotoAndPlay action is ignored, and the gotoAndPlay action in the fourth line is executed. This action sends the playhead back to the frame named Preload (which happens to be frame 1), where the whole sequence is repeated until the MovieStart frame has been completely loaded. In this case, the frames following the Preload frame might contain a simple animation that toggles the word "Loading" between red and black.

Progress Check

1. Do you have to learn ActionScript programming to use the information from the bandwidth profiler to optimize your movie?

2. How could you ensure that a large object would have time to load before the playhead reaches it without using ActionScript?

CRITICAL SKILL

11.3 Putting Your Movies on the Web

Once you have finished developing your Flash movies, you are almost ready to place them on a web page where visitors can come and see them. Doing so is a process known as *publishing* your movie.

As you work on your movie in Flash, you are working with the Flash movie project file—the file with the .fla file extension. This file contains all of the resources that you are using during the creation of your movie. The movie project file is not optimized to reduce the file size, and it cannot be played by the Flash Player.

When you publish your movie, Flash creates a Flash Player movie file—the file with the .swf file extension. This is the file that the Flash Player can actually play, and it is optimized to reduce the size of the file as much as possible. In fact, the published movie file often ends up being tiny compared with the movie project file that it is derived from.

Choosing Settings and Publishing the Movie

There are various options that you can choose when you are ready to publish your movie. These settings can have important implications, so it is a good idea to understand how they may affect you. Let's take a quick look at the options you need to know about.

Choosing the Format Options

A number of options control how the Flash movie file is generated. You can display this dialog box using the File | Publish Settings command. The Formats tab shown here simply enables

---

1. No, learning ActionScript is not necessary.
2. Place the object later in the movie.

you to specify the output formats and filenames for your movie files. I will discuss the options on this tab later in this module.

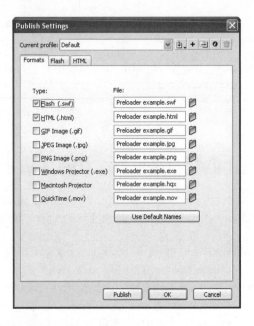

Choosing the Flash Publish Settings

Next, you will want to specify the Flash settings. These settings are available on the Flash tab of the Publish Settings dialog box, as shown here:

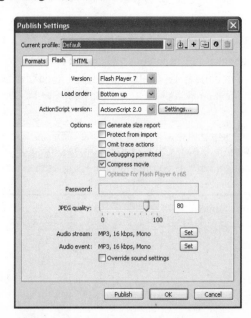

The options on this tab include the following:

- **Version**   This determines the Flash Player version that the movie will be compatible with. Generally, you should select the latest Flash version, but you can select an earlier version if you want to maintain compatibility with older Flash Players. Keep in mind, however, that you will not be able to use any features that were not supported in the older versions.

- **Load Order**   This specifies the load order for the layers and determines what is drawn first when your movie is played. In most cases, you can ignore this setting, since it really affects only the first frame that is displayed.

- **ActionScript Version**   This specifies the version of ActionScript to use in your movies. You will want to choose ActionScript 2.0 unless you need to publish a movie for a version of the Flash Player earlier than 7.

- **Generate Size Report**   You can select this if you want to see a report that shows the size of the various elements in your movie. This can be quite handy if you want to do everything possible to optimize the download and playback characteristics of the movie file.

- **Protect From Import**   This option prevents anyone from importing your movie back into the Flash development environment. When this option is selected, the movie can only be played.

- **Omit Trace Actions**   This option is used along with the Debugging Permitted option to prevent a special window known as the Output window from opening and displaying messages. You can ignore this option.

- **Debugging Permitted**   Choosing this option enables someone else to *debug* your movie. Unless you are having problems with your Flash movie development and have an experienced Flash developer to assist you, it is best not to select this option.

- **Compress Movie**   Choosing this option reduces the size of the published movie file. This option is only available if you publish the movie for Flash Player 6 or later.

- **Password**   This box enables you to specify a password that must be entered in order to debug your movie.

- **JPEG Quality**   This sets the default compression for any bitmap images that are included in your movie. It is usually best to set the compression level for each image separately using the right-click Properties command in the library window.

- **Audio Stream**   This sets the default compression type and level for audio streams, and was discussed in Module 10.

- **Audio Event**   This sets the defaults for audio event sounds and was discussed in Module 10.

- **Override Sound Settings**   Selecting this check box applies the default sound settings to all sounds—even if they were explicitly set to different settings.

Choosing the HTML Publish Settings

The HTML tab of the Publish Settings dialog box also contains a number of important options, as shown here. These settings directly affect the HTML web page that Flash generates when you publish your movie.

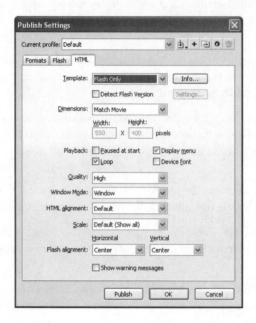

NOTE

To view your Flash movie in a web browser, you need to have an HTML web page that tells the web browser what type of content you want to play and what application should be used to play it. Fortunately, you do not have to learn to program in HTML, since Flash automatically creates the web page for you when you publish the movie.

The HTML tab of the Publish Settings dialog box includes the following options:

● **Template** This specifies which HTML page template is used to create the web page. For now, leave this set at Flash Only (default) so that you get the simplest web page that fully supports your movie.

● **Detect Flash Version** This makes certain that the HTML page will include the proper code to determine if visitors have the correct Flash Player version installed on their system.

- **Dimensions**   This option sets the size of the area for displaying the Flash movie. In most cases, you will want to leave this set to Match Movie so that your movie plays at the size you intended. If you want the movie to scale up or down with the browser window, you might want to choose the Percent option.

- **Paused At Start**   Selecting this option requires the user to start the movie manually rather than having it start automatically.

- **Display Menu**   Selecting this option enables the user to display the right-click context menu to control the movie.

- **Loop**   Choosing this option makes the movie automatically repeat when it finishes playback.

- **Device Font**   Choosing this option enables Windows-based PCs to substitute system fonts for fonts a user might not have installed for the display of static text that appears in your movie.

- **Quality**   Choose an option from this drop-down list box to select a trade-off between image quality and playback performance. In most cases, modern PCs can easily handle the higher-quality settings, but this may not be true for some older computers.

- **Window Mode**   This option selects the way certain versions of Internet Explorer may display the Flash movie. Generally, it is best to leave this set to the default of Window so that the movie appears the same way in all browsers.

- **HTML Alignment**   This option selects the alignment of the Flash movie within the browser window.

- **Scale**   This option determines whether the Flash movie is scaled in one or both directions. Generally, you will want to choose Default (Show All) so that your movie is not distorted.

- **Flash Alignment**   Use this option to change the alignment of the movie within the Flash window. This option is really only effective if the movie is smaller than the Flash window that is displayed in the browser.

- **Show Warning Messages**   Select this option to see any warning messages that tell you if there is a problem with the tags in the HTML web page that Flash generates.

Publishing the Movie

Once you have selected the options for use in publishing your movie, you can proceed with publishing it. To do so, you can click the Publish button in the Publish Settings dialog box, or you can choose File | Publish from the Flash menu.

When you publish your movie, Flash creates the SWF file, which can be played directly in the Flash Player. In addition, Flash generates the HTML web page that is needed to display the movie in a web browser. We will take a brief look at the HTML web page in the next section.

Understanding the HTML Page

Flash automatically generates an HTML web page that contains all of the rather esoteric HTML commands necessary to display your Flash movie. These commands tell a web browser that the movie is a Flash Player movie as well as defining the various parameters that you set in the Publish Settings dialog box. Here is an example of a typical HTML web page necessary to display a Flash movie. Please note that we had to break quite a few lines into multiple lines to fit them into the available space on a page.

```
<!DOCTYPE html PUBLIC "-//W3C//DTD XHTML 1.0 Transitional//EN"
"http://www.w3.org/TR/xhtml1/DTD/xhtml1-transitional.dtd">
<html xmlns="http://www.w3.org/1999/xhtml" xml:lang="en" lang="en">
<head>
<meta http-equiv="Content-Type" content="text/html; charset=iso-8859-1" />
<title>Preloader example</title>
</head>
<body bgcolor="#ffffff">
<!--url's used in the movie-->
<!--text used in the movie-->
<object classid="clsid:d27cdb6e-ae6d-11cf-96b8-444553540000"
codebase="http://download.macromedia.com/pub/shockwave/cabs/flash/
swflash.cab#vers
ion=7,0,0,0" width="550" height="400" id="Preloader example" align="middle">
<param name="allowScriptAccess" value="sameDomain" />
<param name="movie" value="Preloader example.swf" />
<param name="quality" value="high" />
<param name="bgcolor" value="#ffffff" />
<embed src="Preloader example.swf" quality="high" bgcolor="#ffffff"
width="550"
height="400" name="Preloader example" align="middle"
allowScriptAccess="sameDomain" type="application/x-shockwave-flash"
pluginspage="http://www.macromedia.com/go/getflashplayer" />
</object>
</body>
</html>
```

HTML is a *page description* language that uses *tags* to identify pieces of information. Tags are those names you see inside the angle brackets, as in <head> and </head> (the tag with the slash in front of the name ends a tag). In this case, the two most important tags are the <object> and <embed> tags. The <object> tag is used to tell Internet Explorer how to display your Flash movie, and the <embed> tag is used to tell Netscape Navigator how to display it.

TIP

To add the Flash movie to your own web page, copy and paste everything between the <object> and </object> tags.

Progress Check

1. Which file does the Flash Player display?

2. Which file is necessary to display your Flash movie in a web browser?

CRITICAL SKILL
11.4 Exporting Flash in Alternative Formats

As popular and versatile as Flash may be, not everyone has the Flash Player installed, and this fact could prevent some people from viewing your Flash movies. In addition, there may be times when you want to use some animation that you have created in Flash in another type of project that simply does not support Flash movies. Fortunately, Flash provides you with quite a few alternatives.

NOTE

Be sure that you keep in mind that Flash movies that have been exported (or published) in a foreign format may not retain all of the features of a real Flash movie. For example, if you have added any interactivity to your movie, you will find that this is lost when the movie is exported to a different format. In addition, some formats will save only a single image (but this can be an effective way to convert a Flash drawing into a bitmap format for use in other applications that cannot use Flash images directly).

Exporting a Flash movie and publishing Flash movies in foreign formats are quite similar processes. The major difference between the two is that when you export a Flash movie, you create a single file containing the exported content in the alternative format. When you publish a Flash movie in additional formats, you can create several formats at the same time, and you can generate the HTML code necessary to display those additional formats in a web browser.

Next, we will take a look at each of these two processes.

Exporting Movies

If you simply want to create a single file containing some of the content from your Flash movie, you can export your movie into a foreign file format. To do so, you select the File |

1. The SWF published movie file
2. The HTML file

Export | Export Movie command to display the Export Movie dialog box, as shown here. Use the drop-down Save As Type list box to choose the format for the file.

TIP

To save a single frame of the movie as an image file, use the File | Export | Export Image command.

Remember that using the File | Export | Export Movie command does not create the HTML web page that you would need to place the exported movie onto your web site. If you want to generate this file, use the publishing options shown next.

Publishing in Alternate Formats

You can also publish your Flash movies in a number of alternative formats. Publishing movies rather than simply exporting them offers some advantages. For example, by publishing your movies in alternative formats, you gain the following (compared with exporting them in these formats):

● You can have Flash automatically generate HTML web pages so that your movies can be displayed in web browsers.

● You can create files in several formats with a single command.

● You can create stand-alone *projectors* that enable your movies to be played without requiring the Flash Player or a web browser.

To publish your movies in alternative formats, follow these steps:

1. Select the File | Publish Settings command to display the Publish Settings dialog box.

2. Click the Formats tab, shown here:

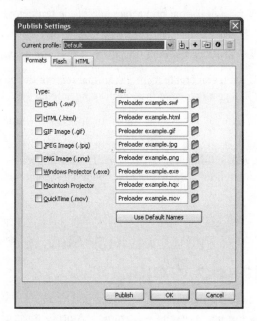

3. Select the file formats that you wish to use.

4. If you want to specify alternative names for the files, enter the names you prefer. To once again use the default names, click the Use Default Names button.

5. To specify an alternative destination folder, click the folder icon to the right of the File text box.

6. Click the Publish button to create the files.

NOTE

For some formats (such as QuickTime), you may need to select a different template on the HTML tab.

Limitations on Using Alternate Formats

Flash, of course, is really intended for creating movies that are published in the Flash Player format. If you choose to export or publish your Flash movies in an alternative format, you should be prepared to live with certain limitations that are inherent in those other formats. Some of these limitations include the following:

- If you choose any foreign format other than one of the projectors or QuickTime, you will lose all interactivity.

- If you choose JPEG or PNG, the resulting file is a static image without any animation.

- If you choose GIF, you can create a simple animation, but the color palette will be limited to 256 colors (or 216 colors, depending on the color model you select).

- Alpha effects often do not survive the transition to another format.

- A Macintosh projector created on a PC will not be seen as an executable program on a Macintosh unless you go through the extra step of converting it using a utility on the Macintosh system. This is a limitation of the Macintosh operating system—not of the Flash publishing process nor of the PC.

Project 11-1 Creating a Stand-Alone Flash Movie Using a Projector

Now it is time to put together the skills that you learned in this module to create a stand-alone Flash movie that uses a projector to show the movie. A projector is essentially a self-executing combination of a Flash movie and the Flash Player. You can use projectors to create animated sequences that can be run on their own or even to create interactive games.

NOTE

If you use a Mac, select the Macintosh Projector option in step 4 of the following project, and then use your Finder in step 7.

Step by Step

1. Open a Flash movie that you would like to convert into a stand-alone application using a projector. Alternatively, create a new Flash movie and add whatever animation and interactivity you want to the movie.

2. Select File | Publish Settings to display the Publish Settings dialog box.

3. Click the Formats tab.

4. Select the Windows Projector (.Exe) option.

5. Deselect all other file format options, as shown here:

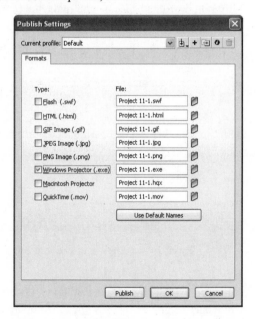

6. Click the Publish button to create the projector.

7. Open Windows Explorer and navigate to the folder where your Flash movie files are stored.

8. .Double-click the projector file you just created to test it.

Project Summary

In this project, you learned how you can create a stand-alone application from a Flash movie. This makes it very easy for you to create all sorts of interesting programs using just the skills that you have learned by developing Flash movies. As you can certainly imagine, this opens up a whole new world of uses for your Flash movies. You could create animated greeting cards complete with a soundtrack, for example.

✓

Module 11 Mastery Check

1. The amount of data that a connection can handle is often referred to as the _____ of the connection.

2. When you create a _____, you are making a stand-alone Flash movie that is self-executing.

3. To produce the Flash Player file for use on a web page, you _____ your movie.

4. You can use the _____ to see how the data will stream as your movie downloads.

5. To see the effects of different download speeds, you make the bit rate selections on the _____ menu.

6. Flash movies begin playing before all of their content is downloaded because they are an example of _____ content.

7. When you are testing the download characteristics of your movie, the red line in the chart represents:

   A. The maximum amount of data that can be downloaded during the frame

   B. The minimum amount of data that can be downloaded during the frame

   C. The average data rate for all frames

   D. None of the above

8. The _____ dialog box enables you to choose the HTML options.

9. You can use the _____ From Import option to prevent other people from importing your movies.

10. A _____ is often used to make the movie display a "Loading" message rather than beginning immediate playback to prevent pauses once the movie begins playing.

11. You need the proper _____ code on a web page in order for a browser to recognize your Flash movie.

12. A visitor to your web site must have a copy of the _____ installed in order to view your movies.

13. If you publish your Flash movie in a foreign format, you will lose any _____ in your movie.

14. You can use the options on the _____ tab of the Publish Settings dialog box to specify if your movie will begin playing automatically.

15. The _____ tab of the Publish Settings dialog box includes a password option that enables you to protect your movies.

Module 12

Learning Basic ActionScript Concepts

CRITICAL SKILLS

12.1 Understand the concepts behind ActionScript

12.2 Know the basic elements of ActionScript

12.3 Recognize the types of data you can use

As you have seen in the earlier modules, it is entirely possible to create quite impressive Flash movies using nothing more complex than tween-based animation sequences. But if you limit yourself to the types of movies that you can create without learning a little bit about ActionScript programming, you will be missing out on some of the most powerful possibilities that exist within Flash.

In this module, you will learn some of the basics of ActionScript, and you will see how even some very simple ActionScript code can really enhance your movies. ActionScript is a fairly simple programming language that is amazingly easy to use even if you spend almost no time learning about it. Often, you will be able to add rather sophisticated behavior to your movies with just a few mouse clicks. In fact, you will soon learn that most of your ActionScript programming will consist of clicking some choices with your mouse. It would be hard to find another programming language that enables you to do so much with so little effort.

Understanding ActionScript

ActionScript is the programming language that you use to control various aspects of a Flash movie. ActionScript is a fairly simple programming language, yet it is capable of some fairly sophisticated actions. As the name "ActionScript" implies, ActionScript is a *scripting* language. Basically, this means that creating a program in ActionScript largely consists of selecting statements and parameters from lists.

Because ActionScript is a scripting language, the program statements tend to be quite easy to understand. Even if you have little or no experience with computer programming, you will likely find that ActionScript programs seem to make sense because the statements generally look an awful lot like ordinary English.

Computers require you to follow certain rules if you want them to understand you. These rules are the *syntax* of whatever programming language you are using. For example, when you are giving the computer a couple of different pieces of information, the syntax must be correct if you want to achieve the desired outcome. That is, if the computer expects you to say something like "change the color of the object named Ball1 to red," it probably won't understand if you change the order of the arguments to say "change to red the color of the object named Ball1." Even though you can easily understand both forms of the statement, altering the syntax to something that the computer does not expect will almost certainly prevent the computer from understanding you. ActionScript is similar to other programming languages in this respect, and you must use the correct syntax to be understood. Fortunately, Flash does its best to make certain that you are using proper syntax in your ActionScript statements.

ActionScript's Origin in JavaScript

Beginning with Flash 5, ActionScript underwent a major change from the previous versions of ActionScript. To make the language more powerful and easier to use, and to base it on an open standard, Macromedia based the newer version of ActionScript on an international specification known as ECMA-262. This specification was created by a group called the European Computer Manufacturers Association (ECMA).

ECMA-262 was an attempt to create a new definition of JavaScript—a programming language that is widely used on web pages. This new definition of JavaScript aimed to make JavaScript an open specification not under the control of one company—a language that everyone would be able to use without fearing that someone's arbitrary decision would render their work incompatible.

By basing ActionScript on the ECMA-262 standard, Macromedia made it very easy for JavaScript programmers to use ActionScript, and for ActionScript programmers to use JavaScript. Essentially, ActionScript would now be a programming language that developers could count on to be quite stable and reliable.

NOTE

With the release of Flash MX 2004, Macromedia created a new version of ActionScript called ActionScript 2. To a very large extent, this new version and ActionScript 1 are identical, and the differences between them are unimportant to most Flash developers. In fact, unless you use Flash MX Professional 2004, you will not have the means to even use most of the new language elements, because Flash MX 2004 lacks an external script editor.

Of course, ActionScript is not identical to JavaScript. ActionScript is intended as a language for controlling Flash movies, and JavaScript is intended as a language for controlling actions on a web page. This difference alone makes certain variations necessary. For example, ActionScript does not support a few JavaScript statements that deal with objects that are never part of a Flash movie. In addition, to allow some older ActionScript programs to run in newer versions of the Flash Player, ActionScript allows certain obsolete syntax constructs to be used in a few instances (although ActionScript also has newer ECMA-262 constructs to replace all of the obsolete items so that you do not have to use those obsolete items in your new ActionScript programs).

NOTE

The ActionScript Reference Guide in the Help panel lists all of the differences between ActionScript and JavaScript if you want to know all of the details. See the section entitled "Differences between ActionScript and JavaScript."

Understanding Object-Oriented Programming

In addition to being a script-based language, ActionScript is also an *object-oriented* language. This means that when you are working in ActionScript, you are dealing with different objects that possess a number of characteristics (or *properties*) that can be easily examined or modified. In addition, those objects have the built-in ability to perform certain actions or to respond to specific events.

If you recall the discussion about button symbol objects in Module 8, you will remember that the button symbol object already knows how to respond to certain mouse events. With absolutely no programming on your part—just a little basic drawing—it was possible for you to create a button that could change color or play a sound when the mouse pointer was rolled over or clicked on the button. This is an excellent example of how object-oriented programming works. You don't have to know anything about what it takes to detect and respond to an event such as a mouse click—you can simply use the fact that the button symbol object knows how to do so.

Even if you have never done any computer programming, you have almost certainly become quite familiar with a very common example of object-oriented programming. Whenever you right-click an object to display a pop-up context menu, you are seeing an example of how an object can respond. The pop-up menu displays a series of options that represent actions that can be applied to the selected object. Everything on that pop-up menu is something that applies to that specific object.

Progress Check

1. What common language is ActionScript largely based upon?

2. What do you call a programming language that has objects with built-in properties and actions?

---

1. JavaScript
2. Object-oriented

12

ActionScript Basic Elements

To understand how ActionScript works, you should start by learning a little about the basic elements of the ActionScript language. Once you understand what the different terms mean, it will be far easier for you to apply the concepts of programming in ActionScript. In the following sections, we will take a brief look at some important elements of ActionScript that you will encounter often.

Functions

Functions are the built-in commands in the ActionScript language. These are the statements that you will use to make something happen in your movie. For example, in this illustration, I have selected one of the functions from the Timeline Control category in the Actions panel. The selected function, gotoAndPlay, tells Flash to move the playhead to a specific frame and then play the movie from there.

Show Code Hint

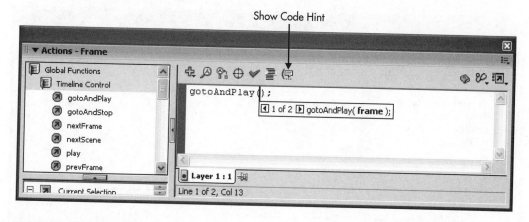

TIP

When you open the Actions panel (using the Window | Development Panels | Actions command), you will notice that there are several subcategories of functions. This breakdown is simply there as an aid to Flash developers.

In previous versions of Flash, the Actions panel had two different modes that determined how you worked in the panel—Normal mode and Expert mode. With the introduction of Flash MX 2004, Macromedia has dropped Normal mode, and you must now enter all of the parameters in the script pane of the Actions panel yourself. Fortunately, you can get a little help with the parameters by making certain that the Show Code Hint button is selected.

NOTE

Macromedia renamed several ActionScript language elements in Flash MX 2004. In previous versions, functions were called "actions."

Because the functions are the ActionScript elements that you will use most often, I will now provide a very brief description of each of the functions. This will help you determine which action you need to use to accomplish your goals.

Timeline Control Functions

The timeline control function category includes various commands that you use to control the movement of the playhead through your movies. This category includes the functions shown here:

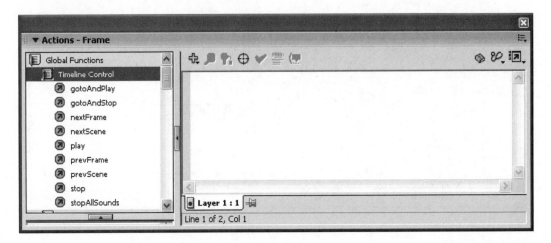

- **gotoAndPlay** Sends the playhead to a specific frame and then begins playing the movie from that point.

- **gotoAndStop** Sends the playhead to a specific frame and then stops the playhead at that frame.

- **nextFrame** Moves the playhead to the next frame in the timeline.

- **nextScene** Moves the playhead to the next scene in the movie.

- **play** Causes the movie to begin playing starting at the current frame.

- **prevFrame**   Moves the playhead to the previous frame in the timeline.

- **prevScene**   Moves the playhead to the previous scene in the movie.

- **stop**   Stops the movie from playing.

- **stopAllSounds**   Stops the playback of the current soundtrack.

Browser/Network Functions

The browser/network functions enable you to control the web browser as well as to load or unload additional movie files. This category includes the functions shown here:

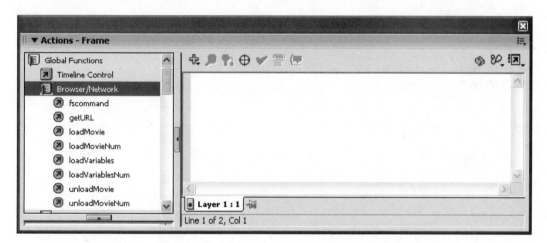

- **fscommand**   Enables you to send commands from your Flash movie to the JavaScript functions on a web page.

- **getURL**   Loads a document from a specified URL and optionally passes the values of the movie's variables to that URL.

- **loadMovie**   Loads a movie clip instance into the movie. This new movie can be added to the current movie, or it can replace it, depending on the format you choose.

- **loadMovieNum**   Loads a movie clip instance into the movie and places it at a specified level.

- **loadVariables**   Loads information from a specified URL into the current movie.

- **loadVariablesNum**   Loads information from a specified URL into the current movie and places it at a specific level.

- **unloadMovie**   Removes a specific movie from the stage.

- **unloadMovieNum**   Removes a movie at a specific level from the stage.

Movie Clip Control Functions

You use the movie clip control functions to control specific movie clip instances that you have added to your movies. This category includes the functions shown here:

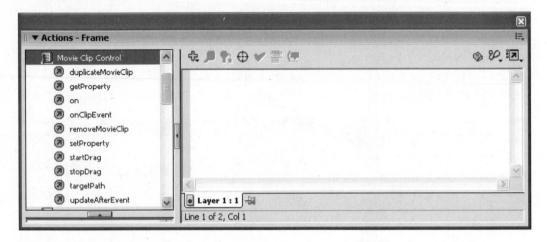

- **duplicateMovieClip**   Creates a new instance of a movie clip and is useful for adding objects to the stage as the movie is playing.

- **getProperty**   Determines the current value of a specified property for the movie clip instance.

- **on**   Executes a series of ActionScript statements when a specific mouse event occurs.

- **onClipEvent**   Executes a block of statements when an event involving a movie clip instance occurs.

- **removeMovieClip**   Removes a movie clip instance from memory and frees up the memory it was using.

- **setProperty**   Modifies a specific property of an object.

- **startDrag**   Enables a movie clip instance to be dragged as the movie is playing.

- **stopDrag**   Prevents a movie clip instance from being dragged.

- **targetPath**   Returns the path to the specified movie clip instance.

- **updateAfterEvent**   Redraws the screen after a mouse event or a clip event.

Printing Functions

The printing functions enable you to provide users with the ability to print various parts of your movies. This category includes the functions shown next:

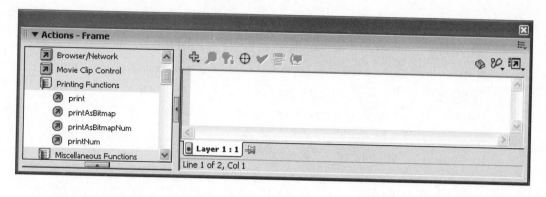

- **print**   Prints frames from your movie based on parameters that you define and on labels that you place in the timeline.

- **printAsBitmap**   Prints frames from the movie as bitmaps rather than as vectors.

- **printAsBitmapNum**   Prints frames from a specified level as bitmaps rather than as vectors.

- **printNum**   Prints frames from a specified level.

Miscellaneous Functions

The miscellaneous functions perform a number of useful tasks that don't easily fall into any of the other categories. This category includes the functions shown here:

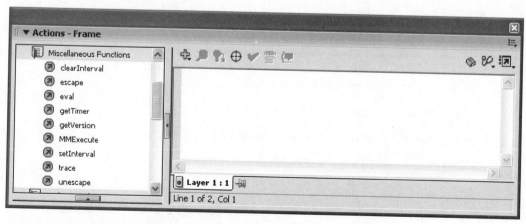

- **clearInterval**   Stops execution of a timed event that was started using setInterval.

- **escape**   Converts text strings into URL-compatible strings.

- **eval**   Determines the value of a variable.

- **getTimer** Specifies the number of milliseconds since the movie began playing.

- **getVersion** Returns the version number of the Flash Player.

- **MMExecute** Enables you to issue Flash JavaScript API commands from within an ActionScript script.

- **setInterval** Starts executing an event at specified intervals.

- **trace** Displays information in the Output window while you are testing your movie so that you can determine what is happening.

- **unescape** Removes the escape characters from a URL-formatted string and returns plain text.

Mathematical Functions

The mathematical functions enable you to perform specific mathematical operations on numbers. This category includes the functions shown here:

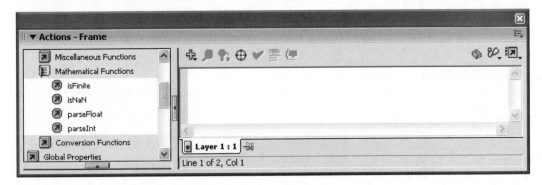

- **isFinite** Tests a number to see if it is finite.

- **isNaN** Tests a value to see if it is not a number.

- **parseFloat** Converts a string into a floating-point number.

- **parseInt** Converts a string into an integer.

Conversion Functions

The conversion functions convert data into a specific type. This category includes the functions shown next:

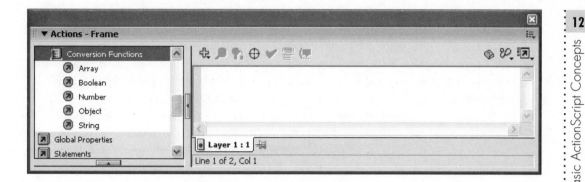

- **Array**   Converts values into an array.

- **Boolean**   Converts values into Boolean (true/false) values.

- **Number**   Converts values into numbers.

- **Object**   Converts values into a specified type of object.

- **String**   Converts values into strings.

NOTE

A number of the ActionScript statements are *deprecated*—which means that they are obsolete statements that are no longer supported and should be avoided. The deprecated statements are subject to being dropped from future versions of the Flash Player.

Progress Check

1. What is another term that describes ActionScript functions?

2. Which panel do you use to add ActionScript statements to your movies?

1. Commands
2. The Actions panel

Events

Events are occurrences that can cause objects to respond. For example, when you create a button symbol and then place an instance of that symbol onto the Flash stage, the button instance responds when users click the button with their mouse. Just how the button responds is up to you, because Flash simply provides the ability to respond to events—not the response itself.

You can use a number of different types of events to trigger actions. For example, this illustration shows the Actions panel when the *on* function is selected in the movie clip control category. As this shows, you can choose from several different mouse events (as well as a key press) to trigger actions:

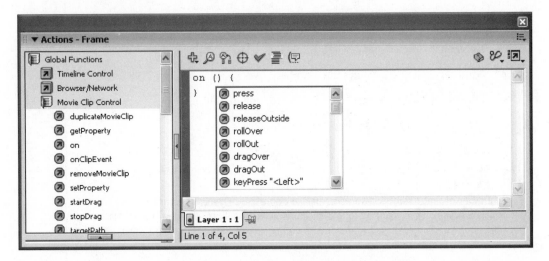

Movie clips can also respond to a number of different events. You use the onClipEvent action as shown here to assign events that you want a movie clip instance to respond to. Notice that movie clip instances have several additional events they can respond to compared with button symbol instances. (In both illustrations, there are additional options that cannot be seen in the drop-down list of options.)

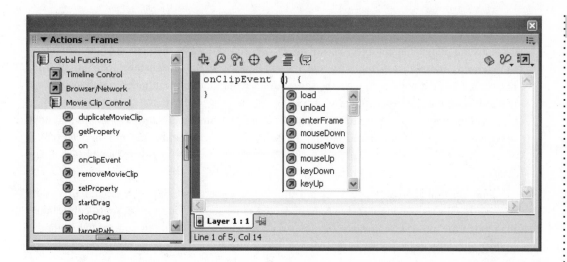

Events are a very important concept in any object-oriented programming language. Unlike older, linear programming methods, object-oriented programming places the intelligence into different objects. Those objects then control how the program works by responding to events. The beauty of this approach is that you don't have to write a program that keeps checking every possibility to see what is happening. All you need to do is to say something like, "If this happens, do this." Then, if that something happens, your objects will respond correctly. This frees you to concentrate on the results you want rather than worrying about all the little housekeeping details that lead up to obtaining those results.

Progress Check

1. What are events?

2. What type of events do buttons typically respond to?

---

1. The triggers that make things happen
2. Mouse events

Methods

Methods are things that an object knows how to do. In most ways, methods are quite similar to functions, except that methods are specifically defined by the objects they are a part of. In most cases, the methods even have the same name as the functions (although functions and methods do use a slightly different syntax).

As an example, consider the following ActionScript statement that uses a function to move the playhead in the current timeline to frame 100 and begins playing the movie from that point:

```
gotoAndPlay(100);
```

This function is pretty straightforward and easy to understand. Suppose, though, that you wanted to tell a movie clip instance to perform the same action. Since you want to control the timeline in the movie clip instance from the main timeline, you would use one of the methods of the movie clip object to perform this same task:

```
MyMovieClip.gotoAndPlay(100);
```

NOTE

To use object methods, in most cases you must first name the object instance using the Properties panel. In the preceding example, the movie clip instance was named MyMovieClip.

Progress Check

1. How do methods compare to functions?

2. What must you do before you can use most methods?

Properties

Properties are the various characteristics that define an object. These include a number of things you already know about, such as the alpha setting, which controls the transparency of an object, and the height property, which defines the height of the object in pixels.

Most object properties can be both read and modified. That is, you can use ActionScript statements to determine the current value of a property and to change the value of the property

---

1. Methods are similar to functions, but they are built into objects.
2. Name the object instance.

to a different value. Some properties, however, are read-only; you can only examine their value, not change it. For example, the _xmouse property returns the current horizontal position of the mouse pointer, but you cannot set the property to a different value using ActionScript commands.

NOTE

In previous versions of Flash, all property names began with an underscore. That is no longer true in Flash MX 2004.

Progress Check

1. What are properties?

2. What types of properties can be viewed but not modified?

Variables

Variables are names that you create so that Flash can use them to store information while your movie is playing. In Flash, variables can hold any type of information you want. You might, for example, store the user's name so that you can use it later in the movie, or you might use a variable to store the score during an interactive game.

In addition to using variables to hold information for use in your movies, you can also send the values of the variables to a URL using one of several ActionScript statements. The getURL function is one of the functions that can use either the GET or POST method of sending information to a server.

Though ActionScript includes a set variable statement, it is generally not necessary to use this statement to set the value of a variable. For example, the following two ActionScript statements both accomplish the same thing:

```
set (MyVar, 100);
MyVar = 100;
```

1. They are the characteristics that define an object.
2. Read-only properties

Expressions

Expressions are ActionScript statements that are used to assign a value to a variable. You are no doubt quite familiar with mathematical expressions—expressions in ActionScript programs work just the same way.

Parameters

Parameters are the arguments that tell various ActionScript actions, functions, and so on, exactly what you want them to do. Parameters provide considerable flexibility by allowing the same statement or function to do different things depending upon variable information that you have provided.

Imagine for a moment how difficult it would be to program a Flash movie using the gotoAndPlay function if the function did not accept parameters. There would be no way to tell the function which frame you wanted to play next.

In virtually all cases, you can specify the parameters using specific values or by using the name of a variable that was defined earlier in the program execution. This makes it possible to add logic to your ActionScript programs, since the program can be controlled by factors that become available only when the program is run. One good example of how you might use this is to load different movie clips depending on which day of the week someone is visiting your web site. Since you don't know in advance when someone might visit, it would be pretty difficult to accomplish this result without using variables to define the parameters.

Progress Check

1. What is another common name for parameters?

2. What are variables used for?

Operators

Operators are the controlling element in an expression. Operators tell Flash just what you want it to do in order to manipulate the objects on either side of the expression.

---

1. Arguments
2. Storing information

ActionScript operators come in many different flavors. The Actions panel toolbox lists some of them immediately under the Operators category, and a bunch more in subcategories under Operators, as shown here. Your old friend the equal sign (=) is actually an *assignment* operator—meaning that using the equal sign in an expression assigns the value that is on the right side of the operator to the variable that is on the left side of the operator.

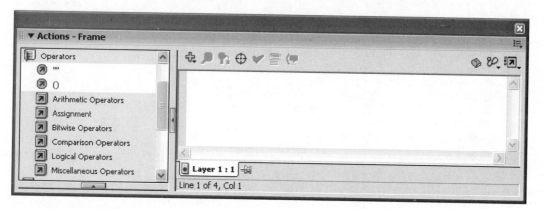

TIP

One of the most confusing things about using operators in ActionScript is that they do not always act exactly the way you may expect from your basic math training. Probably the prime example of this comes about when you want to test to see if two values are equal. In basic math, you would perform this test using the equal sign, but in ActionScript you must use the *equivalence* operator, which is a double equal sign (==). The reason for this is simple—Flash always assumes that the single equal sign is used to assign values rather than to test them.

Looping

Looping is the process of repeating a block of ActionScript statements a number of times based on the results of a conditional test. You can use looping to automate many different tasks in your Flash movies. One example might be to display a countdown timer as your movie is loading. You could create a simple animation that displays steadily decreasing numbers and then begins the main movie playback when zero is displayed.

Several different ActionScript actions can be used to create a loop. These include the *for, for..in, do while,* and *while* actions. Each of these actions creates a slightly different type of loop. In some cases, the conditional test is performed first, and if the test is true, the statements are executed. Some other types of loops perform the test after the first pass through the loop, thus assuring that the statements in the loop will always be executed at least once. The following illustration shows the statements that you use to control loops and to perform conditional tests:

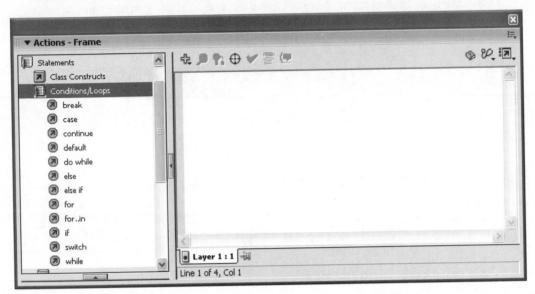

Working with Objects

Objects are key to programming in ActionScript. Virtually everything that you do in your ActionScript programming (or in a Flash movie, for that matter) involves objects. You move objects, change their properties, hide or display them, and so on.

To work with objects using ActionScript, you need to know how to reference them properly. That is, you need to be able to tell the program exactly which object it is that you want to address with an action or a property setting. Fortunately, ActionScript uses a very simple and easy-to-understand method of referencing objects.

As you have seen several times, ActionScript uses a number of rather strange-looking names for actions and other elements of the language. For example, the function that moves the playhead to a new frame and begins playback from that point is gotoAndPlay—without any spaces between the words. Likewise, you are free to use similar naming conventions when you name variables or objects. If you want to call a movie clip something like MyFunnyMovieClip, you are free to do so.

NOTE

ActionScript is picky about capitalization. Thus, you must enter the action name as *gotoAndPlay* because *gotoandplay* simply won't work. You can thank the programmers at Macromedia for coming up with all of these odd capitalization conventions that are so hard to type.

Because ActionScript uses (and allows you to use) such a mixed bag of strange names, it needs a convention that will enable it to recognize where one name ends and the next begins. This convention is known as *dot notation,* and it comes with its own set of rules. In dot notation, the following rules apply:

- All names are separated by dots (periods).

- Dots cannot be used within names.

- A name to the left of a dot is the parent of the name to the right of the dot.

- Object methods appear to the right of the object name, also separated by a dot.

It will be easier for you to understand dot notation by taking a look at an example. In the following, I am using the gotoAndStop method of a movie clip named MyClip to move its playhead to frame 20. But in this case I am calling this method from another movie clip that is in my movie, so I need to fully identify the location of MyClip. Since MyClip is attached to a frame in the main timeline, I can use _root to specify the location because _root is ActionScript shorthand for the lowest level in the movie—just as C:\ would be the lowest level on your main hard drive.

```
_root.MyClip.gotoAndStop(20);
```

It is also possible to address objects that are contained within other objects (as opposed to simply being a part of the main movie). You simply nest the names using dot notation, remembering to start with the highest-level object and work your way inward.

Progress Check

1. What are operators used for in ActionScript?

2. If two names are separated by dots, which name is the parent?

3. What is a looping structure used for in ActionScript?

---

1. Manipulating objects

2. The one on the left of the dot

3. To execute a block of ActionScript statements more than once

Data Type Basics

As you work with ActionScript programs, you will end up using a number of different types of data. Fortunately, using different types of data in ActionScript is easy, since ActionScript is not very strict about data typing (unless you want it to be). In fact, Flash automatically handles any allowable data type without asking you to declare the type of data that a variable may hold.

Many programming languages are known as *strongly typed* languages. This means that before you can use a variable, you must declare the type of data that the variable will hold. Generally, this is done to improve efficiency, since some types of data require more memory to store than do others. When you use variables in ActionScript, you do not have to declare the type of data that the variable can hold. As a result, any ActionScript variable can hold any type of data. Although this programming method is slightly less memory efficient, it is also far easier for most programmers—especially casual ones—to use because you don't generate errors if you forget to declare a variable type, or if you attempt to store a different type of data in a variable. Note, however, that if you publish your movies for Flash Player version 7 or later, Flash MX 2004 allows you to specify the data types for your variables.

Though ActionScript is fairly lax about data types, it is a good idea for you to understand the different types of data that you can use. That way, you can avoid any unpleasant surprises. In the following sections, we will take a quick look at the ActionScript data types that you can use in your movies.

Strings

Strings are the most flexible of all data types. You can store letters, numbers, and punctuation in a string. You enter strings by enclosing them in quotes. (Single or double quotes are acceptable to Flash.)

You can concatenate strings by using a plus sign (+). If you attempt to concatenate a string and a number, Flash simply produces a string result that treats the number as if it were a string. This can be quite handy for building strings using incrementing numbers as a part of the string. For example, if you are loading a series of movie clips, a very effective technique is to number the filenames of the movie clips sequentially. You can then load the movie clips using a *for* loop that builds the filenames by concatenating the value of the loop counter onto the end of the filename.

Although strings can generally hold almost any character, a few characters require some special handling because Flash normally considers these to have special meanings. Here are some of the characters that you must enter using a special notation:

- **Backslash**   Enter as \\
- **Backspace**   Enter as \b
- **Carriage return**   Enter as \r

- **Double quote**   Enter as \"
- **Form feed**   Enter as \f
- **Line feed**   Enter as \n
- **Single quote**   Enter as \'
- **Tab**   Enter as \t

Numbers

Flash treats all numbers as double-precision, floating-point numbers. As a result, all mathematical calculations are done with a high level of accuracy. Double-precision, floating-point numbers require more memory than other types of numerical values, and they also can be a little slower to use in calculations, but since few Flash movies rely on heavy mathematical calculations, you aren't likely to notice the negative impact.

When you want to perform mathematical calculations, you should make use of the Math object, shown here. The Math object has a large range of built-in methods that enable you to manipulate values easily. You simply call the Math object method with the number you are passing as an argument, and the method returns the appropriate value.

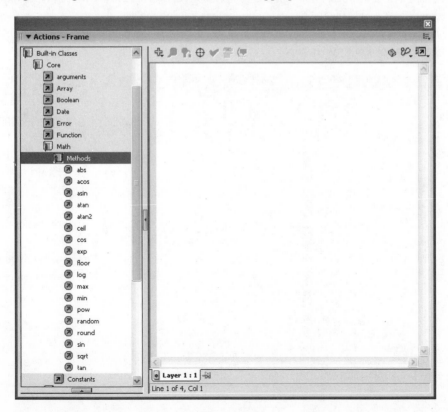

Boolean

The Boolean data type is a quite simple one. Boolean values can be either *true* or *false,* and they are generally the result of a conditional test.

TIP

You can also treat the Boolean value of true as equal to 1, and the Boolean value of false as equal to 0.

There is also a Boolean object that you can use, but generally speaking you are free to use the Boolean data type without resorting to any complicated processes.

Movie Clips

The movie clip data type is actually there for your convenience. This data type enables you to use the methods of the movie clip object to control instances of movie clip symbols in your movies.

Both the movie clip data type and the object data type are a little different in operation from the other data types. Although this has little effect on you, these two data types reference a memory area where the data is stored rather than storing the actual data.

Here is an example of using the movie clip data type to obtain the total number of bytes that are contained in a movie clip:

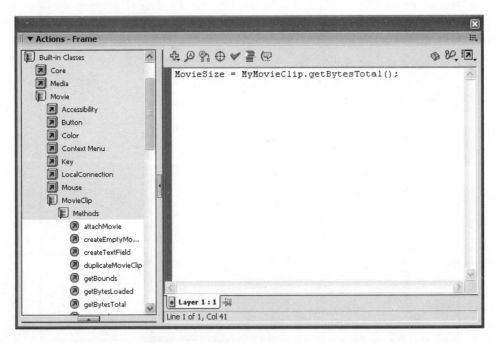

Objects

The object data type is a rather complex data type because it is essentially free-form. That is, the object data type is a custom data type that you define when you want to create an object that does not really fit into any other category. It's unlikely that you will find much use for this data type unless you become a very advanced Flash developer.

When you create a custom object, you must define everything about that object. Every property and method that you want the object to possess must be defined. To learn more about this process, I recommend reading the "Using Custom Objects" topic in the ActionScript Reference Manual.

Arrays

Arrays are not actually one of the ActionScript data types, but they do provide you with a very handy way to store and access data. You might think of arrays as a way to organize information in a very flexible structure in which each piece of information is stored using an index number. To refer to any element of the array, you simply supply the proper index number and access the information.

The Array object has a number of methods that you can use for various purposes. For example, you can easily add a new element to the end of an array using the push method, and you can obtain the final element of the array using the pop method. You can even create a string from all of the array elements using the join method.

NOTE

Arrays are beyond the scope of this book. You may want to refer to my book *Macromedia Flash MX 2004: The Complete Reference, Second Edition* for more information.

Progress Check

1. How do you tell Flash that you are creating a string?

2. How many different Boolean values can there be?

---

1. Enclose the string in quotes.
2. Two: true or false

Project 12-1 Adding Simple ActionScript to a Movie

Now that you have learned some of the basic concepts of ActionScript, it is time to see how you can use some simple ActionScript statements to improve your movies. For example, you will learn how to make your movies stop playing when they reach the end of the timeline rather than repeating endlessly. You will also see how some simple ActionScript programming can control the flow of the playback as your movie is playing so that you are no longer limited to following a strictly linear path from the beginning to the end of the timeline. Now you will have the choice of moving the playhead under program control so that your movie plays the way you want.

Step by Step

1. Open a new, blank Flash movie.

2. Click the Oval tool to select it.

3. Draw a circle near the upper-left corner of the stage.

4. Click the Arrow tool to select it.

5. Double-click the circle so that the fill and the stroke are both selected.

6. Select Modify | Group to group the circle.

7. Click frame 15 in the timeline to select the frame.

8. Use the Insert | Timeline | Keyframe command to add a keyframe to frame 15.

9. Drag the circle to the middle of the bottom edge of the stage.

10. Click the tween frames to select them.

11. Use the Insert | Timeline | Create Motion Tween command to add a motion tween to the selected frames.

12. Click frame 30 in the timeline.

13. Select Insert | Timeline | Keyframe to add a keyframe to frame 30.

14. Click frame 45.

15. Add a keyframe to frame 45.

16. With frame 45 selected, drag the circle to the upper-right corner of the stage.

17. Click the frames between frame 30 and frame 45.

18. Use the Insert | Timeline | Create Motion Tween command to add a motion tween to these frames. This shows an onion skin view of how your timeline and stage should look now:

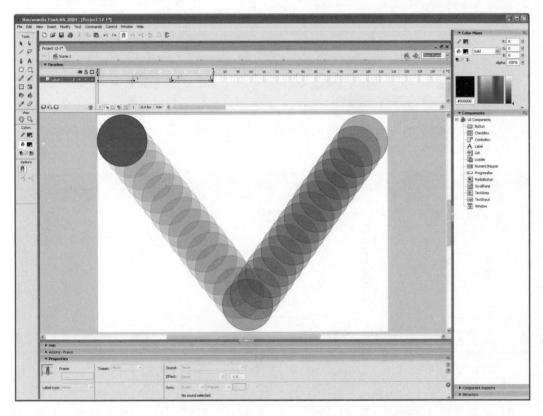

19. Use the Control | Test Movie command to test your movie. At this point, the ball moves down from the left, sits there a while, and then moves up to the right. Clearly, this is not a very convincing bouncing motion.

20. Return to the Flash development environment to continue developing the movie.

21. Click the Insert Layer button to add a new layer for some ActionScript statements to control your movie.

22. Double-click the name of the new layer and name it **Actions** to make the purpose of the layer clear.

23. Click frame 15 in the Actions layer to select it.

(continued)

24. Add a keyframe to frame 15 in the Actions layer.

25. Click frame 30 in the Actions layer.

26. Add a keyframe to frame 30 in the Actions layer.

27. Click frame 15 in the Actions layer again.

28. Select Window | Development Panels | Actions to open the Actions panel.

29. In the Actions panel, double-click gotoAndPlay in the Timeline Control category to add the gotoAndPlay action to the script window (the right pane).

30. In the parameters area, enter **30**, as shown here. This will make the playhead move to frame 30 immediately when it reaches frame 15.

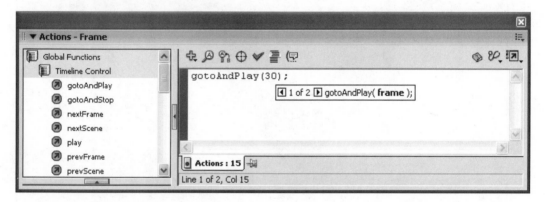

31. Click frame 45 in the Actions layer.

32. Double-click the Stop function in the Actions panel to add it to the script window, as shown here. The Stop action does not accept any parameters and simply stops the movie from playing.

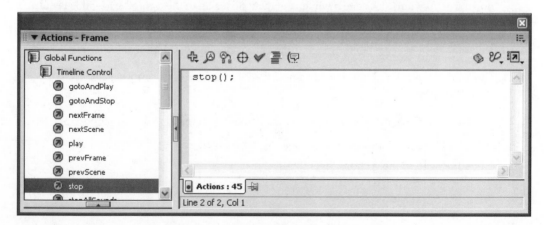

33. Test your movie again using the Control | Test Movie command. Now the ball should bounce without pausing at the bottom of the stage and stop when it reaches the upper-right corner. This shows how your completed movie should look:

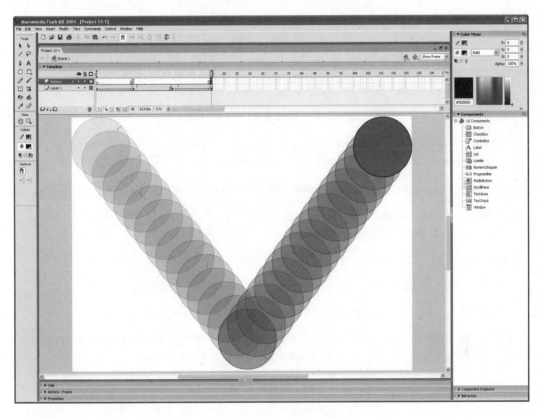

Project Summary

In this project, you learned how to apply some simple ActionScript statements to your movie so that you could gain control over the playback. You saw that even with just a few clicks, you could make a rather big change in the way the movie looked during playback. You will use these same techniques extensively to control your own Flash movies in the future.

Module 12 Mastery Check

1. ActionScript is an _____-oriented programming language.

2. The programming language that ActionScript is most closely related to is called _____.

3. The characteristics of objects that you can examine and modify are called _____.

4. You use the _____ panel to add ActionScript statements to your Flash movies.

5. When you see an ActionScript statement that uses dot notation, the item to the _____ of the dot is the parent of the item on the other side of the dot.

6. The _____ category contains the ActionScript commands you use in Flash movies.

7. When you want to add ActionScript statements to the timeline, you must add them to a _____ in the timeline.

8. The _____ action causes the playback to end immediately.

9. To execute a block of ActionScript statements several times in a row, you use a _____.

10. The _____ data type holds letters, numbers, and punctuation.

11. To get help with the syntax as you add ActionScript code to your movies, make certain that the _____ button is clicked.

12. The _____ functions control the movement of the playhead.

13. The _____ functions enable you to send commands to the web browser.

14. _____ are similar to functions, but are invoked using dot notation.

15. _____ values are always true or false.

Module 13

Learning Basic ActionScript Programming

CRITICAL SKILLS

13.1 Understand how to plan your ActionScript program

13.2 Know where to add the ActionScript statements

13.3 Be able to control properties using ActionScript

13.4 Understand how functions and events are related

Y ou can do a lot with just a little ActionScript programming, but you need to understand how to apply ActionScript to your problem if you want to be effective. You need to know, for example, how to plan your program, where to add the ActionScript statements, and how to make ActionScript do what you want. In this module, you will learn some basic ActionScript programming so that you can begin making your Flash movies even more responsive and impressive.

Applying ActionScript

You probably start out a new Flash movie with an idea of what you want to accomplish. It simply makes good sense to have a plan of action so that you aren't simply wasting your time playing around to see what happens. After all, you likely have an idea what you need before you set off for the grocery store, so doing some advance planning isn't really a foreign idea to you.

As you start to develop Flash movies with more complexity, using ActionScript to control parts of the movie becomes more important. Planning what you want to do with your ActionScript programming becomes an integral part of planning your whole movie.

Planning Your Program

Once you get beyond very simple Flash movies with just one or two tweens to add a little animation, it really helps to sit down and plan things before you begin. There are too many possible areas of conflict not to do so. For example, you will want to consider such things as these:

- How many layers do I need to use in order to avoid unwanted interaction between different elements of the movie?

- What timing-related issues do I need to consider? If I am using several different tweens, where should each begin, and how many frames should each cover to achieve the effect I want?

- Do I want to use a preloader to ensure that playback will be smooth even over a slow dial-up connection?

- What types of interaction do I want to include, and which movie elements should provide that interaction?

- How can I create reusable objects and keep my published movie file size as small and efficient as possible?

Adding ActionScript programming to your movie adds a whole new set of considerations to the planning process. You will almost certainly want to give additional thought to these areas when you are thinking about using ActionScript in your movies:

- What do I want to accomplish with ActionScript programming that I could not do otherwise?

- How will my ActionScript affect the flow of the movie, and will it be necessary to organize things differently because of this?

- Which objects need some ActionScript statements attached to them in order to make them function the way I want?

- What are the appropriate places to add my ActionScript statements?

It is important for you to write down the answers to these questions as well as any other considerations that you feel may affect your movie. It may also help for you to draw a flowchart showing how any ActionScript statements may affect the movie. This is especially true if you intend to add ActionScript statements that use conditional logic to send your movie in different directions depending on things that happen when your movie is played. You certainly will want to make sure that none of the ActionScript statements you add will send the movie into an endless loop or something worse. To avoid this, you will need to test the logic at every possible branch point to make certain you haven't forgotten to account for outcomes you weren't expecting.

Though logical tests can produce only one of two possible results, it is very easy to structure a program so that the results you obtain from performing the test are quite different than what you expect. For example, suppose you added the following ActionScript statements to your movie:

```
if (MyName == "Fred") {
MyLast = "Holabird";
}
MyLast = "Jones";
trace (MyName);
trace (MyLast);
```

At first glance, this set of statements appears as though it should set the value of the MyLast variable to Holabird if the MyName variable is equal to Fred, and set MyLast to Jones otherwise. In reality, though, the result will always be that MyLast is set to Jones, as shown next. How can this be? The first line does perform a conditional test and, if MyName is equal to Fred, executes the second line, setting MyLast equal to Holabird. The problem arises when we reach line 4. Here we are setting MyLast equal to Jones regardless of what happened in the conditional test.

This is because there is nothing in our code sample to prevent line 4 from executing, so it is always executed.

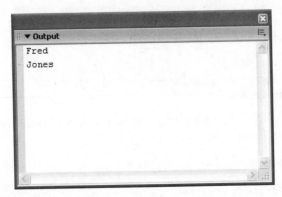

There are several ways to correct this problem. Probably the simplest is to modify the logic by adding an *else* statement, as shown here. This creates a situation where the statement setting MyLast to Jones is executed only if the logical test proves false—rather than always executing it.

```
if (MyName == "Fred") {
MyLast = "Holabird";
} else {
MyLast = "Jones";
}
trace (MyName);
trace (MyLast);
```

As this shows, the simple modification worked:

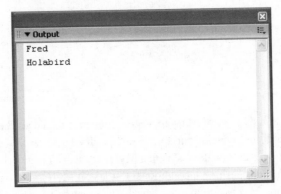

NOTE

These two examples also demonstrate an important tool for helping you determine what is actually happening in your movie. In both cases, the trace actions in the final lines display the value of the MyName and MyLast variables in the Output panel. This is a window that pops up whenever a trace action is encountered in a script while you are testing a Flash movie. The Output panel does not appear when your movie is being played normally in the stand-alone Flash Player or in a web browser window.

Both of these examples were lacking in one important area—there was no mention of just how the MyName variable was initialized. This was done on purpose to demonstrate how you must consider the interactions between all of the elements of your movie. In this case, the intent was to display an input text box in an earlier movie frame, and to ask users to enter their names into that box—and therefore into the MyName variable that you would attach to the input box. The very important point you need to remember here is that even if you get everything correct in one area (the ActionScript programming, in this case), forgetting to plan for other related elements can easily trip you up.

Progress Check

1. Why is it important to step through the logic of your ActionScript programs?

2. Which ActionScript action do you use to display information in the Output panel?

Adding ActionScript to Objects and Frames

One of the areas that Flash developers often find confusing when they start using ActionScript, is deciding where to place the ActionScript statements. Should they be attached to frames in the timeline, or should they be attached to objects such as buttons? And when you attach some ActionScript statements to a button, where do you attach them?

These are good questions, and ones that require some thinking to answer properly. Here are some points you need to consider when determining exactly where you should place your ActionScript statements:

- If an ActionScript statement should be executed automatically when the playhead reaches a specific point in the timeline, you will want to add the ActionScript code to a frame in the timeline.

---

1. To check for logical errors
2. The trace action

- If some ActionScript code is supposed to be triggered by an event such as a mouse click, you will want to attach the ActionScript code to the button symbol instance that the user will click.

- ActionScript code that is attached to a button is always attached to the instance rather than to the main symbol's timeline. This makes it possible for different instances of the same button to perform different actions.

- To control a movie clip instance, you will usually place the ActionScript statements on the movie clip's timeline. Sometimes, however, you may place the ActionScript code on the main timeline or even attach it to a button, depending on what you are attempting to accomplish.

You use the Actions panel to attach ActionScript code both to timeline frames and to objects. In both cases, you open the Actions panel the same way, by selecting Window | Development Panels | Actions.

TIP

Sometimes all the options in the Actions panel are grayed out. This happens when you do not currently have a keyframe or object selected that can accept ActionScript statements. Simply click the keyframe or object where you want to add your ActionScript code to activate the items.

When you open the Actions panel, the title bar of the panel will always indicate where the actions will be applied. This title changes depending on what is selected. It is a good idea to always verify that the panel title is correct for the type of statements that you want to apply.

TIP

When the Actions panel is open, it can cover quite a large area of the screen. To shrink the Actions panel to just its title bar, click the downward-pointing triangle to the left of the panel name. You can use the same technique to redisplay the entire panel. This is often more convenient than closing and reopening the Actions panel.

In Module 12, you also learned that some ActionScript statements are *deprecated*—which means that they are no longer officially supported and should be avoided in your ActionScript programming. These statements remain available primarily to make it possible to support older versions of the Flash Player, but also so that older Flash movies do not need to be rewritten immediately. Macromedia has stated that the deprecated statements may not work in future versions of Flash or the Flash Player, so to make certain you do not encounter this problem, you should avoid using these statements. In every case, there is a more modern, fully supported ActionScript statement that replaces any of the deprecated statements.

Progress Check

1. Where would you attach ActionScript statements that you want to be executed when the user clicks a button?

2. Where would you attach ActionScript statements that must run at a specific time during playback?

CRITICAL SKILL
13.2 Using ActionScript to Control Actions

You will probably use ActionScript functions more than all of the other ActionScript statements put together. In this section, we will look at some of the more basic functions that you are likely to use as you start programming in ActionScript. In this way, you can get a feel for actually using some ActionScript to program your Flash movies.

gotoAndPlay

The gotoAndPlay function is used to move the playhead to a different frame in the timeline and then start playing the movie at that point. You will likely find that gotoAndPlay is one of the most useful of the ActionScript functions since it enables you to play different parts of your movie without simply following the timeline from beginning to end.

gotoAndStop

The gotoAndStop function moves the playhead to a specific frame number or frame label and stops the playback. You would typically use this function when the target frame contained a button that the user could click to resume playback. The most important difference between gotoAndPlay and gotoAndStop is whether the playhead continues to move after the command has been executed.

TIP

If you use either gotoAndPlay or gotoAndStop, it is by far the best to specify a frame label rather than a frame number. Remember, frame labels are adjusted automatically when you add or remove frames from the timeline.

---

1. To a button symbol instance
2. To a keyframe in the main timeline

nextFrame

The nextFrame function moves the playhead one frame to the right and then stops the playback. You cannot specify a particular frame because this function does not accept any arguments.

prevFrame

The prevFrame function moves the playhead one frame to the left and then stops the playback. Like the nextFrame function, the prevFrame function does not accept any arguments, so you cannot use this function to target a specific frame.

play

The play function resumes playback of the movie at the current frame. Typically, you would use this function by attaching it to a button rather than by attaching it to a keyframe. In that way, you could provide users with buttons that they could use to control playback of the movie.

NOTE
The play function does not accept any parameters, so you cannot use it to move the playhead to a different frame. For that purpose, use the gotoAndPlay function.

stop

The stop function stops the playback of the movie. This is another of the functions that you might typically attach to a button so that the user could control the playback. However, this function is also useful in the timeline. For example, you can use the stop function to prevent the movie from looping around back to the start of the movie and playing over again after it finishes its initial playback. The stop function also does not accept any parameters.

stopAllSounds

The stopAllSounds function immediately stops any sounds that are currently playing. This provides the user with a way to mute the soundtrack if you attach this function to a button that the user can click.

It is important to note that this function stops only sounds that are playing when the function is executed. If later frames start a streaming sound, that sound will still play even though the stopAllSounds function has been executed previously. You may want to set a variable when this function is executed, and then check the status of the variable before allowing any further sounds from beginning playback. Otherwise, users will have to click the mute button every time a sound starts in order to have the silence that they are seeking. Remember, you don't want to antagonize your visitors, because then they are far less likely to return to your web site.

The stopAllSounds function does not accept any parameters. The action is applied to whatever sounds may be playing when it is executed.

getURL

You use the getURL function to load a new document from a specific web address. You can use this function for a number of different purposes, including loading another Flash movie.

This function has two optional arguments. The first specifies the type of window or HTML frame in which to display the new document. This argument can take any of the following values:

- *windowname* This is the name of a specific window in which to display the document.
- **_self** This places the document in the current frame.
- **_blank** This places the document in a new window.
- **_parent** This places the document in the parent of the current frame.
- **_top** This places the document in the top-level frame of the current window.

In addition to the window argument, there's also an optional variables argument. You can choose not to send the variables, or you can send them using either the GET or POST method. This can be an effective way to send information from a Flash movie to a server. You can also use a mailto URL to send a message by way of the user's e-mail program.

NOTE

If you send the variables, you send the value of all of the variables in the movie. Depending on the structure of your movie, this may result in your sending far more information than is necessary. A very effective way around this is to use the getURL function from within a movie clip that contains only the variables that you actually want to send.

fscommand

The fscommand function is used to send commands to the Flash Player or the web browser that contains the Flash Player. Most of the commands that you are likely to send would be JavaScript commands. You might, for example, use the following command to play your Flash movie in full-screen mode:

```
fscommand("fullscreen","true");
```

NOTE

If you want to use the fscommand action, be sure to select the Flash with FSCommand template on the HTML tab of the Publish Settings dialog box before you publish your movie. This will add the proper structure to the HTML page so that the command that you send can be executed properly.

loadMovie

The loadMovie function is used to load additional Flash movies. These can be replacements for an existing loaded movie, or they can be additional movies. This function can be very handy if you want to provide the user the option to select particular movies, or if you want to play certain movies according to some condition such as the day of the week.

The loadMovie function has two different formats. These are

- **loadMovie**   You use this format when you want to specify a target movie clip that will be replaced by the new movie clip.

- **loadMovieNum**   You use this format when you want to specify a level on which to load the new movie clip. When you use this format, the new movie does not replace an existing movie clip unless it happens to be on the specified level.

As with the getURL function, the loadMovie function can also send the contents of the current movie's variables. This might be handy if you wanted to send certain information such as the name of the user so that the new movie would also know who was viewing the movie. Other applications of this might be to save the scores of a game or even (with an awful lot of ingenuity on your part) to create a shopping cart.

If you use the first form of the function, loadMovie, the new movie clip that is loaded will occupy the same position as the movie that it is replacing. In addition, it will inherit the same rotation and scale properties as the existing movie. This does not mean, however, that it will necessarily be the same size unless the two movies started out at the same size. Of course, if you use the default size for your Flash movies, this will be the case.

If you use the second form of the function, loadMovieNum, you can load multiple movies by loading them into different level numbers. Keep in mind, though, that whichever movie is loaded into level 0 sets the frame rate, background color, and frame size for all the movies. Also, if you load a new movie into level 0, it will replace the current movie and will unload all the movies that you have loaded onto other levels.

unloadMovie

The unloadMovie function unloads the movie that you specify from memory. You can specify the movie to unload by name or by level number. Once you unload the movie, it can no longer be played.

You may wonder why you might want to use this function. The reason is simple: to free up memory for better performance of the Flash Player. When too many movies are loaded, the Flash Player may require too many resources on the system that is playing your movies.

TIP

The unloadMovie function is especially important if you are developing Flash movies for a platform such as the Pocket PC. Using this function when a movie is no longer needed can have a major positive influence on the performance of the Flash Player.

on

The final function we will look at is labeled "on." In reality, this is not a function; it is a convenient way for you to access the mouse event handler that you can wrap around a block of the ActionScript statements. This function is an object action rather than one that you can add to a keyframe in the timeline.

Notice that there are several different mouse events that you can use to trigger your ActionScript statements (as shown next). In fact, you could select all of the mouse events if you wanted to, but this would make for rather confusing behavior. To select additional mouse events (or key presses), enter a comma between the events.

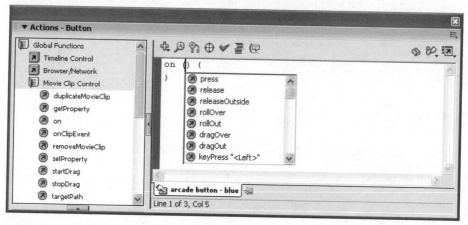

NOTE

In versions of Flash before Flash MX 2004, you did not need to select the mouse event handler, because Flash automatically added this event handler whenever you added actions to a button symbol instance. Flash MX 2004 no longer adds the event handler automatically, so you must remember to add it manually. If you forget to add the event handler when it is needed, you will see an error message in the Output panel when you test your movie or when you click the Check Syntax button in the Actions panel.

Ask the Expert

Q: I tried to test my movie, but instead of playing the movie, the Output panel popped up with a bunch of error messages. What can I do?

A: When you tried to test your movie, Flash identified one or more lines as containing errors. If you cannot figure out how to correct the errors, you can either delete the offending lines or convert them into comments. To convert a line into a comment, add two forward slashes (//) at the beginning of the line. You should also get in the habit of clicking the Check Syntax button whenever you have finished entering a complete block of code. That way, you can find any errors before your movie grows so large that correcting any errors becomes a major task.

Q: When I added a gotoAndPlay function to my script window, I wanted to specify a frame label rather than a frame number, but I guess I must have mistyped the label because I got an error when I tested my program. How can I avoid this?

A: A simple way to avoid these types of errors is to use the copy-and-paste method. Copy the label name from the Properties panel, and then paste it into the argument in the Actions panel. This avoids typing errors and ensures that you are using a valid frame label in the ActionScript statement.

Progress Check

1. Which functions can you use to send the playhead to a specific frame?

2. Which basic functions can send variable information across the Internet?

---

1. gotoAndPlay and gotoAndStop
2. getURL and loadMovie are the most common.

CRITICAL SKILL
13.3 # Using ActionScript to Control Properties

In addition to using ActionScript functions, you will almost certainly need to use ActionScript to control object properties. Controlling properties is not all that different from using ActionScript functions, but there are some subtle variations in the techniques you will use to accomplish your goals.

Understanding Which Properties You Can Set

It is important to remember that some properties are read-only, so any attempt to set the property will fail. For example, you cannot move the mouse pointer under program control, so attempting to set either the _xmouse or _ymouse property will not accomplish anything useful. You can determine if a property is read-only by checking the ActionScript Dictionary in the Help panel. All of the properties can be read, of course, even if they cannot be set.

It can be a little difficult to locate all of the ActionScript properties in Flash MX 2004. The Actions panel does not have a separate category specifically for properties (and there are too many properties to list here), so it helps to understand a few of the tricks for identifying properties. First, you may want to open the ActionScript Dictionary in the Help panel. Then, open the ActionScript Dictionary Overview and click the Contents Of The Dictionary item, as shown here. As you scroll down the contents, you will find an alphabetical listing of the ActionScript dictionary contents.

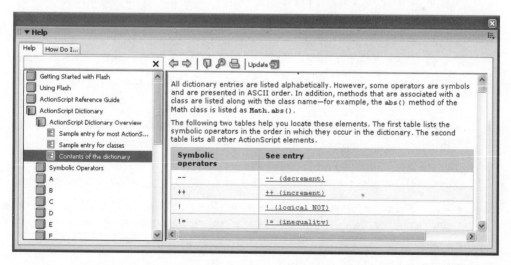

As you look through the ActionScript dictionary contents, you will notice a number of listings that begin with an underscore (such as _alpha). If you click the link to view the help content for these items, you will see that nearly all of them are properties. As you go further down the listing, you will find a number of additional properties that are specific to certain types of objects. To identify which of the entries are object properties, look in the See Entry column. There you will find the object name, a dot, and then the property name with nothing behind the property name. Entries that are followed by a set of parentheses—()—are methods, not properties.

NOTE

A few properties are actually global properties. That is, when you set the value of a property such as the _quality property, the new setting applies to all movies rather than to a single, named movie clip instance.

Here is a listing of some properties that you will find useful:

- **_alpha**   This is the transparency value. The effective range is 0 (transparent) to 100 (opaque), but you can use values outside this range to delay a transparency effect (since only values between 0 and 100 will have a visible effect). Movie clip instances that are transparent are still active.

- **_currentframe**   This is the read-only current frame number of the movie clip's playhead.

- **_droptarget**   This is the read-only name of the movie clip instance where the specified movie clip instance was dropped. Unfortunately, this property is returned using the slash notation from earlier versions of Flash, so you must use the eval function to convert the result into dot notation.

- **_focusrect**   This is a global property that determines if the button that has the focus is surrounded by a yellow rectangle to make it easier for the user to see the active button.

- **_framesloaded**   This is a read-only property that specifies how many of the movie clip's frames have been loaded.

- **_height**   This is the height of the movie clip in pixels. You can both read and set this property.

- **_highquality**   This is a global property that sets the quality of the anti-aliasing that is applied to all movies. You can set this to 0, 1, or 2, with 2 being the highest quality setting.

- **_name**   This is the instance name property of the movie clip. Since you need to know the instance name to access this property, there is really no good reason to use this property.

- **_quality**   This is a global property that is similar to the _highquality property. You can set this property to LOW, MEDIUM, HIGH, or BEST.

- **_rotation**   This property is used to rotate the movie clip instance a specified number of degrees.

- **_soundbuftime**   This is a global property that sets the number of seconds of streaming sound to download before the movie begins playing. The default value is five seconds, which may be inadequate if the user is accessing the Internet via a slow dial-up connection or if there is heavy traffic reducing download performance.

- **_target**   This is a read-only property that specifies the complete target path to the movie clip instance.

- **_totalframes**   This is a read-only property that specifies the total number of frames in the movie clip.

- **_url**   This read-only property specifies the complete URL of the movie clip; it is essentially the same as the _target property.

- **_visible**   This is a Boolean property that determines if the movie clip instance is visible or not. Movie clip instances that are invisible are inactive.

- **_width**   This property specifies the width of the movie clip instance in pixels; it is related to the _height property.

- **_x**   This property specifies the horizontal distance in pixels of the movie clip's registration point (usually the upper-left corner) from the left edge of the stage. If the movie clip is contained within another movie clip and the parent movie clip is rotated, this value still represents the distance from the same corner of the parent movie clip even though the coordinate system is rotated.

- **_xmouse**   This is the read-only x coordinate of the mouse pointer in pixels.

- **_xscale**   This property specifies a percentage to scale the movie clip instance horizontally.

- **_y**   This property specifies the vertical distance in pixels of the movie clip's registration point from the top edge of the stage. The same conditions regarding rotation of the parent movie clip apply as in the case of the _x property.

- **_ymouse**   This is the read-only y coordinate of the mouse pointer in pixels.

- **_yscale**   This property specifies a percentage to scale the movie clip instance vertically.

Progress Check

1. What are global properties?

2. What are read-only properties?

---

1. Properties that apply to all movies
2. Properties you can view but not modify

Setting Movie Clip Instance Properties

You can set the properties of movie clip instances using dot notation and an expression, or you can use the setProperty action to accomplish the task. Either method accomplishes the task equally well, so it is a matter of personal preference on your part. I happen to feel that using dot notation and an expression is slightly more intuitive.

NOTE

In most cases, you can set properties only for named movie clip instances. (You use the Instance panel to name movie clip instances.) The one exception to this rule is if you are setting the property using ActionScript statements that are contained with the movie clip instance itself. In that case, you can use the special name "this" to refer to the movie clip instance.

Setting a movie clip instance property using dot notation and an expression is very similar to setting the value of a variable. In fact, the only functional difference between the two processes is the way that you refer to the movie clip instance using dot notation.

Imagine that you have a movie clip instance named MyClip, and that you want to rotate that movie clip instance 45 degrees whenever the user clicks a button. The following ActionScript example shows how you would go about doing so:

```
on (release) {
MyClip._rotation += 45;
}
```

As this example shows, it is very easy to modify the properties of a movie clip instance. What you may not have expected, though, was the += operator that was used in this case. This operator is known as the *addition assignment* operator. It works by adding the value to the right of the operator to the current value of the expression to the left of the operator. The idea here is that you don't want to set the _rotation property to be equal to 45; you want to increase its value by 45. You will learn more about using the ActionScript operators in Module 14.

It is also just as easy to store the original value of a property so that it can restore the value later, if necessary. To do so, simply assign the current value to a variable, as shown here:

```
originalRotation = MyClip._rotation;
```

CRITICAL SKILL
13.4 Understanding Functions and Event Handlers

Before we conclude this module and move on to the project, let's take a few moments to make certain that you clearly understand two of the more important elements of using ActionScript. Functions and event handlers are parts of ActionScript that you will use in almost every case where you add ActionScript code to a Flash movie, so it is vital that you clearly understand how these language elements work.

Functions

ActionScript functions are what might be called "commands" in some other programming languages. When you use a function such as gotoAndPlay, you are issuing a command to the Flash Player that tells it how you want your movie to be played. Functions cause something to happen immediately when they are executed.

Functions can be attached to keyframes in a timeline, or they can be attached to an object. Where you attach a function has a direct bearing on how (and when) the function is executed:

- If a function is attached to a keyframe, the function is executed when the playhead reaches the keyframe—unless you are using a conditional test that may modify the program flow depending on the results of the test.

- If a function is attached to an object, the function is executed only when the proper event occurs. This is determined by the event handler options you have selected.

Event Handlers

Event handlers function something like traffic signals. That is, a function that is controlled by an event handler can be executed only when the event handler gives the function a go signal. Otherwise, the function will simply sit there and may never be executed.

There are two types of event handlers in ActionScript:

- Buttons use the *on* mouse event handler so that they can respond to mouse events (or keystrokes).

- Movie clips use the onClipEvent handler.

Learning Basic ActionScript Programming

Both types of event handlers can respond to some of the same types of events, but the onClipEvent handler has some additional options, as shown next. The onClipEvent handler can also respond to the movie clip instance being loaded or unloaded, the playhead entering the frame, or to data.

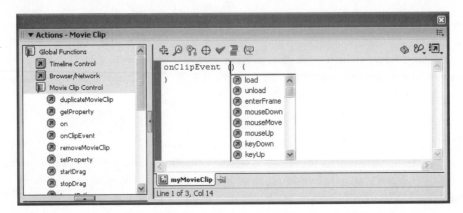

The important thing to remember about event handlers is that they don't actually do anything themselves. They are simply there to provide a trigger to execute some ActionScript code that you have added to an object. But without the proper event, the actions that the event handler is supposed to trigger will never be executed.

Project 13-1 Using Simple ActionScript to Control Movie Flow

Now it is time to apply the knowledge that you gained in this module to actually begin using ActionScript to control your movies. In this project, you will apply some ActionScript code that uses a conditional test to determine how the movie should proceed. This is a technique that you will use quite often in your own Flash movies, so it is important that you understand how you can use conditional tests for this purpose.

Step by Step

1. Open a new, blank Flash movie.

2. Click frame 10 in the timeline to select it.

3. Select Insert | Timeline | Blank Keyframe to add a keyframe to frame 10.

4. Click the Text tool to select it.

5. Draw a text box on the stage, and enter **Frame 10** in the text box.

6. Click frame 20.

7. Insert a blank keyframe at frame 20.

8. Draw a text box and enter **Frame 20** in the text box.

9. Click frame 1 to select it.

10. Select the Window | Other Panels | Common Libraries | Buttons command to open the Buttons library.

11. Drag two instances of a button symbol onto the stage. Make certain they are not overlapping.

12. Click the Insert Layer button to add a layer for your ActionScript statements. You may want to name this layer **Actions** to identify its purpose.

13. Click frame 1 in the Actions layer.

14. Open the Actions panel using the Window | Development Panels | Actions command.

15. Double-click the *if* statement to add it to the script window. You will find this action in the Conditions/Loops subcategory of the Statements category.

16. In the parameters for the *if* statement, enter **MyVar == 1** as the condition to test.

17. Move the insertion point to the end of the line, and press ENTER to move down to the second line.

18. Double-click the gotoAndStop function to add it to the second line in the script window.

19. Enter **10** in the parameters for the gotoAndStop function.

20. Move the insertion point to the end of the line, and press ENTER to move down to the third line.

21. Double-click the *else if* statement to add it to the third line in the script window.

22. In the parameters for the *if* statement, enter **MyVar == 2** as the condition to test.

23. Move the insertion point to the end of the line, and press ENTER to move down to the fourth line.

24. Double-click the gotoAndStop function to add it to the fourth line in the script window.

(continued)

13

Learning Basic ActionScript Programming

Project 13-1

Using Simple ActionScript to Control Movie Flow

25. Enter **20** in the parameters for the gotoAndStop function. The Actions panel should now look like this:

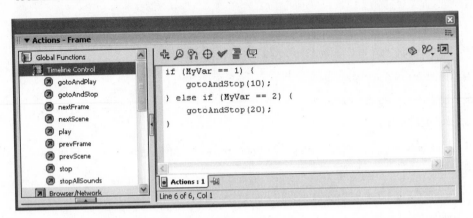

26. Click frame 2 in the Actions layer.

27. Select Insert | Timeline | Keyframe to add a keyframe to frame 2 of the Actions layer.

28. Double-click the gotoAndPlay function to add it to the script window.

29. Enter **1** in the parameters for the gotoAndPlay function.

30. Click the Arrow tool to select it.

31. Click one of the button instances in frame 1. The Actions panel title bar should now say "Actions - Object."

32. In the script pane, enter **MyVar = 1**.

33. Click the other button instance.

34. In the script pane, enter **MyVar = 2**.

35. Use the File | Save command to save your work.

36. Select Control | Test Movie to test your movie. Clicking the button that sets the MyVar variable to 1 should display the frame 10 message, while clicking the other button should display the frame 20 message.

37. Close the test window. You will need to close the test window before you can test the movie again.

Project Summary

In this project, you learned how to use ActionScript statements to do conditional tests and how to make Flash respond appropriately to the results by branching to the correct place in the timeline. In addition, you learned how to add ActionScript statements to buttons so that those buttons could provide controls for your movie. You will no doubt find many uses for these techniques in your Flash movies. Of course, you would probably want to do something more useful than simply display a message indicating where the playhead was, and you would probably want to add labels to your buttons to indicate their purpose, but you now know the basics and can easily make these types of modifications on your own.

✓

Module 13 Mastery Check

1. To add ActionScript statements that must run at a specific time in your movie, you add those statements to _____.

2. To check for errors in the ActionScript statements, click the _____ button in the Actions panel.

3. You must add an _____ when you add ActionScript statements to a button.

4. You cannot modify properties that are _____.

5. Properties that apply to all movie clips are _____ properties.

6. Obsolete ActionScript statements are also known as _____ statements.

7. Conditional tests always produce a _____ result.

8. The actions that control the flow of the movie are found in the _____ subcategory.

9. gotoAndStop and play are examples of ActionScript _____.

10. The _____ function can be used to create a mute button.

11. You use the _____ handler to make movie clips respond to events.

12. You can use the _____ function to move the playhead to the next frame in the timeline.

13. To add ActionScript statements that are triggered by events, you typically add those statements to _____.

14. To avoid the problem of sending the playhead to the wrong frame if your timeline is altered, you should use _____ rather than frame numbers as arguments.

15. To control a movie clip instance from the main timeline, you must assign an _____ to the movie clip.

Module 14

Learning More ActionScript Programming

Y ou have already learned that ActionScript is a powerful programming language that enables you to accomplish a lot with little effort. In this module, you will learn more about using ActionScript to add features to your Flash movies that simply could not be added any other way. By the end of this module, you will know enough about ActionScript programming to create the ActionScript programs you want on your own.

CRITICAL SKILL
14.1 Understanding ActionScript Versions

As Flash has evolved, the version of ActionScript that is included has evolved, too. The newer versions have added features that were not found in the older versions, and Flash developers have found that the power of ActionScript has grown considerably with each new release.

This evolution has made life both easier and harder for Flash developers. The added power and features in the newer versions have made it possible to do far more with a lot less work. But at the same time, those new features have made it necessary for you to consider your audience more carefully, since using the new features means that people who are using old versions of the Flash Player may not be able to play your movies successfully.

NOTE

When you publish your Flash movies, the HTML web page that Flash generates includes information about the required Flash Player version. Depending on the browser that someone is using, visitors to your web site whose Flash Player is too old may receive a message telling them how to upgrade their Flash Player, or else they may be given the opportunity to simply click a link to automatically make the upgrade. In all cases, the upgrade is both free and quick, so you probably don't have to worry too much about whether users have the correct Flash Player. As you will see shortly, there are a few special cases where an upgrade is not available, but these are fairly rare.

Understanding Deprecated Commands

Before Flash version 5, ActionScript was a considerably different language than it is today. When Flash 5 was introduced, ActionScript was changed into a language that was based on the ECMA-262 standard, making it very similar to JavaScript.

Rather than simply throwing out everything that went before, Macromedia chose to update ActionScript while at the same time maintaining a level of *backward compatibility* so that existing Flash movies containing ActionScript programs could continue to run. To accomplish this, a number of elements of previous versions of ActionScript were demoted to deprecated status. This meant that those statements no longer really fit into the modern ActionScript programming concepts, but that they would still function if they existed in an ActionScript program.

Using deprecated ActionScript statements is a risky proposition. Even though Macromedia has continued to allow the deprecated statements to function up until now, the fact that they are deprecated means that the next version of Flash may not support them. Essentially, Macromedia has given Flash developers a little longer to update their programs and quit using the deprecated statements, but they have warned us that you cannot count on that support in the future.

NOTE

Although Flash MX 2004 officially uses a new version of ActionScript called ActionScript 2, this new version is functionally identical to the version of ActionScript that was introduced in Flash MX for most users. The advanced areas of ActionScript 2 that are really only available to Flash MX Professional 2004 users are beyond the scope of this book.

Determining the Flash Player Version

If certain elements of ActionScript are deprecated, you are probably wondering why anyone would continue to use them. Actually, there are a very few instances where using deprecated statements is not only valid but also quite necessary.

Unfortunately, even though new versions of the Flash Player are available for free download for most platforms, there are a few important exceptions. For example, as this is being written, Macromedia has still not released a version of the Flash Player later than version 6 for the Pocket PC platform. There are similar limitations in the Flash Players for certain other operating systems as well. Eventually this will change, of course, but it is a reality for now.

In addition to the problem of platforms where a newer Flash Player is not available, you also have to consider that some people simply may not want to update their Flash Player. For example, a company may have a list of approved software, and newer versions of the Flash Player may not be on the list.

Understanding Browser Differences

Internet Explorer and Netscape Navigator use different types of Flash Players. Internet Explorer uses an ActiveX control, while Netscape Navigator uses a browser plug-in. As a result, the two browsers require different HTML code on the web page as well as different Flash Players.

If a visitor to your web site uses Internet Explorer, the HTML code on the web page directs Internet Explorer to check for the current version of the Flash Player ActiveX control. If your movie requires a newer version of the Flash Player, Internet Explorer may download the new version automatically (or, depending on their security settings, users will be given the option to download the ActiveX control).

If visitors are using Netscape Navigator, a different part of the HTML code offers to direct the users to the download site where they can obtain the newer version of the Flash Player. Depending on the version of their browser, they may be directed to the specific page for downloading the Flash Player, or they may be directed to a generic Netscape Navigator plug-in download page. Visitors using the Opera web browser will have these same options, since Opera uses Netscape Navigator plug-ins.

NOTE

Regardless of the web browser that someone is using, they can decline the download—which means that your movie will not run. In addition, for some older versions of web browsers, there simply may not be a newer version available.

Checking the Flash Player Version Using ActionScript

As I mentioned earlier, the HTML code on the web page does a rudimentary check for the proper Flash Player version. By using a little ActionScript code in your Flash movie, you can perform a more thorough test. Here is an example of an ActionScript program (adapted from an example that is available on the Macromedia web site) that you can use for this purpose:

```
//Begin by initializing the variables
OSName = "";
MajorVer = "";
MajorRev = "";
MinorRev = "";
//Parse for the operating system
i = 1;
while (substring(eval("$version"), i, 1) ne " ") {
    OSName = OSName add substring(eval("$version"), i, 1);
    i++;
}
//Parse for Player's major version number
i++;
while (substring(eval("$version"), i, 1) ne ",") {
    MajorVer = MajorVer add Number(substring(eval("$version"), i, 1));
    i++;
}
//Parse for Player's major revision number
i++;
while (substring(eval("$version"), i, 1) ne ",") {
    MajorRev = MajorRev add Number(substring(eval("$version"), i, 1));
    i++;
}
//Parse for Player's minor revision number
i++;
```

```
while (substring(eval("$version"), i, 1) ne ",") {
    MinorRev = MinorRev add Number(substring(eval("$version"), i, 1));
    i++;
}
//Display values in Output panel
trace ("Operating system: " + OSName);
trace ("Flash Player version: " + MajorVer);
trace ("Flash Player major revision level: " + MajorRev);
trace ("Flash Player minor revision level: " + MinorRev);
```

TIP

If you try this example, publish your Flash movie as a version 4 movie so that it can be properly run in Flash Player version 4. You can do so by selecting Flash version 4 on the Flash tab of the Publish Settings dialog box.

Once you know what version of the Flash Player is available, you can use that information to work around any problems. For example, you could do a conditional test, and load different versions of your movie depending on the version of the Flash Player that is available. Or, you might develop a generic little movie that runs if an older version of the Flash Player is detected and that tells visitors about all the great things they are missing if they don't apply the update.

TIP

If you need to test your Flash movies using earlier versions of the Flash Player, you can download older versions for testing purposes from the Macromedia web site.

Progress Check

1. What are deprecated statements?

2. Why should you avoid using deprecated statements?

3. When would it be necessary to use deprecated statements?

---

1. ActionScript statements that are no longer fully supported
2. They may not exist in future versions of the Flash Player.
3. When you need to support older versions of the Flash Player

CRITICAL SKILL
14.2 Using More ActionScript Functions

In the last module, you learned how to use a few of the ActionScript statements to provide some enhancements for your Flash movies. Now we will look at a few more examples that will show you some additional ways to use ActionScript.

Using Variables

Imagine for a moment how difficult life would be if there were no way to store information for future use. You wouldn't be able to have a bank account, because there would be no way for the bank to keep track of who owned the money. You wouldn't be able to have a telephone, because the phone company wouldn't have a way to know who had which phone number. I'm sure you can think of many other such absurd examples of how the inability to store information would make modern life impossible.

Computers, of course, are masters at storing information. Your PC probably has copies of e-mail messages that you received weeks or even months ago. It is just as likely that there are many other types of information it is storing as well.

There are probably a number of different ways that you could use stored information in your Flash movies. Consider these possibilities:

● You could store the user's name so that it could be used later in your movie.

● You might want to store the initial values of object properties so that they could easily be restored after they had been modified.

● If you create an interactive game, you might want to keep the current score.

● If you are using a soundtrack, you might want to make note of the user's preference so that later streaming sounds don't suddenly start blasting forth after the user has clicked a mute button.

These are just a few examples of how you might choose to store information in your Flash movies. In each case, you would do so by storing the appropriate values in variables.

NOTE

Flash does not provide a means for you to store information on the user's computer for retrieval during a future visit. That is, Flash does not allow you to store "cookies" on someone's system.

Storing information in variables in a Flash movie makes that information available for as long as the movie is loaded. Once the movie is unloaded, the stored information disappears unless you have sent it using one of the ActionScript actions (such as getURL) that can send information to a web server. Unfortunately, simply sending the information to a URL serves no purpose unless you have built a mechanism on the web server to process that information—and that topic is far beyond the scope of this book.

We will now look at a real-world example of how you can store and use information in a Flash movie. Consider the case of a Flash movie that has a couple of different small sound files that are used as a soundtrack for various portions of the movie. Now suppose that you have set up your movie to have a convenient mute button so that visitors can stop the sounds from playing. You might think that simply using the following ActionScript action attached to a mute button would do the job:

```
stopAllSounds();
```

While this action does, indeed, stop any sounds that are currently playing, it has no effect on sounds that might start at some later point in the movie. Here's where you can put a variable to good use. Rather than simply allowing sounds to play, why not use a conditional test to see if the user has indicated that they don't want sounds? For example, you might add the following ActionScript statement to the first frame of your movie:

```
PlaySounds = 1;
```

Then you could change the ActionScript code on your mute button to the following:

```
stopAllSounds();
PlaySounds = 0;
```

Finally, before any sound began playing, you could check the value of the PlaySounds variable, and play them only if the value was 1. Since you *initialized* the variable by setting its value to 1 in the first frame, this would be the default value. If the user had clicked the mute button at any time, the variable would be set to 0, and you would know that they did not want any more sounds to play.

TIP

You could easily extend this example so that the mute button was actually a toggle. Clicking the button once would turn off all sounds, and clicking it again would re-enable them.

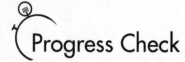

Progress Check

1. Why would you want to initialize a variable?

2. How do you store a cookie with Flash?

Using Conditional Tests

In the previous example, you learned how to set a variable for use in a conditional test. Now we will look a little more closely at how you can set up a conditional test.

In ActionScript, all conditional tests are Boolean tests. This means that there are only two possible outcomes. Either the test proves to be true, or it proves to be false. If the test produces a true result, the statements within the block that follow the test are executed. If the test proves false, the block is skipped and execution continues following the block. Here is the structure of a basic ActionScript conditional test:

```
if (condition) {
//The statements here are executed
//if the test result is true
}
//The execution continues here regardless
```

You may have noticed a problem with the basic conditional test. The statements that follow the block are always executed (unless the block moved the playhead to a different frame). You can work around this problem by adding an *else* block as in:

```
if (condition) {
//The statements here are executed
//if the test result is true
} else {
//This block is executed if the test
//result is false
}
//The execution continues here regardless
```

You can even extend this idea further by nesting additional if tests using the *else...if* structure.

---

1. To make certain that it is defined before it is needed
2. Flash cannot store information on the local system, so cookies cannot be stored.

Now, going back to our mute button example, suppose you had a sound file attached to a movie clip instance named Sound1. At a particular point in the timeline, you could use the following ActionScript statements to determine if the instance should be loaded and played:

```
if (PlaySounds) {
loadMovieNum ("Sound1", 1);
}
```

Notice how simple the conditional test is in this example. If you recall, we used a value of 1 to indicate that the sounds should be played and used 0 to mute them. In ActionScript, a value of 1 is the equivalent of a Boolean true value, and a value of 0 is the equivalent of a Boolean false value.

You could easily argue that the conditional test in this example is too cryptic and therefore too hard to understand at some later point. It would be easy enough to correct this by simply writing the first line of the example as:

```
if (PlaySounds == 1) {
```

TIP

Any computer program can be difficult to understand, and ActionScript programs are certainly not immune to this problem. One very good solution to this is to liberally add comments to your code. Simply add two slashes // and then type whatever comments you feel would be helpful. Comments have no adverse effect on your published movie, since they are stripped out before the movie is published. They do remain in your movie project file so that you can view them in the future, however.

Progress Check

1. What types of values are used in conditional tests?

2. What happens if a conditional test is not followed by an *else* block?

---

1. Boolean
2. The block that follows is automatically executed.

Creating Loops

Now that you understand how powerful a conditional test can be in allowing you to designate specific blocks of ActionScript statements to execute depending on the outcome of certain conditions, we will take a look at a similar type of structure that you will find useful. In this section, we will look at looping structures.

When you set up a block of ActionScript statements that are controlled by an *if* test, the block of statements is executed once if the test result proves true. A looping structure is a similar type of construction, but there is an important difference—the statements within a loop are executed for as long as the conditional test remains true. This produces a very efficient method of repeating a block of statements for as many times as necessary.

NOTE

There is one very important difference between a simple *if* block and a loop. The condition that is used to determine if the loop should execute should be a condition that changes as the loop is executed. Otherwise, the result can be an endless loop where the same block of statements is repeated forever. Needless to say, this is not the type of structure that is desirable, since the end result is generally a computer that is locked up.

ActionScript has four different types of looping actions. In the following sections, we will take a brief look at these four structures.

for

A *for* loop is a very simple type of structure. Here is the basic structure of a *for* loop:

```
for (starting value, test, increment) {
//Place the statements to execute here
}
```

The elements of the *for* loop are as follows:

- **Starting value**   This sets the initial value of the variable that is used in the conditional test. For example, you might specify i = 1 to set the loop counter variable to 1. You can specify any variable name you prefer.

- **Test**   This specifies the conditional test to perform. As long as this test produces a true result, the statements in the loop will be executed. For example, you could test to see that the value is less than 10 using i < 10 as the test.

- **Increment**   This tells Flash how to change the value of the loop counter variable during each pass through the loop. Typically, you would use an operator such as the ++ increment operator, which adds 1 to the value each time. (You'll learn more about the ActionScript operators later in this module.)

It is important to remember that a *for* loop performs the conditional test before the statements in the loop are executed. As a result, it is not a given that the statements will actually be executed.

for...in

A *for...in* loop is quite different from a *for* loop. This type of loop executes once for each element in an array or once for each of the properties of an object. In this type of loop, you do not create a formal conditional test. Rather, Flash performs an internal test on its own to determine how many times to execute the statements in the loop.

The structure of a *for...in* loop looks like this:

```
for (variable in object) {
//Statements to execute
}
```

The variable name you choose is unimportant, since Flash is only using it as a placeholder. The object name is the instance name of the object or the name of the array that you want to process. A typical use for this type of structure is to list all of the elements in an array. Since you don't have to know how many array elements there are in advance, you can execute the loop with the confidence that all of the array elements will be processed.

while

A *while* loop is a type of loop that is fairly similar to a *for* loop. But unlike a *for* loop, a *while* loop places the variable initialization outside of the loop structure and places the burden of remembering to change the value of the variable inside the loop on you. Here is the structure of a *while* loop:

```
while (test) {
//Place the loop statements here
}
```

The conditional test for a *while* loop is the same type of test you use with a *for* loop. The primary differences you need to remember about a *while* loop are these:

- Set the initial value of the variable before the *while* loop begins. This provides you with additional flexibility, since you can use a variable set elsewhere in your Flash movie as the loop controller.

- Change the value of the variable within the statements that are contained in the *while* loop. If you forget to do this, you will create an endless loop that never terminates.

As with a *for* loop, a *while* loop tests the condition before executing the statements in the loop. Therefore, it is entirely possible to create a situation where the statements in the loop will never be executed.

Ask the Expert

Q: I'm having trouble deciding which type of loop to use. How should I make that choice?

A: You should start by considering several factors. First, if you intend to use the value of an existing variable rather than one you create within the loop itself, you'll want to use a *while* or a *do...while* loop. Second, you need to determine if the statements in the loop must always be executed at least once, or if they should be skipped if the first pass through the conditional test is false. A *do...while* loop always executes the statements at least once.

Q: I want to test a value and jump to another frame if the test proves true. But if I follow the *if* block with a gotoAndPlay statement to jump back to the top of the frame and try again, Flash seems to lock up. What is wrong and how can I fix it?

A: When you use a gotoAndPlay statement that jumps to the current frame, Flash has a hard time understanding exactly what you want. To avoid this, add a keyframe to the next timeline frame, and then jump back to the current frame from there.

do...while

A *do...while* loop is very similar to a *while* loop, except that the statements in a *do...while* loop are always executed at least once, since they are executed before the conditional test is performed. Here is the structure of a *do...while* loop:

```
do {
//Place the block of statements here
} while (test);
```

As with a *while* loop, a *do...while* loop requires that you initialize the variable before the loop and that you modify the variable's value within the loop.

Progress Check

1. What happens if you do not change the value of the loop variable in a *while* loop?

2. What type of loop should you create if you want to be certain the loop executes at least once?

---

1. You create an endless loop.
2. A *do...while* loop

CRITICAL SKILL
14.3 Using ActionScript Operators

Operators provide a convenient shorthand method of specifying different types of operations that you want Flash to perform. Using the proper operator can make your ActionScript code far more compact and efficient. For example, the following two ActionScript statements produce exactly the same result:

```
MyVar = MyVar + 1;
MyVar++;
```

The ActionScript operators fall into several different categories. These can be broken down into the following general areas:

- **Arithmetic**   These operators perform simple mathematical operations such as addition and subtraction.

- **Assignment**   These operators assign new values to variables.

- **Bitwise**   These operators manipulate numbers as 32-bit binary values.

- **Comparison**   These operators compare values in a number of different ways, such as determining if one value is less than another value.

- **Logical**   These operators compare Boolean values, thus allowing you to create complex conditional tests that compare more than two values.

- **Miscellaneous**   These operators perform various actions that simply don't fit into any of the other categories.

You are probably already pretty familiar with the way the arithmetic and comparison operators work. These categories of operators are virtually identical to the equivalents that you likely learned about in math classes. The bitwise operators are a class of operators that you are unlikely to use unless you start doing some pretty fancy mathematical operations in your Flash movies. Therefore, it makes the most sense to look at examples of how you can use some of the operators that may not be familiar to you.

Progress Check

1. What type of operator would you use if you wanted to perform more than one test in a single statement?

2. What type of operator enables you to check to see if two values are equal?

---

1. A logical operator
2. A comparison operator

Using Logical Operators

The logical operators make it possible for you to combine two or more conditional tests into a single ActionScript statement. This can make for some pretty efficient ActionScript code, since a single statement can do the work of a number of statements. For example, look at this sample of ActionScript code:

```
if (x < 10) {
    if (y > 5) {
        gotoAndPlay (100);
    }
}
```

In this case, I have nested two *if* statements to test if the value of x is less than 10 and then to test if the value of y is greater than 5. If both tests prove true, the gotoAndPlay statement is executed. By using a logical operator, I could combine the two tests and end up with more compact code, as shown here:

```
if (x < 10 && y > 5) {
    gotoAndPlay (100);
}
```

Now imagine how many lines of nested code you would need if you wanted to test four different values. By using logical operators, I can still write the entire block in three lines, as shown here:

```
if (x < 10 && y > 5 && a == 1 && b <= 3) {
    gotoAndPlay (100);
}
```

In addition to the logical AND operator (&&), you can also use the logical OR (||) and logical NOT (!) operators in any combination necessary to produce the results you need.

TIP

You may need to use parentheses to group the tests when you are using logical operators. Any expressions within a set of parentheses are treated as a single result that is evaluated before the expressions outside of the parentheses.

Using Assignment Operators

ActionScript has a number of operators in this category that are used to both manipulate a variable and assign it a new value. For example, both of the following lines of ActionScript code increase the value of a variable named HighScore by 25:

```
HighScore = HighScore + 25;
HighScore += 25;
```

One of the hidden benefits of using the assignment operators in this way is that you reduce the potential for errors in your ActionScript statements. Suppose, for example, that I made the following typing error in the first format:

```
HighScore = HigScore + 25;
```

Since the correct variable name is "HighScore," not "HigScore," this typing error could result in my ActionScript program not working correctly because the HigScore variable would be undefined. This type of error is hard to spot, and it is even more difficult to find when you discover that your ActionScript is not working as you had expected. Remember that Flash has no way to determine if you have made a typing error on a variable name, so this would not be considered a syntax error. As a result, Flash would not flag this as an error, and you would be left on your own to determine just what was wrong.

Progress Check

1. What is the operator you use to check to see if either of two tests produced a true result?

2. Which operator would you use to test if two values were exactly equal?

Using Additional Functions in ActionScript

If you have ever used a spreadsheet program, you are familiar with the concept of functions. The built-in ActionScript functions are not identical to the various mathematical functions that you would find in a spreadsheet, but the basic idea is similar. Essentially, functions provide a means to accomplish certain tasks without the requirement that you program them yourself.

Using Built-in Functions

The built-in functions make it easy for you to access information and perform some specialized tasks. For example, you can use the getProperty function to access the properties of objects. As an alternative to the example shown earlier in this module, you could use the getVersion function to determine the Flash Player version that is in use. If you are creating an interactive

---

1. A logical OR operator (||)
2. The equivalence operator (==)

game in Flash, you will probably use the hitTest function to determine if two objects have collided.

Many functions take arguments. These represent the information that the function needs in order to do its work. For example, the following ActionScript statement uses the getProperty function to determine if a movie clip instance is visible. This function requires two arguments—the instance name of the object and the property that you want to examine.

```
CanSee = getProperty (MyClip1, _visible);
```

As this example shows, the results that are returned by functions are often assigned to a variable. In fact, it is a good idea to save the current value of a property before you set it to a different value, and saving the current value in a variable is the way that you do this.

If you do not enter the correct number of arguments, you may create a problem that shows up when you attempt to run your movie. If a required argument is not specified, the value of that argument is undefined, and the results will be unpredictable. If you specify too many arguments, Flash will simply toss out the excess information. This can mean that your movie may not be processing information that you expected it to be processing.

Using Custom Functions

In addition to using the built-in functions, you can create your own custom functions. This is something you might do if you were going to use the same calculations a number of times in a movie—by creating your own custom function, you make it far easier to perform those calculations.

Custom functions do not have to be complex. Often they are used to perform a fairly simple calculation. For example, suppose you wanted to calculate the shipping charge on items that people were buying from your web site. You might have several different places where that same calculation would be used, and you would (of course) want the calculation to always come out the same no matter where it was done. By using a custom function, you could be sure that the calculation was always performed exactly the same way.

To create a custom function, you use the function statement followed by a definition of the function, as shown here:

```
function Shipping(OrderTotal) {
    return  OrderTotal * .05;
}
```

Then, to call your function and obtain the result, you call the function by name, passing any necessary arguments, as shown here:

```
ShipAmt = Shipping(OrderAmt);
```

Notice that you do not have to use the same argument names when you call the function that you used when you defined the function. All Flash cares about is that you pass the proper arguments, regardless of their names.

TIP

You may want to create your own library of custom functions for reuse in your Flash movies. That way, you won't have to re-create them every time you want to use them in a new movie.

Progress Check

1. What happens if you don't include enough arguments in a function call?

2. What happens if you include too many arguments in a function call?

Setting Properties

You have seen several examples of using ActionScript statements to set object properties. Any property that is not read-only can be set using ActionScript. All properties can be read, of course.

You can set properties using the setProperty action, or you can do so directly using dot notation. Using dot notation seems a little more straightforward, but either way will work.

It can sometimes be a little confusing to determine the best way to set a property. Let me show you an example. Imagine that you have a movie clip instance on the stage that is named MyCB. You can examine the _x and _y properties of the movie clip instance to determine the x and y coordinates of the instance. Now, suppose you want to create a one-frame movie that uses ActionScript statements to move the movie clip instance across the stage as the movie continues to loop through the frame. You might reasonably expect that the following ActionScript statement would move the instance horizontally across the stage:

```
MyCB._x = MyCB._x + 10;
```

Although this statement appears to be correct, you would soon find that the movie clip wasn't moving as you had expected. Why is this so? Remember that this is a single-frame movie, and each time the movie loops back to frame 1, the movie clip instance is restored to its

---

1. The results will be undefined and cause an error.
2. The extra arguments are ignored.

original position. There is, however, a way around the problem. If you create a separate variable, increment its value, and add that value to the _x property value, the movie clip will move as you intended. Here is how to modify the ActionScript code to accomplish this:

```
Step += 10;
MyCB._x = MyCB._x + Step;
```

If you try this set of ActionScript statements, you will find that the movie clip instance does move across the stage. The important point to take away from this example is that you need to consider more than what appears in your ActionScript statements—the entire Flash movie can have an influence on how your ActionScript code actually works.

TIP

Although the _x property is a pretty straightforward property to understand, it is easy to become confused by the corresponding _y property. The reason for this is simple—Flash uses the upper-left corner of the stage as the 0, 0 point. Therefore, moving a movie clip instance upward results in lower—not higher—values of the _y property. You must keep this in mind as you work with these properties in your movies.

In the previous examples, we have assumed that the ActionScript statements that were being used to control movie clip instances properties were attached to keyframes in the main timeline. As a result, it was possible to simply address the movie clip using its instance name. Suppose, though, that you wanted to control the movie clip instance from another movie clip rather than from the main timeline. If you tried to use the same form of the ActionScript statements shown earlier, your code would fail to accomplish your goals.

The reason for this failure is that the controlling movie clip would be looking in the wrong place for the movie clip instance that it was trying to control. With only the instance name to go on, the controlling movie clip would assume that you wanted to address an instance that it contained. To address another movie clip instance whose parent was the main timeline, you would need to add _root to the name, as in:

```
_root.MyCB._x = _root.MyCB._x + Step;
```

If this seems confusing, just consider the way the filenames and folders work on your hard drive. You can have two different files with the same name as long as they are contained in different folders. If you want to address the file that is in a different folder, you need to tell your computer exactly where to find that file. This is precisely how object naming works in Flash (except that Flash uses dots rather than slashes between the names).

Progress Check

1. What type of properties cannot be set using ActionScript statements?

2. In addition to using the setProperty statement, how else can you set properties?

Using Behaviors

Now that you have learned some of the fundamentals of creating ActionScript programming for your movies, I am going to briefly introduce a feature that may make it possible for you to add all of the ActionScript you need automatically, without any manual programming. *Behaviors* are prewritten scripts that you can add to objects in your Flash movies simply by making a few selections in dialog boxes.

You add behaviors using the Behaviors panel, as shown next. In this case, I have selected the option to add a command to go to a specific frame and then play the movie from there. You display the Behaviors panel using the Window | Development Panels | Behaviors command.

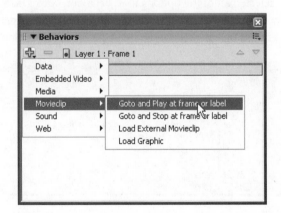

1. Read-only properties
2. Using dot notation

Each behavior has options that are specific to the selected behavior. In this example, you need to choose the options to specify which movie clip you want to control, the form of addressing to use, and the destination frame, as shown here:

Once you have selected all of the options for a behavior, click OK to add the resulting ActionScript statements to the object. This shows the ActionScript code that Flash added to the keyframe as a result of the choices shown in the previous illustration:

TIP

Examining the ActionScript code that Flash adds when you use the Behaviors panel can be an excellent method of learning more about ActionScript programming. In some cases, the ActionScript code that Flash adds contains elements that are not strictly necessary (such as the *this.* in the example), but you can be sure that the code will function properly.

Project 14-1 ## Using ActionScript to Fade an Object In and Out

Now it is time to apply your skills to a useful project. In this case, you will create a Flash movie that has a movie clip instance that you can fade in and out by clicking buttons. This project will demonstrate several useful techniques that you can apply to your own Flash movies.

Step by Step

1. Open a new, blank Flash movie.

2. Select Insert | New Symbol to open the Create New Symbol dialog box.

3. Name your symbol **Fish**.

4. Select the Movie Clip option button.

5. Click OK.

6. Draw an object that looks like a fish.

7. Optionally, add some animation so that the fish appears to be swimming.

8. Click the scene name above the timeline to close symbol editing mode.

9. Select Window | Library to open the Library window.

10. Drag a copy of the Fish Movie Clip symbol onto the upper half of the stage. Make certain that the registration point is approximately centered between the right and left edges of the stage.

11. Select Window | Other Panels | Common Libraries | Buttons to open the Buttons library.

12. Drag an instance of a button symbol onto the lower-left side of the stage.

(continued)

13. Drag an instance of a button symbol onto the lower-right side of the stage. The stage should now look something like this:

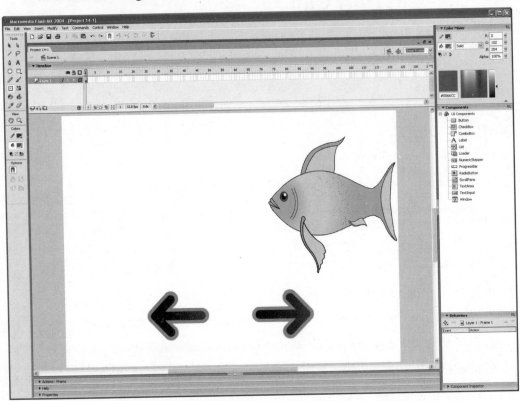

14. Click the Fish Movie Clip symbol to select it, and then use the Window | Properties command to display the Properties panel.

15. Enter **MyFish** in the Name text box, as shown here. Remember, you need to name the instance in order to control its properties using ActionScript statements.

16. Close the Properties panel.

17. Click the left arrow symbol to select it.

18. Select Window | Development Panels | Actions to open the Actions panel.

19. Add the following ActionScript code to the script pane, as shown:

```
on (release) {
    IsVis = MyFish._alpha;
    if (IsVis >0) {
        MyFish._alpha = MyFish._alpha - 20;
    }
}
```

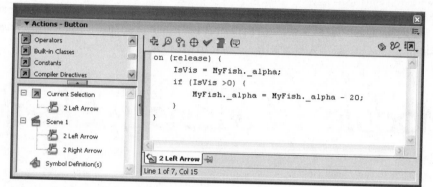

20. Click the right arrow symbol to select it.

21. Add the following ActionScript code to the script pane:

```
on (release) {
    IsVis = MyFish._alpha;
    if (IsVis < 100) {
        MyFish._alpha = MyFish._alpha + 20;
    }
}
```

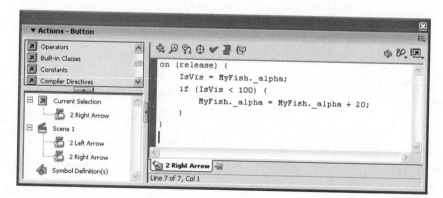

22. Use the File | Save command to save your work.

(continued)

23. Select Control | Test Movie to test your movie. Clicking the left arrow button several times should make the fish go transparent, and clicking the right arrow button several times should return it to opaque.

Project Summary

In this project, you learned how to control the properties of a movie clip instance using ActionScript statements attached to buttons. You saw that you could store the current value of the property and then use a conditional test to determine if the property was within an acceptable range before allowing it to be further modified. In addition, you learned how to combine several different ActionScript actions to accomplish your goal.

✓ Module 14 Mastery Check

1. In some cases, you may need to use _____ ActionScript statements to support older versions of the Flash Player.

2. You can use the _____ operator to increase the value of a variable by one.

3. To add the value that is to the right of the operator to the current value of a variable, you can use the _____ operator.

4. You can use _____ tests to control movie flow.

5. A _____ loop always executes the statements at least once.

6. A loop that does not change the value of the loop variable can become an _____ loop.

7. The _____ operators enable you to combine more than one test.

8. You must use the _____ action to create your own custom functions.

9. The _____ function returns the value of an object property.

10. To address a movie clip instance that is a child of the main timeline and not a child of the current movie clip, you use the _____ name to address the main timeline.

11. You use the _____ panel to add ActionScript code to objects automatically.

12. You can store information in _____ while your movie is running.

13. You use the _____ statement to prevent the ActionScript code following an *if* block from executing automatically.

14. An object must have an _____ if you want to control it from another object.

15. _____ perform calculations that you have defined.

Appendix

Answers to Mastery Checks

Module 1: Understanding Flash MX 2004

1. The area in Flash MX 2004 where you draw objects you want to appear in your movie is the _____.

   stage

2. The tool that you use to select objects is the _____ tool.

   Arrow

3. Which of the following is not something you can do with Flash MX 2004?

   C. Lay out a trip route using a GPS receiver

4. To create a perfect circle with the Oval tool, you hold down the _____ key.

   SHIFT

5. The dialog box–like objects that you use to set options in Flash MX 2004 are called _____.

   panels

6. The two types of tweens you can create in Flash MX 2004 are _____ and _____ tweens.

   motion, shape

7. If you want to animate two objects independently of each other, you would place them on separate _____.

   layers

8. Before you can place an object in frame 24 of the timeline, you must insert a _____.

   keyframe

9. When a button in your movie responds to a user's mouse click, that response is known as _____.

   interactivity

10. To draw a box on the stage, you would use the _____ tool.

    Rectangle

11. The _____ panel enables you to change the characteristics of drawn objects.

    Properties

12. If you use the standard settings, a 48-frame movie will take _____ seconds to complete.

    four

13. **You can reverse most actions that you have performed in Flash MX 2004 by using the _____ command.**

    Edit | Undo

14. **The view of the stage that shows how an animation will appear over the span of several frames is called the _____ view.**

    onion skin

15. **For someone to view a Flash MX 2004 movie that you have placed on your web site, they must have a copy of the _____ installed on their computer.**

    Flash Player

Module 2: Learning the Flash Tools Panel

1. **The area of the Tools panel where you can choose settings for some of the drawing tools is the _____.**

   Options pane

2. **The _____ tool enables you to draw Bézier curves.**

   Pen

3. **Once you have drawn a curved line, you can use the _____ tool to modify the shape of the curve.**

   Subselect

4. **To select objects by drawing a selection box, you use the _____ tool.**

   Arrow

5. **Which of the following is not one of the Pencil tool modes?**

   B. Kink

6. **To select an irregular area, you use the _____ tool.**

   Lasso

7. **To draw a perfectly horizontal line, you hold down _____ as you draw the line.**

   SHIFT

8. **You need to enter _____ as the value in the Rectangle Settings dialog box to create square corners.**

   0

9. **To create a text box with a fixed width, _____ with the Text tool.**

   drag

10. The _____ tool enables you to paint an area with a gradient fill.

Brush

11. To make objects automatically align with nearby objects as you draw them, you select the _____ icon in the Options pane.

Snap To Objects

12. To remove the fill from an object, select the _____ option before you click with the Eraser tool.

Faucet

13. In addition to using the Properties panel, you can use the _____ menu to choose the font size.

Text | Size

14. If you want to continue the same gradient fill across multiple objects, you select the _____ option.

Lock Fill

15. To duplicate an existing color, you can click that color with the _____ tool.

Dropper

Module 3: Learning the Flash Panels

1. The Flash panels are similar to _____ in many other programs.

dialog boxes

2. The _____ panel enables you to change the style of lines.

Properties

3. You use the _____ panel to view the help information for ActionScript statements.

Help

4. When you drag a panel so that it is free floating, the panel is _____.

undocked

5. You can add a new scene to your movie by using the _____ panel.

Scene

6. To return the panels to their normal layout, you use the _____ command.

Window | Panel Sets | Default Layout

7. The panels appear on the _____ menu.

Window

8. If you want to set an object to a very specific height and width, you can use the _____ panel.

Transform

9. To add a shape tween, you must open the _____ panel.

Properties

10. The _____ panel enables you to add ActionScript statements.

Actions

11. To replay a set of actions, you use the _____ panel.

History

12. Error messages are displayed during testing of a movie in the _____ panel.

Output

13. You can add ActionScript code to objects automatically using the _____ panel.

Behaviors

14. You use the _____ panel to add labels and comments to timeline frames.

Properties

15. You use the _____ panel to make it possible for screen reader programs to describe objects in your movies.

Accessibility

Module 4: Using the Timeline and Layers

1. You can add objects only to _____ in the timeline.

keyframes

2. To add labels and comments to a frame, you use the _____ panel.

Properties

3. If you want to add a comment rather than a label, you add _____ to the label.

two slashes (//)

4. To view several frames of an animation at the same time, you use _____ view.

onion skin

5. When there are two or more layers in the timeline, the layer that is _____ in the timeline list appears in front of the other layer.

   higher

6. You can use a _____ layer to create a window onto another layer to control what will be seen as the movie plays.

   mask

7. _____ layers are used to direct a motion tween along a path.

   Guide

8. Flash has _____ types of layers.

   three

9. The different types of layers are _____.

   ordinary, mask, and guide

10. Adding extra layers to your movie has which of the following effects:?

    D. It makes no difference to the size or speed.

11. When you add a motion guide to a Flash movie, that motion guide is _____ when the movie is played.

    invisible

12. If you allow a Flash movie to play at normal speed, _____ frames will be needed for a 10-second movie.

    120

13. If you want to prevent changes to a layer, you can click the _____ column.

    Lock layer

14. To view just the strokes for the objects on a layer, you can click the _____ column.

    Outline view

15. Keyframes that contain content can easily be identified in the timeline because they contain a _____.

    black dot

Module 5: Drawing Objects

1. You can use gradients for the _____ of an object.

   fill

2. **If you want to use a _____ tween, you must group the object.**

   motion

3. **If you want to warp a gradient fill, you use the _____ tool.**

   Fill Transform

4. **To apply precise rotation, skew, or scale settings to an object, you would use the _____ panel.**

   Transform

5. **To make an object partially transparent, you adjust the _____ property.**

   alpha

6. **You can create your own gradient fills using the _____ panel.**

   Color Mixer

7. **Which of the following is not a fill style option:?**

   C. Vector gradient

8. **Warping an object by dragging one of the side rotation handles is known as _____.**

   skewing

9. **If you want to bend the side of an object using a single curve between two of the corners, you would use the _____ tool.**

   Arrow

10. **You can apply a new fill to an object by using the _____ tool.**

    Paint Bucket

11. **Another name for a line is a _____.**

    stroke

12. **To draw a rectangle without a fill, you click the fill color selector and then the _____ button.**

    No Color

13. **A _____ gradient flows outwards from a central point.**

    radial

14. **To change the size of an object, you select the Modify | Transform | _____ command.**

    Scale

15. **To rotate an object, you drag a _____ handle.**

    corner

Module 6: Creating Animations

1. You can apply shape tweens to _____ objects.

   ungrouped

2. If you want an object to slow down as it reaches the end of a tween, you use _____.

   easing

3. To control the visibility of an object, you would use a _____ tween.

   motion

4. When you create a tween, you can use the _____ panel to control various aspects of the tween.

   Properties

5. To help Flash create a better shape tween, you can add _____.

   shape hints

6. You can add a _____ tween using the Insert | Timeline menu.

   motion

7. By default, Flash displays _____ frames per second.

   12

8. Timeline frames that have a tween applied are designated by an _____ in the timeline.

   arrow

9. You can change the color of an object with:

   C. Both (a shape tween and a motion tween)

10. You can place a copy of an object that you have copied into the same location using the Edit | _____ command.

    Paste In Place

11. Flash animations actually consist of a series of _____ images.

    still

12. The only type of tween you can apply to a symbol instance is a _____ tween.

    motion

13. When you add a shape tween to the timeline, the type of frame you will most likely want to add to the end of the tween is a _____.

    blank keyframe

14. If you use a negative easing value, the tween will _____ as it plays.

accelerate

15. A dotted line in the timeline indicates a _____ tween.

broken

Module 7: Using Guides and Masks

1. You use a _____ to make a motion tween follow a curved path.

motion guide

2. A _____ serves as a window onto a masked layer.

mask

3. A guide layer appears _____ the guided layer in the timeline.

above

4. If you want the object being guided to rotate so that it stays perpendicular to the motion guide, you select the _____ option.

Orient To Path

5. To create a scrolling text banner, you apply a motion tween to the _____.

text box

6. When you use a mask, you can apply a tween to:

D. Both (the mask and the masked layer)

7. Which of the following cannot be used as a mask?

C. A line

8. When you create a mask, the _____ in the mask serves as the window onto the masked layer.

fill

9. To view the mask effect in Flash, you must _____ the mask layer.

lock

10. How many different motion tweens can use the same motion guide?

C. As many as you want

11. In addition to using a motion guide, it is possible to make a tween follow a curved path using _____ animation.

frame-by-frame

12. The mask is _____ when the movie is played.

    invisible

13. To create a horizontally scrolling text banner, the mask must be at least as _____ as the text box.

    tall

14. To modify a mask, you must first _____ the mask layer.

    unlock

15. To create a news-ticker effect, you use _____ scrolling text.

    horizontally

Module 8: Creating Symbols and Using the Library

1. When you create symbols, they are stored in the _____.

   library

2. Which of the following is not one of the Flash symbol types?

   B. ActionScript object

3. A _____ symbol has the built-in ability to react to mouse events.

   button

4. When you place copies of symbols into your movie, those copies are called _____.

   instances

5. The button symbol has _____ frames in its timeline.

   four

6. The _____ symbol uses the main movie timeline.

   graphic

7. The _____ symbol has a timeline that is independent of the main timeline.

   movie clip

8. To use the pre-built symbols that come with Flash, you open one of the _____.

   common libraries

9. Modifying a master copy of a symbol in the library affects which instances of the symbol?

   C. All instances no matter when they are added to the stage.

10. To use symbols from another movie, you can open that movie's library using the File | Import | _____ command.

    Open External Library

11. You can add interactivity to a symbol instance using the _____ panel.

    Behaviors

12. A button symbol instance needs some _____ code in order to do anything useful.

    ActionScript

13. Using symbol instances rather than copies of ordinary objects _____ the size of the published Flash movie file.

    reduces

14. You should add any text you want on a button to _____ of the button symbol.

    an instance

15. The _____ frame of a button symbol defines the area a user can click.

    Hit

Module 9: Using Imported Graphics

1. The native graphic format for Flash is _____ graphics.

   vector

2. JPEG images are an example of _____ graphics.

   bitmap

3. You use the File | _____ command to bring in graphics from other sources.

   Import | Import To Stage or Import | Import To Library

4. To use text as graphics, you must first use the Modify | _____ command.

   Break Apart

5. To turn a bitmap image into a vector-based graphic, you _____ the bitmap image.

   trace

6. To use a bitmap image as a fill, you _____ the bitmap image.

   break apart

7. You use the _____ tool to select a bitmap as a fill.

   EyeDropper

8. _____ images can be scaled up without reducing their quality.

   Vector

9. Reducing the size of a bitmap image by throwing away some of the detail is a process known as _____.

   compression

10. The _____ tool ceases to be effective on a block of text that has been broken apart.

    Text

11. Vector graphics are a type of image that can be scaled without losing quality because a vector image is defined by a _____ expression.

    mathematical

12. Macromedia _____ is a vector graphic editor that can create images that you can use in your Flash movies.

    FreeHand

13. When you trace a bitmap, larger Color Threshold values will tend to _____ the resulting image.

    posterize

14. If you choose a larger Minimum Area value when you are tracing a bitmap, the result will be a _____ file size.

    smaller

15. You use the _____ dialog box to adjust the JPEG settings for an imported bitmap image.

    Bitmap Properties

Module 10: Adding Sounds to Your Movies

1. The _____ rate refers to the number of data points that are recorded each second.

   sampling

2. The _____ file format typically offers the best compression ratio for sound files in Flash.

   MP3

3. The process of adjusting volume levels to make it appear as though the sound were moving is known as _____.

   fading

4. _____ sounds play until they are finished, even if the movie has ended.

Event

5. To make a sound play just as long as the animation, you set the sync option to _____.

Stream

6. To make a sound play more than once, you set the _____ option.

Number Of Times To Loop

7. Selecting a lower bit rate _____ the size of your movie file.

reduces

8. The settings you make in the Properties panel apply to an _____ of the imported sound file.

instance

9. The Edit Envelope dialog box enables you to adjust the _____ of a sound.

volume

10. Sounds you add to button symbols are _____ sounds.

event

11. Stereo sounds take _____ the space of mono sounds.

double

12. You use the _____ panel to set most options for imported sounds.

Properties

13. You can use the options in the _____ dialog box to override the individual sound settings.

Publish Settings

14. To make a button produce a sound when someone clicks the button, you add the sound to the _____ frame.

Down

15. Adding a sound to the _____ frame of a button would play the sound after the mouse button was released.

Up

Module 11: Publishing Flash Movies

1. The amount of data that a connection can handle is often referred to as the _____ of the connection.

   bandwidth

2. When you create a _____, you are making a stand-alone Flash movie that is self-executing.

   projector

3. To produce the Flash Player file for use on a web page, you _____ your movie.

   publish

4. You can use the _____ to see how the data will stream as your movie downloads.

   bandwidth profiler

5. To see the effects of different download speeds, you make the bit rate selections on the _____ menu.

   View | Download Settings

6. Flash movies begin playing before all of their content is downloaded because they are an example of _____ content.

   streaming

7. When you are testing the download characteristics of your movie, the red line in the chart represents:

   A. The maximum amount of data that can be downloaded during the frame.

8. The _____ dialog box enables you to choose the HTML options.

   Publish Settings

9. You can use the _____ From Import option to prevent other people from importing your movies.

   Protect

10. A _____ is often used to make the movie display a "Loading" message rather than beginning immediate playback to prevent pauses once the movie begins playing.

    preloader

11. You need the proper _____ code on a web page in order for a browser to recognize your Flash movie.

    HTML

12. A visitor to your web site must have a copy of the _____ installed in order to view your movies.

Flash Player

13. If you publish your Flash movie in a foreign format, you will lose any _____ in your movie.

interactivity

14. You can use the options on the _____ tab of the Publish Settings dialog box to specify if your movie will begin playing automatically.

HTML

15. The _____ tab of the Publish Settings dialog box includes a password option that enables you to protect your movies.

Flash

Module 12: Learning Basic ActionScript Concepts

1. ActionScript is an _____-oriented programming language.

object

2. The programming language that ActionScript is most closely related to is called _____.

JavaScript

3. The characteristics of objects that you can examine and modify are called _____.

properties

4. You use the _____ panel to add ActionScript statements to your Flash movies.

Actions

5. When you see an ActionScript statement that uses dot notation, the item to the _____ of the dot is the parent of the item on the other side of the dot.

left

6. The _____ category contains the ActionScript functions you use in Flash movies.

Global Functions

7. When you want to add ActionScript statements to the timeline, you must add them to a _____ in the timeline.

keyframe

8. The _____ action causes the playback to end immediately.

   Stop

9. To execute a block of ActionScript statements several times in a row, you use a _____.

   loop

10. The _____ data type holds letters, numbers, and punctuation.

    string

11. To get help with the syntax as you add ActionScript code to your movies, make certain that the _____ button is clicked.

    Show Code Hint

12. The _____ functions control the movement of the playhead.

    Timeline Control

13. The _____ functions enable you to send commands to the web browser.

    Browser/Network

14. _____ are similar to functions, but are invoked using dot notation.

    Methods

15. _____ values are always true or false.

    Boolean

Module 13: Learning Basic ActionScript Programming

1. To add ActionScript statements that must run at a specific time in your movie, you add those statements to _____.

   keyframes

2. To check for errors in the ActionScript statements, click the _____ button in the Actions panel.

   Check Syntax

3. You must add an _____ when you add ActionScript statements to a button.

   event handler

4. You cannot modify properties that are _____.

   read-only

5. Properties that apply to all movie clips are _____ properties.

   global

6. Obsolete ActionScript statements are also known as _____ statements.

   deprecated

7. Conditional tests always produce a _____ result.

   Boolean

8. The actions that control the flow of the movie are found in the _____ subcategory.

   Timeline Control

9. gotoAndStop and play are examples of ActionScript _____.

   functions

10. The _____ function can be used to create a mute button.

    stopAllSounds

11. You use the _____ handler to make movie clips respond to events.

    onClipEvent

12. You can use the _____ function to move the playhead to the next frame in the timeline.

    nextFrame

13. To add ActionScript statements that are triggered by events, you typically add those statements to _____.

    objects

14. To avoid the problem of sending the playhead to the wrong frame if your timeline is altered, you should use _____ rather than frame numbers as arguments.

    labels

15. To control a movie clip instance from the main timeline, you must assign an _____ to the movie clip.

    instance name

Module 14: Learning More ActionScript Programming

1. In some cases, you may need to use _____ ActionScript statements to support older versions of the Flash Player.

   deprecated

2. You can use the _____ operator to increase the value of a variable by one.

   increment (++)

3. **To add the value that is to the right of the operator to the current value of a variable, you can use the _____ operator.**

   addition assignment (+=)

4. **You can use _____ tests to control movie flow.**

   conditional

5. **A _____ loop always executes the statements at least once.**

   do…while

6. **A loop that does not change the value of the loop variable can become an _____ loop.**

   endless

7. **The _____ operators enable you to combine more than one test.**

   logical

8. **You must use the _____ action to create your own custom functions.**

   function

9. **The _____ function returns the value of an object property.**

   getProperty

10. **To address a movie clip instance that is a child of the main timeline and not a child of the current movie clip, you use the _____ name to address the main timeline.**

    _root

11. **You use the _____ panel to add ActionScript code to objects automatically.**

    Behaviors

12. **You can store information in _____ while your movie is running.**

    variables

13. **You use the _____ statement to prevent the ActionScript code following an *if* block from executing automatically.**

    else

14. **An object must have an _____ if you want to control it from another object.**

    instance name

15. **_____ perform calculations that you have defined.**

    Custom functions

Index

INTERNATIONAL CONTACT INFORMATION

AUSTRALIA
McGraw-Hill Book Company
Australia Pty. Ltd.
TEL +61-2-9900-1800
FAX +61-2-9878-8881
http://www.mcgraw-hill.com.au
books-it_sydney@mcgraw-hill.com

CANADA
McGraw-Hill Ryerson Ltd.
TEL +905-430-5000
FAX +905-430-5020
http://www.mcgraw-hill.ca

GREECE, MIDDLE EAST, & AFRICA
(Excluding South Africa)
McGraw-Hill Hellas
TEL +30-210-6560-990
TEL +30-210-6560-993
TEL +30-210-6560-994
FAX +30-210-6545-525

MEXICO (Also serving Latin America)
McGraw-Hill Interamericana Editores
S.A. de C.V.
TEL +525-1500-5108
FAX +525-117-1589
http://www.mcgraw-hill.com.mx
carlos_ruiz@mcgraw-hill.com

SINGAPORE (Serving Asia)
McGraw-Hill Book Company
TEL +65-6863-1580
FAX +65-6862-3354
http://www.mcgraw-hill.com.sg
mghasia@mcgraw-hill.com

SOUTH AFRICA
McGraw-Hill South Africa
TEL +27-11-622-7512
FAX +27-11-622-9045
robyn_swanepoel@mcgraw-hill.com

SPAIN
McGraw-Hill/
Interamericana de España, S.A.U.
TEL +34-91-180-3000
FAX +34-91-372-8513
http://www.mcgraw-hill.es
professional@mcgraw-hill.es

UNITED KINGDOM, NORTHERN,
EASTERN, & CENTRAL EUROPE
McGraw-Hill Education Europe
TEL +44-1-628-502500
FAX +44-1-628-770224
http://www.mcgraw-hill.co.uk
emea_queries@mcgraw-hill.com

ALL OTHER INQUIRIES Contact:
McGraw-Hill/Osborne
TEL +1-510-420-7700
FAX +1-510-420-7703
http://www.osborne.com
omg_international@mcgraw-hill.com

Sound Off!

Visit us at **www.osborne.com/bookregistration** and let us know what you thought of this book. While you're online you'll have the opportunity to register for newsletters and special offers from McGraw-Hill/Osborne.

We want to hear from you!

Sneak Peek

Visit us today at **www.betabooks.com** and see what's coming from McGraw-Hill/Osborne tomorrow!

Based on the successful software paradigm, Bet@Books™ allows computing professionals to view partial and sometimes complete text versions of selected titles online. Bet@Books™ viewing is free, invites comments and feedback, and allows you to "test drive" books in progress on the subjects that interest you the most.

Mc